New Issues in International Crisis Management

New Approaches to Peace and Security

Richard Ned Lebow, Series Editor

Increasing anxiety about conventional and nuclear war has triggered a corresponding interest in books that treat these themes. This burgeoning literature is largely descriptive and narrowly technical and often reflects a prodefense bias. This series, by contrast, will address broader theoretical and policy questions associated with conflict and conflict management. On the whole, its perspective is critical of conventional wisdom in the realm of both policy and theory. The overarching goal of the series is to help lay the intellectual foundations for alternative approaches to thinking about security.

Titles in This Series

New Issues in International Crisis Management, edited by Gilbert R. Winham

Arms Control and U.S.-German Relations, Gert Krell

About the Book and Editor

A comprehensive overview of the state of crisis management in international affairs, this book focuses primarily on the U.S.-USSR relationship. For most of the postwar period, the U.S. superiority in nuclear weapons shaped the political structure within which international crises occurred. This edge began to deteriorate by the late 1970s, leading to a new and potentially more dangerous structure within which the superpower rivalry is now conducted. Arguing that the shifting nuclear balance has created a new dimension for crisis management, the contributors analyze such issues as the informal norms of diplomatic behavior that have evolved during the extended superpower rivalry, the tendency of both superpowers to engage in activities that progressively reduce crisis stability, and various concrete measures such as risk reduction centers that might enhance the current system for crisis management. The book also includes case studies of crisis management among non-superpowers. Taken together, these papers address the important question of how human control can be maximized in situations of international crisis.

Gilbert R. Winham is professor and chairman of the Department of Political Science, Dalhousie University, and former director of the university's Centre for Foreign Policy Studies. He is the author of *International Trade and the Tokyo Round Negotiation* (1986) as well as other books and articles and is the coeditor (with Denis Stairs) of *The Politics of Canada's Economic Relationship with the United States* and *Selected Problems in Formulating Foreign Economic Policy* (both 1985).

New Issues in International Crisis Management

edited by
Gilbert R. Winham

Westview Press / Boulder and London

New Approaches to Peace and Security

Copyright © 1988 by Westview Press, Inc.

Published in 1988 in the United States of America by Westview Press, Inc.; Frederick A. Praeger, Publisher; 5500 Central Avenue, Boulder, Colorado 80301

Library of Congress Cataloging-in-Publication Data
New issues in international crisis management.
  (New approaches to peace and security)
  Bibliography: p.
  Includes index.
  1. International relations. 2. Crisis management.
3. Nuclear crisis control. 4. United States—Foreign
relations—Soviet Union. 5. Soviet Union—Foreign
relations—United States. I. Winham, Gilbert R.
II. Series.
JX1391.N49 1988   327.1'1   87–3452
ISBN 0–8133–7295–X

Printed and bound in the United States of America

The paper used in this publication meets the requirements of the American National Standard for Permanence of Paper for Printed Library Materials Z39.48-1984.

10   9   8   7   6   5   4   3   2   1

Contents

Preface ix

1 Introduction, *Gilbert R. Winham* 1

PART ONE
THEORY AND PRACTICE

2 Crisis Management: A Critical Appraisal,
   James L. Richardson 13

3 Clausewitz, Loss of Control, and Crisis Management,
   Richard Ned Lebow 37

PART TWO
SUPERPOWER RELATIONS

4 U.S.-Soviet Global Rivalry: Norms of Competition,
   Alexander L. George 67

5 Arms Control Negotiations and the Stability of
   Crisis Management, *Karen Patrick MacGillivray*
   and Gilbert R. Winham 90

PART THREE
NUCLEAR CRISIS MANAGEMENT

6 Enhancing Crisis Stability: Correcting the Trend
   Toward Increasing Instability, *Charles F. Hermann* 121

7 Approaches to Nuclear Risk Reduction,
   Joseph S. Nye, Jr., and William L. Ury 150

PART FOUR
CRISIS MANAGEMENT IN REGIONAL CONTEXT

8   The Managed and the Managers: Crisis Prevention
    in the Middle East, *Janice Gross Stein*   171

9   Alternative Attempts at Crisis Management:
    Concepts and Processes, *I. William Zartman*   199

10 Conclusion, *Gilbert R. Winham*   225

About the Contributors   233
Bibliography   237
Index   251

Preface

Crisis is a long-standing concern to scholars of international relations, and there is a substantial literature, both of the case study and theoretical variety, that deals with this subject. The diplomacy associated with crisis has an equally long-standing intellectual tradition. Much of diplomatic history, which can begin with a reading of the politics between warring Greek city-states recounted in Thucydides' *Peloponnesian Wars*, is an analysis of the exchanges between governments during periods of international tension and crisis.

Despite the fact that scholars have long been concerned about diplomacy during crisis, the sub-field of crisis management has had a short history. Essentially, crisis management is the practice of attempting to avoid an outcome in interstate relations that leads to violence or war, without abandoning at the same time one's position. This practice has become of increasing importance in international relations since World War II because the prospect of nuclear war has made violence a more costly mechanism for resolving conflict. Similarly the literature on crisis management has developed mainly since World War II and includes landmarks such as Buchan (1966), Bell (1971) and George *et al.* (1971), as well as an international collection of essays edited by Frei (1978). A lively journal literature now exists on this subject and has been reviewed by Tanter (1975) and Gilbert and Lauren (1980).

In preparing for its XIIIth World Congress in Paris in July 1985, the International Political Science Association established a section entitled "New Forms of Crisis Management" under the direction of G. R. Winham of Canada and A. Yakovlev of the USSR. The focus of this section was on crisis management between the superpowers, which is the area of greatest concern from the perspective of world security. Other selected aspects of crisis management outside the main lines of East-West confrontation were also included. The academic papers presented at the IPSA World Congress in Paris served as the catalyst for this edited volume.

This book could not have been completed without the assistance of others. The editor wishes to thank the contributors to this volume, as well as those who participated at the 1985 IPSA meeting. Financial support for this volume was received from Professor Robert Boardman, director of the Centre for Foreign Policy Studies at Dalhousie University, and from the Faculty of Graduate Studies at that university. The administrative work associated with the IPSA meeting was carried out by Mrs. Doris Boyle, former secretary to the centre. Nina Winham edited the papers and the final manuscript and prepared the bibliography and index. The arduous tasks of typing and coding the final manuscript were cheerfully accomplished by Paulette Chiasson, administrative secretary to the Department of Political Science. To these people I owe an enormous debt of gratitude.

Gilbert R. Winham
Halifax, Nova Scotia

New Issues in International Crisis Management

1

Introduction

Gilbert R. Winham

In 435 B.C. the Greek city of Epidamnus, a colony of Corcyra suffering internal unrest and external hostilities, appealed for military assistance from its mother country. It was rebuffed. It took its case to Corinth; and the Corinthians, motivated in part by hatred of Corcyra, which was in turn a colony of Corinth, agreed to come to the assistance of Epidamnus. The Corcyreans reacted violently to this action, and hostilities commenced between Corinth and Corcyra.

In the ensuing brief struggle, Corcyra appealed to Athens for assistance. The Athenians, recognizing Corcyra's strategic position and not wanting the Corcyrean navy to pass into Corinthian hands, forcibly prevented Corinth from defeating Corcyra. The Corinthians regarded the Athenian action as a cause for war, and a breach of the treaty between Athens and the Peloponnesians.

Anticipating Corinthian hostility, the Athenians took the defensive action of insisting that Potidae—a Corinthian colony subject to Athenian rule—dismantle its naval fortification. The Corinthians attempted to thwart this action, and hostilities again resulted. The Corinthians carried their grievances to Sparta, and together with other allies who feared Athens, tried to convince Sparta that the Athenians had broken the thirty year truce between them. The Spartans deliberated, and then voted the treaty had been broken and declared war on Athens: " . . . not so much because they were influenced by the speeches of their allies as because they were afraid of the further growth of Athenian power" (Thucydides, 1954: 87). So began the Peloponnesian War, an event which Toynbee described as the "breakdown" of the Hellenic Civilization.

On June 28, 1914, Archduke Franz Ferdinand, heir to the Austrian throne, was assassinated with his wife in Sarajevo, Serbia. This action inflamed public opinion in Austria-Hungary. Austrian leaders, who had long felt Serbia's presence exacerbated the internal threat to the Austrian Empire from Slavic nationalism, seized on the incident as a pretext to suppress Serbia. After nearly a month of internal deliberations and diplomacy, on July 23, 1914, Austria delivered an exceptionally strong-worded ultimatum to Serbia.

Austria-Hungary acted on the strong encouragement of Germany. Its actions, however, were opposed by Russia, which saw itself as the defender of Slavic interests in Southeast Europe. This pattern of antagonism was not new. Five years earlier, with German support, Austria had annexed Bosnia-Herzogovina over the strong opposition of both Serbia and Russia. The Bosnian crisis had humiliated Russia, and left the Russians with the resolve to increase their military preparedness and to decrease their diplomatic isolation. At the opposite extreme, the earlier crisis motivated Germany to recommend a belligerent policy to Austria-Hungary in 1914.

Serbia responded to the Austrian ultimatum on July 25, 1914, accepting most conditions. Meanwhile Germany, having miscalculated Russian resolve and the support Russia would have from its allies France and Britain, vacillated in its support of Austria-Hungary. However, control over events was quickly lost. Military leaders in all capitals—sensing war was imminent—began urging their political leaders to mobilize forces, which in the technology of the day was tantamount to a declaration of war. Russia commenced military preparations against Austria-Hungary.

On July 31, believing Russia to be mobilizing, Germany activated its own mobilization plans and dispatched an ultimatum to Russia. The ultimatum was rejected the following day, and Germany declared war on Russia. In response, France commenced mobilization. On August 2, pursuant to an inflexible military strategy (Schlieffen Plan), the German army invaded Luxembourg and one day later, invaded Belgium. France and Britain quickly declared war, and commenced hostilities. The resulting war killed over eight million soliders, wounded about twenty million more, and devastated Europe.

A more recent case of crisis produced an entirely different outcome. On October 15, 1962, the President of the United States was presented with photographic evidence that the Soviet Union was placing intermediate range nuclear missiles in Cuba. American intelligence sources estimated the missiles would be operative in seven to ten days, after which they could strike most locations in the United States. The Soviet action represented an unexpected and dramatic bid to shift the strategic balance of power. This was unacceptable to the U.S. Government.

The motivation for the Soviet action lay in the perception that the balance of power had turned sharply against them. Despite widely publicized claims in the United States of a "missile gap" with the Soviet

Union, U.S. satellite reconnaissance in 1961 confirmed that the Soviets lacked sufficient ICBMs to provide a credible retaliatory capability against the United States. After pondering the implications of this information, the U.S. Government informed the Soviet Union that it knew of the latter's weakness, in an effort to restrain Soviet Cold War diplomacy. This ended over a half-decade of highly-successful strategic deception by the Soviet Union. The Soviet action in Cuba was an attempt to reverse a deteriorating strategic situation brought about by the collapse of the missile gap myth, and by the increased military expenditures of the U.S. Government after 1960.

Despite the obvious danger of precipitating a war between the superpowers, the United States quickly determined it would take military action to effect an early withdrawal of the missiles. In a now-celebrated example of crisis management, the American Government carefully deliberated the alternatives of a naval quarantine or an air strike. On October 24 the United States initiated a quarantine. Soviet ships carrying missiles declined to challenge the quarantine and turned back, but not before several tense encounters between Soviet submarines and American patrol vessels.

U.S. attention then turned to the missiles already in Cuba, which would be operational shortly. On October 27, a Soviet ground-to-air missile destroyed a U.S. reconnaissance plane over Cuba. Amid sharply escalating tension, the United States announced it would take military measures to safeguard reconnaissance flights, and it recalled 24 troop carrier squadrons to active duty. On October 28, just as the U.S. Government was preparing to consider new measures, an agreement was reached: the Soviet Union agreed to withdraw all offensive missiles from Cuba, in return for the United States' pledge not to invade Cuba. The crisis was over.

The previous three cases are examples of international crises. Crises are not uncommon in the international system, but few result in full-blown war. Many do not involve hostilities at all. Thus the Cuban missile crisis is more representative than either the 1914 case or the Peloponnesian War. However, when war does occur the results can be devastating. Moreover, the knowledge that few crises result in war provides little reassurance when contemplating the prospects for crisis between superpowers armed with nuclear weapons. Clearly, any hostilities today that involved nuclear weapons would produce calamitous results for the parties involved, and possibly for the entire human race. The incomprehensible cost of nuclear war has enormously escalated the need to manage international crises below the threshold of war. In this sense crisis management is an unavoidable subject.

Crisis and crisis management have been defined in academic literature, and are reviewed in this volume (Richardson, 1987). The requirements for successful crisis management are also well analyzed (George, 1984) and the literature may have gone as far as it can go in prescribing rules and mechanisms for avoiding violent conflict in crisis situations. The problem, however, is that national leaders often do not want to avoid crises and they are willing to manipulate the risk inherent in a crisis to promote political interests. Crises can create change, and change is sometimes seen as necessary. The incentive for policy-makers to pursue crisis diplomacy is the need to preserve the interests of the nation, and these interests occasionally come into sharp conflict with the interests of other nations.

Crisis management involves difficult decision-making. The basic dilemma is that there would be no crisis if parties were willing to forego their objectives, but this can involve unacceptable costs to nations and/ or their leaders. The central problem of crisis management has been well summarized by Snyder and Diesing (1977: 10), namely, " . . . to achieve an optimum blend of coercion and accommodation in one's strategy, a blend that will both avoid war and maximize one's gains or minimize one's losses." Put in these terms, crisis management is nothing more than an extreme form of diplomatic behavior, for all diplomacy necessarily involves judgments about how much one should contest, or accommodate, the interests of other states.

There is enormous variety in the crises which have occurred in the international system, which limits the capacity of analysts to establish generalized rules for crisis management. Fortunately, scholars have responded to this empirical challenge. Since the early 1970s, several major studies have examined international crises on a comparative case study basis. These works include George and Smoke (1974), Snyder and Diesing (1977), Lebow (1981), various articles by Brecher (esp., Brecher and Winfield, 1982), and a government analysis published by Hazlewood *et al.* (1977). Findings from these studies provide a context for any current examination of crisis management.

As one might expect, there was substantial variation in the cases included in these studies. For example, using a "low threshold" definition of crisis, Hazlewood *et al.* examined 289 cases involving the U.S. Government over the period 1946–76; while Lebow, using a higher threshold, selected 26 cases of international crisis from the 20th century. Despite the differences in sampling techniques, it is apparent that most of the incidents that these scholars described as crisis did not end in war. This reinforces the point that crisis is a common and inescapable part of international politics, and that crisis management is a necessary tool of diplomatic statecraft.

The case study literature provides useful advice on three important questions about international crises: (i) why they arise; (ii) how they are resolved (short of war); and (iii) what main problems are associated with their resolution. On the first point, the variety in types of crises makes it difficult to pinpoint any one set of variables as being a general cause of crisis. Crisis can arise in situations ranging from a fundamental military challenge to the balance of power, to an insignificant border dispute that escalates into a major confrontation. Common factors in such different circumstances are not easy to find. However, Lebow's analysis of the aggressive policy behavior that usually accompanies international crises suggests this behavior arises more out of the domestic *needs* of the parties than the *opportunities* that might be presented in the external arena. As Lebow (1981: 276) puts it: "we discovered a good opportunity for aggression (i.e., a vulnerable commitment) in only about one third of our cases but found strong needs to pursue an aggressive foreign policy in every instance. This suggests that policymakers . . . are more responsive to internal imperatives than they are to external cues."

Lebow's findings go some distance to explain why compromise may be difficult to achieve in crisis situations. Parties in crisis usually focus on the external actions taken by their adversaries; they are rarely in a position to appreciate, let alone to accommodate, the internal needs of their opponents. The main policy pursued in crises is deterrence, especially crises involving superpowers, but deterrence is more directed to limiting the external options of an adversary than to understanding the constraints or pressures that might make those options necessary in the first place. There have been some examples of parties in crisis taking account of the other side's political position, such as the effort by the U.S. Government to avoid humiliating the Soviets in the Cuban missile crisis. However, these examples stand essentially as exceptions, and the more general rule may be that of an imbalance between the largely internal motivations that lead to crisis, and the largely external means by which they are handled in the international system.

The second question is how crises are resolved. In a study of sixteen crises, Snyder and Diesing (1977: 248) found that backing down was a more common means of resolving crisis than compromise. As they put it: "In 9 or 10 of our fourteen crisis cases that did not lead to war, the accommodative process was mostly one way—i.e., one party did virtually all the accommodating, after realizing it was the weaker in bargaining power. Most settlements, in other words, were a clear win for the stronger party, with sometimes a face saving concession being awarded to the loser to make it possible for him to accept defeat." These findings are also consistent with those of Lebow and with Wilkenfeld and Brecher (1982). The latter authors note that in crises in which the United States or the USSR are involved, decisive outcomes (victory or defeat) occur more than twice as often as ambigious outcomes (compromise or stalemate). The relative absence of compromise in such cases makes even more stark the pressures faced in crisis situations.

The mechanisms of accommodation in cases that ended decisively was usually an "imbalance of bargaining power" (Snyder and Diesing, 1977: 248) that emerged during the crisis. As crisis clarifies the situations for the parties, the weaker party comes to recognize its weakness, and it backs off rather than pursue war. As elaborated by Snyder and Diesing, bargaining power is a function of resolve, which in turn is determined by relative military strengths and the interests engaged in the confrontation. With regard to military strength as being a determinant of bargaining power, the question arises whether nuclear weapons, which are unusable in any conventional sense, might nevertheless confer an advantage in bargaining power. On this point, Snyder and Diesing (1977: 462) state: " . . . there are theoretical and some empirical grounds for believing that absolute quantitative superiority in nuclear power can be a bargaining asset in crises, although how valuable an asset is unclear."[1] The authors further note that although some national decision-makers might be indifferent toward nuclear weaponry, whether this would cancel out the benefits that nuclear superiority might confer in a crisis is "problematical."

The third question deals with the problems associated with crisis resolution. Many analysts note that perception and information processing are often faulty in crisis decision-making, and that parties are subjected to a great number of "ambiguous signals" (Bell, 1979: 166). This results in an unrealistic view of the adversary's position and interests, and can also lead to an unrealistic view of the costs of war. It takes time to establish an accurate assessment of the adversary, which is usually done through analysis of behavior during the crisis. A further problem is that of the threat of loss of control. Lebow has noted (1981: 264): "In crisis, nations may have to demonstrate willingness to go to war in order to prevent war." This is a behavior Schelling (1966: 92–125) has identified as a competition in risk taking. This kind of crisis diplomacy always entails two kinds of risks: one is that the parties will at some point decide war is inevitable, and then, like Tsar and Kaiser in 1914, commence preemptive actions to put themselves in the best possible position in the impeding conflict; the other is that the parties will lose control of the situation and inadvertently stumble into war. How much difference actually exists between these two processes may be conjectual. With regard to loss of control, Snyder and Diesing report that although decision-makers usually feared (sometimes quite intensely) that a crisis they were involved in might go out of control, in fact these fears were highly exaggerated. This assertion does not seem to enjoy wide support in the literature. Instead, most analyses have viewed loss of control as a serious problem of crisis management, and they feel this problem has grown more severe with the increasing complexity of modern military machines.

There are indications that crisis management between the superpowers may have become more problematic in the 1980s, which which calls for increased attention to this subject. Over the period of the Cold War a fundamental shift has occurred in the military balance of power between the United States and the USSR. For the first two decades of the Cold War, the United States had an overwhelming strategic superiority over the Soviet Union. Although the U.S. nuclear monopoly was broken as early as 1949, it was not until the mid-1960s that the Soviets were able to threaten the U.S. homeland with a significant nuclear strike.

For most of the 1960s real military expenditures rose in the United States. However, in response to the public reaction to the Vietnam War, U.S. real military expenditure declined substantially over the period 1968–76. Meanwhile military expenditures of the USSR continued to grow by about two to four percent per year, and the Soviets embarked on an ambitious program to build a navy and increase their ICBM forces. The result was that by the early 1970s, it was assumed the forces of both sides possessed essentially equivalent capabilities, and by the late 1970s public opinion in the United States was inflamed over an alleged "window of vulnerability" posed by Soviet heavy ICBMs. What had occurred over this period was a fundamental change in the military balance of power between the United States and the Soviet Union. The reason this change was not more evident is that the international system had been bipolar in political terms, resulting in part from the U.S. policy of exaggerating the Soviet threat and from the Soviet policy early in the Cold War of concealing Soviet strategic weakness.

What is the effect of this shift in the prospects for crisis management? The answer depends somewhat on how one views history and the operation of the balance of power. In the theory of balance of power, it is often assumed that roughly equivalent power between individual nations (or alliances of nations) produces stability and preserves the independence of nations from each other (e.g., Morgenthau, 1961: 174). Because a balance of power system was coterminus with long periods of international peace since 1648, and especially in the 19th century in Europe, it was assumed that the system produced peace as well. Organski (1961) has disputed this interpretation of history. He claims that longer periods of peace in the international system were due not to a balance of power among contending nations, but by a preponderance of power exercised by a leading nation and its compliant allies. This argument led Organski to posit a theory of war that was dependent on power shifts in the international system. War occurred when a disatisfied nation (the "challenger") grew strong enough to challenge the *status quo* established by a preponderant power. As Organski (1958: 297) put it: "A balance of power does not bring peace. On the contrary, the greatest wars of modern history have occurred at times when one of these challengers most nearly balanced the power of the preponderant nations or when through miscalculation a challenger *thought* that its power was as great as that of its rivals."

Organski's analysis has worrisome implications for the current superpower relationship. What creates even greater concern is the apparent support given to the theory from sources as disparate as public officials and behavioral scientists. In a widely quoted speech in 1980, former secretary of state Henry Kissinger (1981: 279) stated that " . . . it can no longer be seriously denied that the overall military balance is shifting sharply against us." Kissinger argued this circumstance created an unprecedented vulnerability, and it created a period of maximum danger for the country in the modern period. Kissinger's fear was not of an imminent nuclear attack, but rather of " . . . an increased Soviet willingness to run risks in local conflicts." As he put it: "Rarely in history has a nation so passively accepted such a radical change in the military balance. Never in history has an opponent achieved as large an advantage in so many significant categories of military power without attempting to translate it into some political benefit" (1981: 280).

Kissinger's statement in itself lends support to Organski's analysis that an equivalence of power between a preponderant nation and its challenger promotes international conflict. Moreover, his suggestion about Soviet risk-taking in local conflicts identifies the mechanism whereby such conflict could be brought about. The capacity for local conflicts to engage the interests of larger powers, and then to stimulate a wider conflict, is well understood in history. It was exactly this mechanism, for example, that initiated the Peloponnesian War in ancient Greece and the First World War in Europe.

Further evidence on Kissinger's proposition about military power being translated into political benefit comes from the data gathered on superpower crisis management behavior by Wilkenfeld and Brecher. These authors examined 39 cases of crisis for the United States, and 20 for the USSR over the period 1945–75. Both superpowers suffered relatively few "defeats" in these cases, but whereas the USSR was not involved in any examples of U.S. defeats (N = 5), the United States was involved in all cases of USSR defeats (N = 5). Furthermore, in those cases coded by the authors as "military-security" as opposed to "political-diplomatic"—that is, cases where one might expect military force to have had a bearing on the outcome—the United States was considerably better able to manage crises to its advantage than was the Soviet Union. The reason given by the authors was that the United States had a capacity to translate its general military superiority into a bargaining advantage. In their words: "Once again, the existence of a U.S. preponderance of power during most of the period under consideration helps explain the greater success of the United States in achieving agreements in crises typified by military-security issues than in those characterized by political-diplomatic issues" (1982: 202).

Where does this leave us regarding crisis management in the 1980s and beyond? First, it is clear that the United States has lost the strategic superiority it enjoyed in the first two decades of the Cold War, and the result will be a certain loss of margin for maneuvering in U.S. strategic planning. This could lead the United States to pursue a more offensive diplomacy in an effort to define and protect interests it feels are threatened by increased Soviet power. Along with this the United States might take a more offensive strategic posture regarding any possible future hostilities with the Soviet Union. The current maritime strategy of the U.S. Navy is an example of such an offensive posture (Beatty, 1987).

Second, strategic equivalence may encourage the Soviets to challenge the United States more frequently in the "gray areas" (George, 1987) outside the central arenas of superpower conflict. This could take the form of direct involvement of Soviet diplomatic or military activities, or simply support for a third party hostile to U.S. interests. This would increase direct U.S.-USSR competition, and in turn it might increase the probability of a major superpower crisis developing from a regional conflict.

Third, strategic equivalence could increase the prospects that a severe crisis would produce a preemptive strike, that is, a first strike taken in the belief that the enemy was just about to attack. In a situation of substantial power disparity, it is questionable whether the interests of the weaker party would be served by preemption, especially if the other side had retaliatory capability, while the stronger party would likely have less need for a preemptive strategy. Preemption is more likely to occur between parties of equal power, because equality maximizes the uncertainty of outcome of any conflict between them.

The conclusion then is that changes have occurred in the nuclear balance since the 1970s which make a fresh examination of crisis management necessary. The current military balance between the United States and the Soviet Union constitutes a potentially more dangerous structure than that which existed for most of the Cold War. This could force adjustments in the way the superpowers conduct their rivalry in the future. At a minimum, it is likely to put increased demands on the crisis management capabilities of their governments.

This book explores four important areas of crisis management. The papers in the first section, "Theory and Practice," review the definition and principles of crisis management, and analyze the prospects for the loss of government control over policy in the context of international crisis. A second section on "Superpower Relations" analyzes the diplomatic groundrules, and lack thereof, in the U.S.-Soviet relationship, and examines one area of that relationship—namely, arms control negotiations—for its impact on superpower crisis management. The third section on "Nuclear Crisis Management" looks at the threat posed to crisis stability by current practices of the superpowers, and it proposes a range of policies that could improve the prospects for crisis management between these two countries. Finally the last section on "Crisis Management in Regional Contexts" examines the capacity of the superpowers to manage crises outside the North Atlantic context where their interests are most sharply engaged. For contrast, the section also analyzes several cases of crisis management and diplomacy outside the superpower rivalry.

Notes

1. In a footnote Diesing dissents from this statement, which underscores the controversial nature of this judgment.

PART ONE

Theory and Practice

2

Crisis Management: A Critical Appraisal

James L. Richardson

There is no longer any such thing as strategy, only crisis management.
—Robert McNamara, 1962

After twenty years of smooth crisis management, doubts are being raised as to the allegedly infinite capacity of modern diplomacy to cope with the increasing crises.
—Daniel Frei, 1982

The two decades following the Cuban missile crisis witnessed a high degree of optimism. Despite the turbulence in many regions of the world and the persistence of serious differences between the two nuclear super-powers, the feeling was that those powers had achieved a degree of mutual understanding and had come to accept norms of crisis management which were adequate to keep the ultimate dangers of the nuclear age at bay. This optimism has been rudely challenged in the 1980s by the peace movement, a challenge to which scholars in international relations have been slow to respond. But even if one does not adopt the perspective of the peace movement, an examination of contemporary ideas on crisis management suggests that the public confidence of the 1960s and 1970s rested on weak foundations.

This chapter[1] first examines the concept of crisis management that, like most political concepts, is used imprecisely and in different senses. The second section discusses the principles of crisis management advanced in the scholarly literature: this reveals a sufficient measure of consensus that one may reasonably speak of a contemporary doctrine of crisis management. The third section considers a number of criticisms of this doctrine, the fourth takes up certain issues which arise from the critique, and the final section attempts a balance sheet: to what extent has progress in understanding been achieved, to what extent are new approaches being explored, to what extent do the problems of crisis diplomacy nonetheless remain elusive?

The focus of the discussion is the academic writing on the subject. This has been greatly influenced by the ideas of policy-makers, especially American policy-makers in the Cuban missile crisis. The chapter does not seek to explore the extent to which this academic writing may in turn have influenced policy. It is unlikely to have done so directly, but in view of the multiple links between policy-makers and international relations scholars, especially in the United States, it is likely that it exercises some influence over the assumptions which enter into policy-making. That influence is in the direction of reinforcing, rather than questioning, the ideas which were first articulated at the time of the Cuban crisis.

The Concept

Whereas the concept of crisis has been extensively discussed in the literature, and the rival merits of highly general *versus* specific international relations definitions, or systemic *versus* decision-making definitions have been frequently debated, the concept of crisis *management*, and in particular the justification for the use of the term "management" has received little attention. In the present context it is not necessary to review the discussions of the concept of crisis (see e.g., Robinson, 1972: 20–27; Tanter, 1975: 73–77; Williams, 1976: 19–26; Eberwein, 1978: 126–133); a specific definition such as that adopted by Glenn Snyder and Paul Diesing adequately identifies the phenomenon with which the paper is concerned, without precluding the adoption of one or other of the theoretical frameworks with which many of the rival definitions are associated. Their definition is as follows:

> An international crisis is a sequence of interactions between the governments of two or more sovereign states in severe conflict, short of actual war, but involving the perception of a dangerously high probability of war. (1977: 6)

No author explicitly defends the introduction of the term "management." Daniel Frei is not alone in tacitly qualifying the term by juxtaposing it with the very different connotations of crisis "coping": Thomas Milburn had done so ten years earlier,[2] and the studies in the International Crisis Behavior Project, edited by Michael Brecher, use the term "coping," not "management" (Brecher with Geist, 1980; Shlaim, 1983; Dowty, 1984). Whereas the latter term would implicitly raise the question whether decision-makers can indeed cope with the pressures of crisis, the chosen term offers tacit assurance that they can not only cope but exercise control. Few discussions of crisis management have addressed the inappropriateness of the terminology: an exception is provided by Coral Bell, who notes that the overtones of the word "imply a rational, dispassionate, calculating, well considered activity, conducted with judgment and perhaps even at a leisurely pace" and observes that "actual crisis decision-making is not usually at all like that: it is improvised at great pressure of time and events by men working in a fog of ambiguity" (1978: 51). While it would be tempting to speculate on the reasons for the introduction and general acceptance of the term, such as the need for reassurance that the ultimate disaster will not take place, this would require too great a digression in an already lengthy analysis. Since it has become standard usage, however, I shall for the most part use the term "crisis management" in the first sections of the chapter, where frequent reference is made to existing discussions, but where appropriate will adopt the term "crisis diplomacy," which avoids the above connotations and is used in a broad sense to include decision-making as well as communication and bargaining.

Crisis management is often defined in terms of restraint, i.e., measures to reduce the risk of war in a crisis. For example, Hanspeter Neuhold refers to measures taken in order to isolate and mitigate crises: "a crisis can be regarded as managed if its intensity has so far been reduced that major armed hostilities can reasonably be ruled out" (1978: 4). While this is in accordance with the primary concern of avoiding nuclear war, it is open to the criticism that it isolates a single dimension of what is essentially a two dimensional problem. That is to say, the central feature of crisis diplomacy is that each of the parties seeks to pursue simultaneously two potentially competing goals, to prevail over the adversary or at least to avoid being the manifest loser, while at the same time avoiding war.

This central dilemma can be conceptualized in two ways. One is to emphasize the distinction between the two kinds of goal and the measures conducive to each, as George, Hall and Simons do by distinguishing between "crisis management"—all those measures directed towards restraint and limitation of conflict, against provocation and escalation—and "coercive diplomacy"—those measures directed towards inducing the adversary to accept one's essential goals (1971: 8–11, 18–19). Alternatively, as Snyder and Diesing propose, the term "crisis management" may be taken to refer to the whole of the process whereby the adversaries each seek to reconcile the competing goals (1977: 207). The differences among these authors raise no issue of substance but merely of convenience of terminology. The Snyder-Diesing terminology appears the more convenient in that while there is no problem in distinguishing between the two kinds of goals, the strategies and measures chosen by the parties may be directed towards both goals; crisis management and coercive diplomacy may be distinct ideal types, but actual decision-making and bargaining processes cannot readily be classified as one or the other, often including a mixture of both.[3] On the other hand, issues of substance are raised if an author proceeds on the basis of a one-dimensional concept of crisis management as restraint, neglecting the second dimension of the problem: the acuteness of the conflicts which precipitate crises and may render restraint (otherwise self-evidently desirable) so difficult to achieve.

A further matter of conceptual convenience is the distinction between crisis management and the more ambitious goals of crisis avoidance and conflict resolution. The study of crisis diplomacy may well lead to heightened awareness of the importance of these goals and a corresponding dissatisfaction with policy which fails to address them. However, it is no service to policy or research to blur distinctions between goals and processes which raise quite different problems. Crisis avoidance raises a wide range of issues concerning international order and procedures as well as knowledge of specific conflicts, which extend far beyond the problems of crisis management, even though there is some overlap (see e.g. George, 1983). Crisis signifies *inter alia* some kind of breakdown and poses dilemmas which need to be resolved if the game is to continue into a new phase in which opportunities for conflict resolution and the avoidance of future crises can be realised. It may be that crisis diplomacy can be conducted in ways that open up rather than foreclose such opportunities—a neglected aspect of crisis management taken up below—but the primary task in crises is to survive.[4]

A more difficult conceptual problem for the definition of crisis management is raised by the diversity of goals that governments actually pursue. Not all decision-makers are committed to the goal of avoiding war. Among great power leaders of this century Hitler provides the extreme example, but international relations have often shown the characteristics which Ali Dessouki notes in relation to the third world at the present time:

> Crisis management research should not assume that crisis avoidance or deescalation is necessarily a desirable goal of all participants . . . crises can be and are planned, engineered and steered by some states to achieve their national interests . . . crisis management does not necessarily mean the avoidance of the use of force . . . It follows that managing a crisis does not always mean deescalating it . . . The concept of "management"

refers to a way of handling or success in accomplishing one's objectives. (1982: 87–88)

Should crisis management be understood restrictively, limited to those cases where adversaries recognize an imperative to avoid war even while engaging in brinkmanship, or should it be extended to include the full range of goals and priorities? Neither option is entirely satisfactory. If the broader definition were adopted, crisis management coming to mean success in achieving an actor's goals in a crisis, irrespective of what they are, Hitler for example would be one of its most successful exponents. This usage departs so radically from the nuclear-age preoccupations which lay behind the introduction of the term that it must surely be rejected. Yet Dessouki's comments serve to underline the point that crisis management in the narrower sense is by no means typical of all crisis behavior. It does not apply in the case of actors who envisage war as a means to the achievement of their goals, or even in the case of many of the actions of the superpowers, since the imperative of restraint applies only to their mutual relationship. The realm of coercive diplomacy is far more extensive than the realm of crisis management. The latter is not restricted to the relations of the nuclear powers, but it is restricted to crises in which the adversaries place a high value on avoiding war.

Principles

Discussions of crisis management reveal a high degree of consensus on principles that were first articulated at the time of the Cuban missile crisis. This is not to claim that they originated then: some have been traced back to earlier cold war crises, and some were developed by strategic theorists in the years preceding the Cuban crisis. It has been suggested by some scholars that they may be regarded as conventions that have come to be accepted by the superpowers to assist them in exercising restraint (Bell, 1971, 1978; Williams, 1976). Nonetheless, the Cuban crisis served as a catalyst for the emergence of a doctrine of crisis management, some of the elements of which had been "in the air" for some time, that has been refined but not substantially modified since then. A number of "revisionist" analyses have questioned whether American policy in the Cuban crisis was in reality shaped in accordance with these principles. The present paper does not address this issue; irrespective of whether they influenced policy or were largely ratio-nalization, it was these claims which dominated the contemporary view of the crisis and the generalizations deriving from it.

The following analysis is not exhaustive, but is based on the most systematic discussions of crisis management in the academic literature:

in addition to Bell and Williams cited above, Holsti, 1972a; Milburn, 1972; Neuhold, 1978; Chang, 1982. In view of substantial overlap, the study on coercive diplomacy by George, Hall and Simons (1971) is also included, and the discussion incorporates an earlier analysis by the present author (1979). Seven agreed principles of crisis management are identified; significant differences emerge with respect to two issues outside what might be termed the core of the crisis management doctrine.[5] The extent of the agreement among these authors is noteworthy and surely reflects an unusual degree of consensus in the (western) scholarly and policy-making communities. The agreed principles are as follows:

The Decision-Making Process: Multiple Advocacy

I believe our deliberations proved conclusively how important it is that the President have the recommendations and opinions of more than one individual, of more than one department, and of more than one point of view. Opinion, even fact itself, can best be judged by conflict, by debate. There is an important element missing when there is unanimity of viewpoint.
—Robert Kennedy, 1969a: 109

Whether the Executive Committee of the National Security Council which advised the President during the Cuban crisis deserves its reputation for encouraging vigorous expression of different viewpoints has come to be questioned. However, the desirability of a decision-making process that is structured to promote the serious canvassing of alternatives has been widely endorsed in discussions of foreign policy-making in general, not only with respect to crisis management (see e.g. George, 1972). Questions have been raised about the feasibility of this procedure when a crisis erupts suddenly without warning, or its compatibility with the styles of some decision-makers, but its desirability is endorsed on a number of grounds. It is considered essential if the rigidities and simplifications which are part of normal cognitive processes and organizational behavior are to be corrected, and even more so as a check on the more pathological cognitive processes characteristic of high levels of stress. As an extension of this principle it is agreed that decision-makers should not rely on any one single source of information but should draw on as many varied channels as time and resources permit.

The Implementation of Policy: Close Political Control

The President was also determined to manage the crisis himself—and he did so, in all its exquisite detail. There was not going to be any possibility for someone down the line to push events any faster or further than he judged necessary. It was the President who decided what ships would be stopped and when, how the announcements would be made, what would be said publicly and privately.

—Hilsman, 1967: 213

Already before the Cuban crisis the discussion of strategy in the nuclear age had led to wide acceptance of the principle that in view of the momentous consequences that would follow from any military move in a nuclear crisis, the responsible political leadership should exercise much closer control over military operations than had been normal in the past. The need to ensure that military operations serve well-defined political goals is a major theme in contemporary strategic studies. Further, it is generally accepted that contingency plans should not be allowed to dictate responses in a crisis, but should be regarded as subject to revision in the light of circumstances. Acceptance of these principles does not prevent sharp conflict between political and military leaders in specific cases, such as the celebrated clash between Defence Secretary McNamara and the Chief of Naval Operations, Admiral Anderson, in the Cuban crisis. More generally, the precise division of responsibilities between the political and military leadership remains inevitably an issue in any political system, subject to subtle rethinking with each change of personalities. The general principle however remains unchallenged in its own terms and may be taken as presupposed or tacitly endorsed by those authors who do not explicitly advance it.[6]

The Limitation of Objectives

Defining a clear and limited objective, he moved with mathematical precision to accomplish it.

—Schlesinger, 1965: 715

Kennedy's limitation of his objective to the withdrawal of the missiles, ruling out, for example, the potential goal of overthrowing the Castro regime, was often contrasted at the time with Britain's failure to define a clear-cut and limited objective in the Suez crisis. A well-defined, restricted objective can serve as a basis for a settlement in a way that diffuse, opportunistic objectives cannot. In the superpower context the logic of limiting crisis objectives in order to avoid challenging interests vital to the adversary has been regarded as compelling. Chang argues that one way in which this may be done is by defining issues in terms of conflicts of interest rather than of principle (1982: 203, 207) and endorses the concept of the "fractionating" of conflicts. Milburn warns *inter alia* against the temptation to increase one's demands in response to perceived successes or concessions by an adversary (1972: 276).

Maintaining Flexible Options

> McNamara helped the Attorney-General mightily with his now-celebrated argument on "maintaining the options." . . . Let blockade be the first option, the contraband list limited at the start to offensive weapons. If that failed, the President would then have a choice of responses. He could decide to deny the Cubans other kinds of cargo, petroleum for example, or he could move up the scale to an air strike, even, at the far end, to invasion. If one form of pressure failed in its purpose, then another, more severe pressure could be applied. . . . . The clinching argument in favor of the blockage was that it could be applied without losing the option to launch an air strike later. If, however, the air strike was to be the first step, other options would be closed.
>
> —Abel, 1966b: 78

A major theme in contemporary strategic studies, the principle of flexible or graduated response is included in all eight discussions of crisis management. The crucial argument for the blockade in preference to the air strike was that it left both sides with a range of options, whereas the air strike would have posed a stark choice between a humiliating defeat or a hazardous escalation. Kennedy, like many commentators, had in mind the situation of July, 1914, when rigid mobilization plans had denied such a range of options to the decision-makers. Contemporary discussion reveals a number of variations regarding this principle. In some cases it is the military aspect—local, proportionate or graduated response—which is emphasized. Others stress the political principle of maintaining freedom of action, which applies equally to non-military measures such as those taken by both sides in the case of the Berlin blockade, and comment with approval on the tendency of decision-makers to act on this principle in nuclear-age crises (Young, 1968: 217–243; Williams, 1976: 119–134).[7]

Time Pressure

> 'If we had had to act on Wednesday in the first twenty-four hours,' the President said later, 'I don't think probably we would have chosen as prudently as we finally did.'
>
> —Schlesinger, 1965: 686

> Against the advice of many of his advisers and of the military, he decided to give Khrushchev more time. 'We don't want to push him to a precipitous action—give him time to consider . . . '
>
> —Robert Kennedy, 1969a: 71

The goal of maintaining freedom of choice can be negated not only by actions that preclude a range of options but also by time pressure such that one or another party is unable to examine its options, either because of absolute time contraints or because the heightened stress imposed by time pressure tends to reduce the awareness of options. The contrast between the effects of stress in July, 1914 and the attempt to reduce time pressure in the Cuban crisis has been extensively noted (e.g. Holsti, 1972b), and although the principle of reducing acute time pressure is less prominent than some of the others in the analyses of crisis management, its importance for the practice of crisis diplomacy is sufficient justification for its inclusion.

Perception of the Adversary

> During the crisis President Kennedy spent more time trying to determine the effect of a particular course of action on Khrushchev or the Russians than on any other phase of what he was doing. What guided all his deliberations was an effort not to disgrace Khrushchev, not to humiliate the Soviet Union, not to have them feel they would have to escalate their response. . . .
> —Robert Kennedy, 1969a: 122

Two different principles are involved under this heading. The first and more important is that in order to avoid lapsing into stereotypes, crisis decision-makers should make every effort to see the situation through the eyes of the adversary. This may well be the most difficult of the principles to implement; while there is no fundamental difficulty in decision-makers' considering how they would act if *they* were in their opponents' situation, the problem is that of achieving what Holsti has termed "sensitivity to the adversary's frame of reference" (1972a: 222), which, as he observes, is "a skill in short supply." In the Cuban instance, great weight was placed on the advice of an experienced former ambassador to Moscow, Llewellyn Thomson, but this technique presupposes that the ambassador is one of those with the rare skill in question. There are many examples to the contrary.

The second principle is more limited but unfortunately more emphasized in the discussion of crisis management, *viz.* that the adversary should be offered a face-saving line of retreat, or as Bell expresses it, "golden bridges" should be built to facilitate his withdrawal (1978: 540). This encourages policy-makers to see themselves as potential victors, but in many cases there is no victor, and cases where each side perceives itself as the victor magnanimously offering to save the other's face are rare. The more difficult skill is to minimize one's losses, having recognized in advance that there will be losses. Moreover, face-saving presupposes the first principle: without some awareness of the adversary's frame of reference one may misjudge what will prove face-saving, or how it should be appropriately offered.

Communication

> Always he asked himself: Can we be sure that Khrushchev understands what we feel to be our vital national interest? . . . President Kennedy dedicated himself to making it clear to Khrushchev by word and deed— for both are important—that the United States had limited objectives and that we had no interest in accomplishing these objectives by adversely affecting the national security of the Soviet Union or by humiliating her.
> —Robert Kennedy, 1969a: 123

Problems relating to communication in crises are among those most extensively studied, both before and after 1962 (see, e.g., Schelling, 1961: 53–80, 119–161). Perhaps the lesson most frequently drawn from the crisis was the need to maintain lines of communication with the adversary, above all at moments of greatest tension; although communication was relatively close, compared with many earlier crises, policy-makers on both sides perceived a need for a more direct channel. Hence the agreement on the "hot line" some months later. Almost as prominent in the literature, though less salient to decision-makers, is the danger of communication overload and the ensuing difficulty of distinguishing the important signals from the mass of background "noise." General remedies for this are not easily arrived at, but one practical recourse is that important communications should be clear and precise, reiterated if necessary and supported by accompanying signals and actions, not inadvertently undermined by them (Holsti, 1972a: 224–225; Chang, 1982: 201–203). This is also relevant to certain other problems of communication, such as the tendency on the part of recipients of messages to misperceive the intentions behind them and more generally to perceive, or misperceive, new information in terms of their expectations (Jervis, 1976), but there is no general corrective to the distorting effects of such general psychological propensities.

Two further topics are addressed in most of the analyses without giving rise to agreed principles. The first is the tension noted earlier between the two goals of crisis diplomacy, avoiding defeat and avoiding war, and thus between coercive diplomacy and restraint. This tension is discussed by several of the authors and is a central theme in George, Hall and Simons and in Snyder and Diesing's (1977) study of crisis bargaining, where it is discussed as a series of dilemmas not admitting any general solution. Reflecting the conceptual divergence noted earlier, some of the authors place the emphasis heavily on the dimension of restraint, but only in Chang does this reach the point that the competing imperative is scarcely acknowledged.

The second topic concerns the role of allies and third parties, and here there is a clear divergence among the authors. At one pole, Chang urges the desirability of third-party intervention and mediation and Neuhold more cautiously advocates the desirability of a broad base of international support (Chang, 1982: 203–204; Neuhold, 1978: 11–13). At the other pole, Bell, although noting some exceptions, endorses the general practice whereby "the powers will not allow their signals to become infected with excess or misleading ambiguities through consultation with allies" (1982: 261) and Holsti draws attention to dangers rather than advantages of commitments to allies in crises (1972a: 217–221).

A number of further principles of crisis management are advanced by individual authors. Some of these are noted here in order to show that thinking on crisis management is not exhausted by the consensus doctrine outlined above. Some are relatively uncontroversial while others point towards problems neglected by the orthodox doctrine.

For example, Bell sees the tacit acceptance of each superpower's sphere of influence as one of the earliest conventions of the cold war period but notes that Soviet policy in the Caribbean raises questions for its continued observance. Perhaps as an extension of this basic convention, the superpowers do not interrupt one another's delivery of arms and supplies to client states (1978: 55–56). Williams, similarly seeking to identify patterns of restraint observed by the superpowers, notes their avoidance of the more dangerous tactics open to them, in particular their refraining from overt acts of violence against one another, and argues that the power with less at stake has been and should be prepared in the last analysis to concede the issue in dispute to the power with more at stake (1976: 101–113; 153–164; 173–182). Neuhold argues for greater attention to the precedents created in crises and is almost alone among the analysts of crisis management in arguing for the significance of international law in this context (1978: 13–15).[8] Milburn offers a wealth of specific proposals or "decision rules," most of which represent operational applications of the principles discussed above, but some of which break new ground: for example, that policy should discriminate among different types of crisis, that decision-makers should deal with only one crisis at a time and that they should look beyond the immediate present, consciously avoiding the contraction of time perspective which has been shown to be one of the effects of stress (1972: 272, 274).

Critiques

Four themes are prominent in the critical discussion of the crisis management doctrine: i) its neglect of the prior question, i.e., which crises are manageable?; ii) the over-generalized and over-simplified character of its recommendations; iii) its neglect of all but extremely short term considerations; and iv) its neglect of fundamental political and psychological constraints. Such criticisms are advanced *inter alia* by Schroeder (1974), Groom (1978), Lebow (1981) and many of them are drawn together by Gilbert and Lauren (1980).

Which Crises Are Manageable?

At the outset, some critics argue that the conceptual difficulties of the term "crisis management" were understated in the earlier discussion. Gilbert and Lauren refer to the British and French leaders before 1939: "Unlike their 1914 counterparts, they managed to avoid war and to defuse the various crises that threatened Europe during this period" (1980: 648). If the appeasers are not regarded as successful crisis managers, the reason must lie in the rejection by subsequent commentators of their values or their definition of the situation. However, this raises difficulties for the conventional usage according to which a successfully managed crisis is one in which war is avoided at an acceptable cost. The cost was acceptable to the relevant decision-makers and to majority opinion in both countries at the time.

In accordance with this usage, a crisis is unmanageable—war cannot be avoided—if one party sees advantage in fighting or if two or more adversaries are prepared to fight over the issue in dispute and the situation admits no compromise. Or a situation may be beyond control for less readily definable reasons: "If a man with a record of near-fatal accidents starts a car with worn-out brakes and faulty steering down a steep mountain road, the fact that he does not want to crash and believes that he can somehow steer his way through does not entitle us to attribute the resulting crash to his mishandling the car en route" (Schroeder, 1974: 538).

Decision-makers cannot know whether a crisis is manageable, or with what degree of difficulty, though they may perceive a situation with greater certainty than is warranted by the available evidence, and this in turn may affect the manageability of the crisis, usually adversely. Even with hindsight and with full documentation, historians' interpretations of some of the major crises, such as the origins of the Crimean war or July 1914, differ over the unravelling of complex causal links to an extent that there is no agreement on how manageable they were (cf. Gilbert and Lauren, 1980: 649–651).

It follows that the criterion suggested earlier, whereby the term "crisis management" should be restricted to cases where the adversaries place a high value on avoiding war, is necessary but not sufficient for the meaningful use of the concept, but the sufficient conditions for crisis manageability are not yet understood. Gilbert and Lauren's suggestion that the adversaries must be resolved to avoid war at all cost will not do: in such cases there would be no problem. In the Crimean crisis, most of the decision-makers placed a high value on avoiding war, but a few became persuaded that it was inevitable and did little to resist the momentum of events towards war. In such cases perceptions of inevitability enter the causation of war, but precisely in what ways remains unclear. They may be related to the overall context: the condition of the road, the slope, the car, the brakes and so forth—or to the perceived intentions of specific actors. It may be concluded that there are some contexts—which may be defined in "structural" terms or as immediate conflicts over values—in which crisis management, however sound its principles, cannot achieve success and that in others the margin for error, or bad luck, is perilously slight.

Over-Generalized and Over-Simplified

The harshest comment on crisis management is that its prescriptions are "about as useful as general advice to hospital emergency room personnel—keep calm, have equipment ready, make no premature diagnoses" (Schroeder, 1974: 539). The problem, however, is that they are not banal truisms but are specific enough to be dangerous if regarded as general rules to be applied universally, as the principle of graduated response appears to have been in the case of some U.S. policy-makers in the Vietnam war. Gilbert and Lauren characterize them as "epigrammatic homilies" and note that such homilies are useful only if one can recognize by other means the circumstances in which they are or are not applicable (1980: 658). Williams sees the principles of crisis management as "little more than an elaboration of some of the basic canons of statecraft" (1976: 200). Traditional rules of statecraft, like everyday maxims and homilies, are useful only if applied with discrimination and judgment. They are stronger in the negative form, in that it is dangerous to neglect the rule, but offer no positive assurance that observing the rule will bring success. The danger is that the connotations of "crisis management" may encourage over-confidence in the general validity of its rules and thus their indiscriminate application.

The rules of crisis management resemble the maxims of everyday life in that at times it may be the opposite rule that is appropriate to the circumstances. The tension between the goals of restraint and the achievement of vital interests was noted earlier, a tension which can appear in complex and paradoxical forms in the tactical choices that confront decision-makers. Reducing time pressure is often appropriate, but it may be necessary to increase time pressure in order to prevent a slow but dangerous deterioration; a well-judged coercive move may offer the best or only way of terminating a crisis or avoiding a loss of control over escalatory pressures. There is considerable literature on the conditions under which threats may be effective and on their adverse side-effects, which perhaps fortunately has not been boiled down into a rule of crisis management.

The other principles require similar qualification. The limitation of objectives, for example, represents only one dimension of a complex issue. A limited goal needs to be defined shrewdly in relation to one's own and the adversary's larger interests. If pursued unconditionally it may introduce rigidities and unwanted side-effects. It is apparent that the capacity to *reformulate* objectives may be crucial, but this in turn is subject to a variety of constraints: objectives which are perceived as tentative, on the one hand, or as open-ended, on the other, may introduce new problems. The formulation of objectives reflects a series of dilemmas no less (though less studied) than the choice of strategies and tactics. To take a further example, comprehending the adversary's frame of reference, although an unexceptionable principle, is frequently perceived in the heat of conflict as being excessively soft, or appeasing or accepting the adversary's demands. The psychological resistance to the practical acceptance of this principle warrants further study.

The close link between the rules of crisis management and contemporary American strategic thought was noted in a number of cases, suggesting two problems with the body of rules as a whole. The first is whether the other superpower, the Soviet Union, subscribes to similar principles, especially in the light of the hostile stance of Soviet commentators towards American strategic doctrine. There is no question that Soviet policy in major crises has shown appropriate caution with respect to dangerous options, but it is likely that the rationale for Soviet crisis diplomacy is related to Soviet strategic thought and if drawn together as an "operational code," might show quite different emphases from American thinking on crisis management, as recent studies imply (Adomeit, 1982; Hart, 1984).

The second problem, if the principles of crisis management are viewed as a body of general maxims distilled from a particular phase of historical experience, is that in reflecting salient issues of a particular time and place they may neglect issues that are central in other times and places. The Cuban crisis, as has been recently argued, was atypical in important respects:

> . . . we should ask whether the crisis itself can and should serve as an appropriate model either for those studying policy or for those conducting it. We must, in short, ask ourselves whether the uniqueness of the crisis

does not destroy its value as an archetype, or worse, make it a profoundly misleading subject for reflection. (Cohen, 1986: 5)

The problems confronting Neville Chamberlain, for example, were in a sense prior to the kinds of choices to which the contemporary rules of crisis management are addressed: they included basic choices over values (what issue would justify going to war) and dilemmas over means (how if at all could Germany be induced to limit its objectives?). Even in the case of a major contemporary crisis such as that over Berlin (1958–62), the rules of crisis management are of only very limited relevance to the problems confronting decision-makers.

The conclusion is not that the principles of crisis management are of no value. As hard-won lessons of experience they are indeed of some value, especially in their negative form, but only if their limitations are acknowledged.

Too Short-Term a Perspective?

A further limitation of crisis management doctrine is its preoccupation with the short term, the immediate outcome, the securing of one's limited but essential objectives without recourse to war. Although it was argued earlier that crisis management should be distinguished conceptually from conflict resolution, and that in a crisis survival goals should come first, survival may reasonably be extended beyond surviving the immediate crisis to include improving the chances of survival after the crisis—or at least not reducing them. The case against the 1930s appeasers is that they unwittingly neglected this, and it is often suggested that although the crises preceding World War One were resolved peacefully, they tended to exacerbate the tensions between the powers and thus increased the subsequent probability of war. Bell's concept of the "crisis slide" refers to cases where successive crises, like boulders rolling down a mountainside, "not only come thick and fast, but seem, as it were, to repercuss off each other until the whole mountainside, or the whole society of states, begins to crumble," and decision-makers come to "see the options available to them steadily closing down to the single option of war or unlimited defeat"(1971: 14–15).

This topic requires far more investigation than it has received. In particular, it raises questions of the relationship between systemic determinants of crisis slides and determinants at the level of policy choices and crisis outcomes. John Groom, adopting a systemic perspective, offers some preliminary suggestions on "counter-crisis strategies" (1978: 112–115), still at some distance from operational policy options. Richard Ned Lebow compares the outcomes of several pre-1914 crises that exacerbated hostilities with two cases that opened the way towards improved relationships between the protagonists, Fashoda (1898) and Cuba (1962), identifying a number of factors relevant to the differing outcomes: the choices among coercive bargaining tactics, the initiator's apparent willingness to accept war, the extent of post-crisis military preparations, the impact on domestic politics, the re-evaluation of foreign policy assumptions, the settlement of related issues, and the promotion of empathy or trust (1981: 315–317, 326–333). Such a disaggregated analysis, based on induction from a small set of cases, offers a promising first step towards identifying *desiderata* and pitfalls, but no more than that.

It is clear that the criteria for successful crisis diplomacy need to be expanded to include a positive impact on the overall movement of relationships but that there has been very little systematic examination of this dimension of the topic in the existing literature.

Psychological and Political Constraints

The fourth line of criticism is that the doctrine of crisis management suffers from a fundamental lack of realism in its neglect of the constraints which may render it unlikely or even impossible for decision-makers to act in accordance with its recommendations. These may be of three kinds, and may combine and reinforce one another. First, many decision-makers may lack the unusual intellectual and imaginative capacities, and the soundness of judgment, to achieve the level of performance that is required (Gilbert and Lauren, 1980: 655–656). Second, the pressures of acute crisis may impair the level of performance even of decision-makers who in other contexts show outstanding qualities of leadership: they may be subject to cognitive weaknesses that render them irrationally resistant to unpalatable information, insensitive to the available options and lacking in realism in appraising the adversary. Third, these cognitive weaknesses appear most intractable when the crisis coincides with acute domestic political pressures or, for other reasons, the decision-maker's political position is precarious. In such situations unshakable commitment to a chosen course of action can become fatally attractive: because achievement of the goal is necessary, it must be possible. Lebow, reviewing the findings of several case-studies, concludes that "learning during a crisis is likely to be hindered by the same impediments that caused the initiator to misjudge his adversary's resolve in the first place," and that "those policy-makers with the greatest need to learn from external reality appear the least likely to do so" (1981; 272–273).

Decision-makers in this frame of mind are unlikely to be capable of acting in terms of the principles of crisis management. They will resist any advice that challenges the assumptions on which policy is based; they will be blind to evidence that the objective to which they are committed is unacceptable to the adversary. There will be no awareness of the adversary's frame of reference: communication will have broken down. Thus, it follows that there are crises that in principle are open to management (i.e. the parties are strongly averse to war and their basic interests are not irreconcilable *ab initio*) but in which crisis management fails because of psychological and political pressures that lead decision-makers to become committed to incompatible courses of action, and unable to correct their misperceptions or reconsider their goals in the way that crisis management would require. Lebow makes a very convincing interpretation of certain of his cases along these lines, especially the Sino-Indian crisis of 1962 and the U.S. miscalculation of China's intervention in Korea in 1950. His pessimistic analysis offers a salutory corrective to the optimistic assumptions underlying the crisis management doctrine.

On the other hand, Snyder and Diesing's case studies show that there have been a wide variety of circumstances in the twentieth century in which the bargaining process during crises has enabled decision-makers to correct their misperceptions or reformulate their immediate goals in order to avoid becoming locked into a collision course (1977: 323–339; 389–398). The presence of even a few counter-examples, however, is sufficient to show that there can be cases in which decision-makers are unable to act with this kind of flexibility. An awareness that crises can prove unmanageable for these kinds of reasons should heighten interest in the question of crisis avoidance and the establishment of relationships less crisis-prone than has been the experience of the nuclear powers up to the present.

Assessment

Before attempting a final balance sheet of crisis management, an additional two inter-related issues need to be addressed: the weakness of the theoretical foundations of the crisis management doctrine and the question of what conditions are conducive to successful crisis diplomacy.

The doctrine of crisis management exemplifies George and Smoke's suggestion that policy-oriented theories in international relations tend to consist of "free-floating generalizations and isolated insights" (1974: 620). The basis for these generalizations, as they are usually presented, appears to be the author's reading of recent historical experience, even though for certain of the authors they also reflect one or another of the contemporary theories relating to crisis behavior or international conflict.

These theories, however—most prominently, theories of bargaining and theories of cognitive psychology and the effects of stress—have been developed at a relatively high level of generality and thus principles derived from them are likely to be too generalized to be of very much direct relevance to policy-making. George and Smoke indeed argue that the goal of policy-oriented theory, as distinct from empirical theory which strives for hypotheses of the widest scope and generality, should be to formulate contingent or differentiated generalizations (1974: 616–642). This suggests that the existing body of theory is unlikely to provide rationales for the kinds of distinctions which, it was argued above, are required if the rules of crisis management are to overcome the excessive generality which afflicts them in their present form.

Snyder and Diesing (1977) offer an example of such differentiated theory in their analysis of the way in which different structures of the international system and value structures of the actors give rise to different bargaining situations that may in turn be approached through differing styles of information-processing and decision-making. They do not formulate a systematic account of the policy implications of their analysis; whether this is because they do not consider it possible to make any general normative suggestions, or because of the complexity of those which appear to follow from their analysis, is not clear. It would appear however, if such implications were sought, that they would tend to reinforce some of the above principles of crisis management, such as multiple advocacy, political control, and perception of the adversary, and would tend to qualify others such as flexible options and time pressure.

More fundamental than the gap between general empirical theory and applied, differentiated theory is the persistence of unresolved differences over which theories should provide the basis for policy thinking. One problem is the link between different levels of analysis, in particular between the systemic and decision-making levels, which is only infrequently addressed. Even more serious are the fundamental differences among theories at the latter level, between those which focus on rational choice and bargaining and those which focus on non-rational cognitive psychology and stress. It is not helpful to suggest, as Raymond Tanter does (1975: 87) that the latter are empirical, the former normative: there have been extensive empirical studies of crisis bargaining (Young, 1968, as well as Snyder and Diesing, 1977) and even if this were not the case it would be a major theoretical problem to link an empirical theory framed in terms of one set of concepts with a normative theory framed in terms of quite different concepts. This problem is present in the work of most of those who have analysed crisis behavior in terms of cognitive psychology and stress: their normative recommendations are directed to the achievement of a standard of rationality that they take to be atypical of actual decision-making. While this is not logically excluded, it is nonetheless surprising and calls for a clear account of the link between the two dimensions of the analysis, a reconciliation of the apparent paradox. This is not offered: the policy recommendations remain "weakly linked to the theoretical analyses that purportedly fathered them" (Kinder and Weiss, 1978: 728; see also Lebow, 1981: 296, 298).

When theory and policy analysis are so tenuously linked, it is not surprising that there has been little systematic discussion of the issue, noted above, of constraints which may impede the successful conduct of crisis diplomacy, or more positively, conditions which may be conducive to its success. Success, in the light of the foregoing discussion, should be understood to include not only the avoidance of war but also the achievement of an outcome which reduces tensions or at least does not increase subsequent pressures for war, which implies that it enjoys a degree of acceptance amounting to legitimacy on the part of the most important of the parties affected.

Lebow, who takes the first principle of crisis management— an "open" decision-making process permitting the genuine consideration of different views—as fundamental, suggests that the preconditions for such decision-making are the existence of a legitimate authority, consensus within the policy-making elite with respect to fundamental political values, and a degree of insulation from domestic political pressures (1981: 305). However, while it is clear that the absence of any of these will reduce the chances of effective crisis diplomacy, they do not appear to represent absolute prerequisites. For example, it is arguable that the second and third conditions were not present during the Nixon Administration, or at least not fully present, yet it is not clear that its approach to crises was less effective than that of other recent U.S. administrations. Moreover, these conditions are often matters of degree, and they are limited to the national decision-making level.

The range of considerations which may be conducive to successful crisis diplomacy in a variety of contexts, and of constraints which may militate against it, is likely to be unmanageably great if one proceeds inductively from an examination of cases. An alternative may be to proceed deductively to seek to identify absolute prerequisites, a procedure that is likely to be limited to the generation of ideal types imperfectly reproduced in actual situations. Thus, for example, at the level of the international system, the conflicts among the major actors must not be so acute and so immediate as to permit no resolution short of war; at the national level, the relevant governments must place a high value on avoiding war, and at the individual level, decision-makers must have the capacity to devise policies which support such a value structure.

Beyond this, it may be that the more specific conditions sometimes referred to such as Lebow's should be regarded as conducive to successful crisis diplomacy but not absolute prerequisites. For example, the existence of a "legitimate" international order, accepted as such by the principal actors, such as occurred during the Concert of Europe, promotes the acceptance of norms and procedures which reduce the incidence of major crises and assist in their peaceful regulation when they prove unavoidable. But the example of the Cold War shows that crises can be coped with in the absence of such agreement on legitimacy. Some authors have argued that despite the lack of agreement at the ideological level, in practice the superpowers have come to accept a number of conventions, tacitly agreed procedures which assist them in exercising restraint in crises (Bell, 1971; Williams, 1976). It is beyond the scope of this paper to examine the soundness of this important interpretation of the super-power relationship.[9] In the present context the point is that while the acceptance of such conventions would be a major step towards successful crisis diplomacy, it would not be a *necessary* prerequisite—nor of course would it be sufficient. Its evident importance serves to underline the need to include considerations at the system level as well as the national level in any account of conditions favorable and unfavorable to crisis diplomacy.

Conclusions

A Balance Sheet

Whether a particular crisis is manageable cannot be known to decision-makers and is partially dependent on their own actions. The outcome of many crises proves that they were manageable, but in the case of some of those which led to war there is room for continuing disagreement over the extent to which this was due to "mismanagement." While it is meaningful conceptually to regard crises as occuring along a spectrum of degrees of manageability, the position of a particular crisis on the spectrum cannot be established with certainty even with hindsight, and never at the time.

While certain very general prerequisites for successful crisis diplomacy can be identified, these are seldom totally present or totally absent in the states in question and in the international system as a whole; instead, they are present in some degree. At a more concrete level of analysis the range of considerations which render crises less or more manageable is only partially understood. Certain conditions have been identified, through a combination of theoretical analysis and historical case studies, which generate strong pressures towards war in situations where the basic value structures of the actors, considered in isolation, appear to point towards a different outcome. Such cases and their implications are of particular concern to the study of crisis diplomacy.

The formulation of rules for crisis management is likely to be counterproductive if these are understood as general precepts to be followed indiscriminately, and the terminology of crisis management is itself counterproductive in view of its overtones of controllability, predictability and high confidence in success. The discussion of rules for crisis diplomacy can be fruitful only if these are understood to be conditional, relevant in some circumstances but not in others, and if this discussion is part of a wider discussion of the dilemmas of crisis diplomacy. As such, it can make a positive contribution to the intellectual background for foreign policy-making, especially if it stimulates greater interest in the avoidance of crises. The principles of crisis management discussed earlier may be regarded as a sound starting point for such discussion, especially in their negative form, but no more than that.

One important area of policy omitted from the contemporary doctrine of crisis management is the effect of crisis outcomes on future relationships. In different historical contexts, the pressures that may induce a "crisis slide" will be open to influence by policy decisions in varying degrees, as yet little understood. Although it appears to be asking a great deal of policy-makers that they add another dimension to their already difficult balancing of goals in crises, it may well be that in practice it already enters into their thinking more than is recognized. This was surely the case in the Cuban crisis—it may be a case of examining a neglected strand in crisis decision-making rather than introducing a new element.

This is not to imply that the problems of diplomacy within crises are well understood. Brecher and Wilkenfeld, after citing many of the principal crisis studies, commented: "Together, these pioneering studies illuminated *some* aspects of *a small number* of international crises" (1982: 381, emphasis added). Continuing differences of interpretation of individual crises and major differences over the theoretical explanation of crisis phenomena demonstrate the tenuous state of existing knowledge. Crisis studies, which raise many of the central theoretical issues in international relations, are far from providing secure foundations for policy thinking on crisis diplomacy.

The Way Forward?

No rapid breakthrough is in sight. The concept of crisis management has been refined—where it has not been replaced altogether by concepts such as coping—in ways that suggest the need for more differentiated principles than those of the received doctrine, but a sound basis for these has not yet been identified. In this situation the theoretical eclecticism evident in recent policy-oriented studies, permitting insights from a range of different perspectives, is preferable to a rigid adherence to any single framework. Even so, a major advance in the understanding of crisis diplomacy is likely to require a strengthening of the theoretical foundations.

The present analysis has emphasized perennial politico-military considerations bearing on crisis diplomacy which remain relevant in changing strategic contexts. Much recent writing has had the opposite emphasis, as analysts seek to come to terms with changes in the global strategic context in the 1980s and beyond, and in particular with the implications for crisis decision-making of accelerating modifications and increasing complexity of military technology, coupled with ever shorter reaction times. These changes threaten to render crises unmanageable beyond a certain point in a confrontation. An overview of these emerging problems is provided by Hermann (1985); some of the problems stemming from command-and-control dilemmas in a nuclear crisis are explored by Steinbruner (1981–82) and in greater depth by Bracken (1983); questions raised by strategic alerts in the new environment are discussed by Sagan (1985); and the implications for "crisis stability" are generally acknowledged as a major issue in the burgeoning literature on President Reagan's strategic defense initiative (e.g. Glaser, 1984).

Proposals have been advanced in a number of areas for coping with these developments. Landi and colleagues (1984) emphasize improved communications links; new channels of communication, more regular use of existing channels and a variety of other measures including fuller briefings for the political leadership are proposed by Nye and Ury (1985); George (1984b) draws attention to the importance of rules of engagement in the context of a wide-ranging discussion of conflicts among diplomatic and military priorities; Schelling (1984) suggests ways of enhancing mutual confidence in the new strategic environment. George (1985b) and Zartman (1985b) develop new analyses of the negotiation process or diplomatic norms which may enhance the awareness of pre-crisis and crisis options.

The new tone of urgency in the strategic analyses of the mid-1980s, reminiscent of the writings a quarter-century ago, may be seen as a response to similar conditions: the emergence of potential destabilizing elements in the strategic environment and the *laissez-faire* attitude of governments towards developments in military technology. Identifying the new dangers and devising means to cope with them are urgent tasks, but it is also important that the weaknesses of the traditional doctrine of crisis management not be lost from view. If they are, habits of thinking may be perpetuated which may compound the dangers of the future strategic environment.

Notes

1. This paper was originally presented at the XIIIth World Congress of the International Political Science Association.

2. "Crises and their management or mismanagement are omnipresent in human society. . . . The need for ability to cope with crises may be most unmistakable, however, when they involve nations and may precipitate international war" (1972: 259).

3. More recently George appears to have adopted the latter terminology. Discussing the conflicting goals of crisis management—"to do what may be necessary to protect one's most important interests but, at the same time, to avoid actions that may result in undesired costs and risks"—he suggests that: "indeed, 'crisis management' can be usefully defined as embracing the task of resolving this policy dilemma" (1984: 224).

4. This is reflected in the title of Bell's most recent contribution, "Managing to Survive" (1986).

5. Principles (i) (ii) (v) and (vi) are endorsed by five of the eight studies, principle (iii) by seven, and principles (iv) and (vii) by all eight.

6. A partial exception may be found in Hazlewood, Hayes and Brownell (1977: 100–102). Although the authors do not explicitly challenge the principle that the President should control the implementation of policy in crises, they note that the President was involved in decisions in 73% of the crises sampled, even though this was legally required in only 22% of the cases, and claim that "presidential decision-making and bureaucratic coordination slowed the response so much that military crisis management problems arose in a substantial number of cases." The consideration of the domestic or international political impact of actions proposed by the military is characterized as a form of constraint which produced crisis management delays (1977: 101).

7. The most prominent statement of an opposing view is that of Henry Kissinger: "In my view what seems 'balanced' and 'safe' in a crisis is often the most risky. Gradual escalation tempts the opponent to match every move; what is intended as a show of moderation may be interpreted as irresolution; reassurance may provide too predictable a checklist and hence an incentive for waiting, prolonging the conditions of inherent risk. A leader must choose carefully and thoughtfully the issues over which to face confrontation. He should do so only for major objectives. Once he is committed, however, his obligation is to end the confrontation rapidly. For this he must convey implacability. He must be prepared to escalate rapidly and brutally to a point where the opponent can no longer afford to experiment" (cited in Sagan, 1985: 124).

8. This comment does not imply that international lawyers have not concerned themselves with international crises, but points to the subordinate role ascribed to international law by contemporary students of international politics. A series of volumes on *International Crises and the Role of Law*, sponsored by the American

Society of International Law, was published between 1974 and 1978. Although the focus of these studies differs from that of the crisis management literature, there is considerable' overlap, especially in the case of the volume by Roger Fisher (1978), which anticipates some of the criticisms discussed in the following section.

9. Some reasons for questioning whether such conventions have been accepted may be noted. While there is much evidence in each major crisis of careful consideration of risks in relation to the specific circumstances, there is little direct evidence of awareness of conventions. There is some awareness of precedents, but convention implies more than precedent. There is even less indication that policy-makers pass on to their successors an awareness of specific rules or conventions, apart from a general commitment to prudence. Furthermore, the efficacy of even widely recognized conventions in restraining parties involved in acute conflict may be questioned: Australian politics provides some recent illustrations in which disputes over conventions may have exacerbated tension, and references to the "rules of the game" by American participants in the Cuban crisis, for example, referred to alleged violations by the adversary (intervening in the U.S. sphere of influence) but not to rules which might constrain U.S. actions.

3

Clausewitz, Loss of Control, and Crisis Management

Richard Ned Lebow

Loss of control is a principal theme of several recent studies of crisis management (Bracken, 1983; Lebow, 1987b). These studies stress the unforeseen and possibly disastrous consequences of strategic nuclear alerts. They make a strong case for the difficulty of controlling the complex and tightly coupled alert and warning systems of the superpowers. In doing so, they offer a much needed corrective to the strategic community's fixation on guaranteed retaliation, something that over the years has made the command and control problem more acute. At the same time, concern for command and control should not blind us to other causes and manifestations of loss of control that could prove just as destabilizing in crisis. This article[1] will explore three of these: civilian-military conflict, emotions, and political sabotage. It will analyze their mediating conditions, their implications for crisis management and what, if anything, could be done to minimize their disruptive effects.

Friction, Emotion, and Policy

A useful starting point for this analysis is the classic study of war by Carl von Clausewitz. The great Prussian strategist believed war to be dominated by two opposing tendencies. The first of these, friction, consists of all the organizational, logistical and human factors that limit the application of force or its rational direction. According to Clausewitz, friction was the primary cause of military failure. "Countless minor incidents," he wrote, "—the kind you can never really foresee—combine to lower the general level of performance, so that one always falls short of the intended goal." Friction could be to some degree overcome by "iron will-power" but only at the price of wearing down the military machine (Clausewitz, 1976: 119–21).

The abortive mission to rescue the American hostages in Iran gives vivid testimony to the decisive influence of friction on the outcome of contemporary military operations. The technical causes for the mission's failure can be traced to the cumulative effect of a number of oversights and bad judgments. Among these were the failure to equip the helicopters with sand screens to protect their hydraulic systems, the decision to load all of the spare parts for the hydraulic systems aboard one heli-copter—the one that had to turn back because of a sandstorm, the unexpected encounter with a bus full of pilgrims on the supposedly deserted Iranian airstrip, and the fatal collision of a helicopter with an airplane in the course of the force's withdrawal. These problems typify the kinds of "SNAFU's" that Clausewitz described under the rubric of friction (Joint Chiefs of Staff, 1980).

Friction is opposed by the "natural tendency" of war to seek its most extreme expression. War is a test of wills. Each side employs force to demonstrate its own resolve and to bend or break that of its adversary. Escalation by one side compels the other to follow suit. "A reciprocal action is begun," Clausewitz wrote, "which must lead, in theory, to extremes" (1976: 77). In crisis or war this can take the form of runaway escalation despite efforts by leaders on both sides to keep the conflict in check.

Clausewitz attributed runaway escalation to the interplay of institutions and emotions. Violence arouses the passions of leaders and public opinion alike. If, as often happens, elite and public judgment becomes captive to these emotions, the government can lose sight of the goals for which war was begun. A limited objective is then likely to become transformed into the more general one of defeating the enemy, whether or not this serves any political purpose. Political leaders who want to keep a war limited may be helpless in the face of mounting institutional and political pressures for a wider war.

World War I provides the best illustration of this process. Conceived as a limited war by Austria and Germany, it quickly became a European and then a world war. A military stalemate prolonged the conflict for four years despite the realization of many political leaders on all sides that a costly war of attrition was contrary to their individual or collective national interests. The tremendous loss of life and associated hardships on the home front compelled political leaders in every country to commit themselves publicly to war aims commensurate with these sacrifices. Far-reaching objectives of this kind prevented any negotiated settlement.

A primary objective of Clausewitz's study, lost upon most of his contemporaries, was to warn of the dangers of modern warfare. After

1815, most European statesmen and military men were convinced that the genie of modern war had been put back in the bottle and the stopper firmly inserted in its place with the exile of Napoleon to Elba, and finally to St. Helena. Clausewitz disagreed. Napoleon, in his view, had merely been the first leader to foresee the possibilities of modern warfare; he was not its cause. The "nation in arms" was an expression of European industrial, administrative and political development. It was a phenomenon that would not go away. Renewed attempts to wage war in Europe would, of necessity, require mass support and sacrifice. There was a real danger that they would become wars *à l'outrance* regardless of leaders' intentions to keep them limited.

Clausewitz's argument seems to stand in direct opposition to his frequently quoted assertion that "war is a continuation of political activity by other means" (1976: 87). Like many contemporary strategists he was contending that war had become increasingly impractical. The cost of general war was so great, he warned, that there were few, if any, political goals commensurate with it. Limited war, which he still thought feasible, nevertheless threatened to escalate into general war because of the difficulty of controlling it. Caution and restraint were the order of the day.

The seeming contradiction between Clausewitz's political message and his famous aphorism can be reconciled when we realize that Clausewitz couched his narrative in terms of the dialectic, a philosophical construct very much in vogue in Germany at the time. The dialectic was ideally suited to Clausewitz's intention of distinguishing between war in theory and war in practice. The "thesis," war in theory, described war as it ought to be waged. Its purpose was to achieve political objectives that were unattainable by diplomacy or other means. War accomplished this by bending or breaking the adversary's will to resist through the measured application of force. In this sense, war was an extension of politics by other means.

In the real world, Clausewitz recognized, the relationship between means and ends was not so straightforward. Friction and emotions intervened to retard or escalate a conflict. Because of this the means of war sometimes bore only the vaguest relationship to its ends. Administrative, financial, political, and human obstacles at times made it impossible for leaders to apply force in the degree or manner required to achieve their objectives. On other occasions, these same constraints conspired to push war toward its extremes, by far the greater danger according to Clausewitz. War in the real world was therefore imprecise, difficult to wage and to control, and above all else, unpredictable. This was Clausewitz's "antithesis."

In the dialectic, the synthesis resolves the tension between thesis and antithesis. For Clausewitz, the synthesis was the soldier-statesman who understood war in theory and from experience. As far as possible, he would resolve the contradictions between them. Failing that, he would at least be guided by the lessons of both perspectives instead of viewing war only through the prism of one of them. A soldier-statesman would never lose sight of the broader political objectives of war but his choice of objectives and the military means by which they were to be achieved would be shaped and tempered by an understanding of the problems, pitfalls, and uncertainties of war. In the nineteenth century, Bismarck most closely approached this Clausewitzian ideal. Not so his successors, or the other general staffs of Europe, whose narrow conception of strategy as a technical military problem was to a great extent responsible for the tragedy of World War I.

Clausewitz's message was lost on most of his contemporaries. This may have been due in part to the difficulty of piecing together a complex and layered argument from an unfinished manuscript. It was also the result of motivated bias. Throughout the nineteenth century, readers took from *On War* what they wanted to and glossed over its apparent contradictions, if they even noticed them. Military men especially, who were committed to warfare as a way of life, revered Clausewitz for his military lessons—e.g., his emphasis on boldness, surprise, concentration and economy of force and the significance of decisive engagements— and entirely ignored his more important strategic and political insights.

For Clausewitz, the essential dynamic of war was the ever-present tension between the forces restraining war and those pushing it toward its most extreme expression. In the eighteenth century, the force of friction dominated and war was of necessity limited in its aims, scope, and duration. This changed with the French Revolution. Technological and administrative advances encouraged European governments to become far more ambitious in the scope of their military efforts. Even more important, according to Clausewitz, was the political change that the revolution brought about. "The people," he observed, "became a participant in war; instead of governments and armies as heretofore, the full weight of the nation was thrown into the balance." Once this happened, war took on a completely different character. Its sole aim became the overthrow of the opponent. "Not until he was prostrate," Clausewitz lamented, "was it considered possible to pause and try to reconcile the opposing interests. War, untrammeled by any conventional restraints, had broken loose in all its elemental fury" (1976: 592–93).

Since Clausewitz's day, the balance between the forces restraining and expanding war has evolved even further in the direction of the latter. The same is true of crisis. Nuclear weapons are the most important new factor affecting both but they are not the only development responsible for this trend. Some of these other factors would be recognizable to Clausewitz in principle, if not in detail. Let us examine them and their implications for crisis management.

Civilian Control of the Military

Civilian-military conflict can have many different causes. Here, I treat only those that are institutionally based. Political leaders are likely to face two very different kinds of problems in this connection. The first is conflict arising from clashing civilian-military perspectives, a problem that has long been recognized in crisis literature (Allison, 1971: 127–31; Betts, 1977: 12–15; Lebow, 1981: 285–88). Political leaders are likely to show great concern for minimizing the risks of war associated with alerts, shows of force, or limited military operations. Even when sympathetic to this objective, military leaders will also be committed to maintaining their institutional independence and reluctant to expose their forces to what they consider to be unnecessary risks. As Graham Allison documented in his study of the Cuban missile crisis, military officials may oppose and even resist directives that threaten these traditional military concerns (Allison, 1971: 127–31).[2]

The lessons of Cuba are sobering; nevertheless, they may be an inappropriate guide to the future. It was the American military's first experience with civilian "micromanagement"; generals and admirals were predictably outraged. Today's military leaders, while still intent on maintaining service integrity and safeguarding their forces, also realize the dangers of nuclear war and often show greater recognition than civilian officials do of the extraordinary measures war avoidance requires. They are more willing than Admiral Anderson and his contemporaries to run risks to preserve the peace. Many military men may be more committed to doing this than their civilian counterparts (Betts, 1977: 14–15).

The more serious civilian-military problem is the lack of insight and knowledge that each community has about the worldview, objectives, and operational environment of the other. Military plans formulated in a political vacuum compounded by political ignorance of those plans and their requirements can contribute to loss of control and disaster in crisis. The mobilization and war plans of the great powers in 1914, especially the infamous Schlieffen Plan, remain the classic manifestation of this problem. These plans, the broad outlines of which were widely known or guessed at, constituted a major cause of pre-war tension and then a principal impediment to attempts to resolve the July crisis

(Albertini, 1952, II: 479–85; Levy, 1986: 193–222; Snyder, 1984; Lebow, 1987b).

In the United States, civilian-military ignorance of each other's milieu and operating environment is most pronounced on the civilian side. With rare exceptions, elected and appointed officials have little or no knowledge of any of the details of crisis management, military alerts, or operations, nor of the kinds of constraints that affect them. Top-ranking military leaders by contrast tend to know a lot more about the political side of crisis management. Most of them have attended war colleges where they have been exposed to the civilian point of view. They may also have "hands on" experience with the problem in previous tours of duty that involved them in crisis planning or the actual management of the kind of low level crises that have become fairly regular occurrences.

Senior officers are nevertheless likely to be ignorant of the details of strategic alerts or other military measures about which they would be expected to give the president advice. In the Cuban crisis, the Joint Chiefs of Staff learned just how difficult it was to control all military activity with the aim of preventing any gratuitous provocations of the Soviet Union (Allison, 1971: 136–42; Sagan, 1985: 99–139). In the 1973 Middle East crisis, Henry Kissinger was "shocked" that the DEFCON III alert was immediately picked up and reported by the media (Kissinger, 1982: 591). The Joint Chiefs had assured him that the alert could be kept secret (Sagan, 1985: 128).

The field grade officers and their civilian counterparts who design conventional and nuclear alerting procedures, devise SIOP options, and select the targets for them, suffer from a different kind of myopia. They are ignorant of the broader political purposes that any of these military options would be expected to serve. General Richard H. Ellis, former director of the Joint Strategic Target Planning Staff, reports that the officers involved in updating the SIOP used to read speeches by the president and secretary of defense in the hope of finding some hints about what to do with their weapons (1980: 6–7). Since 1974, the Office of the Secretary of Defense has regularly provided guidance to targets but all of the available evidence indicates that alert procedures, crisis deployments and SIOP options are still largely shaped by narrow technical criteria (Powers, 1982a: 82–110).

The ignorance of top political and military leaders of the details of alerts and war plans which themselves have been formulated in a political vacuum does not bode well for crisis management. It courts loss of control in the form of runaway escalation or, failing that, puts leaders at the mercy of pre-planned options that probably bear no relationship to their political needs of the moment. The danger of the former is magnified by the inappropriate conceptions that have dominated American thinking about crisis management since the Cuban missile crisis of 1962.

Top American political officials and their advisors give evidence of approaching crisis management in terms of a stereotyped understanding of the Cuban crisis. Like Kennedy, they would aspire to make the Soviet Union back down by demonstrating their resolve to use force. This would be accomplished by means of visible military preparations coupled with verbal threats. American officials, military and civilian, also tend to think of crisis escalation as a series of discrete, controllable, and reversible steps up a clearly demarcated ladder. In practice, military alerts, the American currency of resolve, are by no means the surgically precise instruments they are envisaged to be. Experience indicates that they are complex and often unwieldy organizational routines that may have major unforeseen and undesired consequences (Bracken, 1983; Lebow, 1987b: Chapter 3).

The most dangerous attribute of strategic alerts is that they can prompt adversaries to initiate military preparations of their own as a hedge against attack. The American strategic alerts of 1962 and 1973 did not provoke Soviet counter-alerts. In 1962, the Soviets were at a severe strategic disadvantage and may have feared American preemption (Berman and Baker, 1982: 36–38, 86–89; Meyer, 1985: 167–205). In 1973, a Soviet response was unnecessary because a cease-fire—the immediate Soviet objective in the crisis—was going into effect at the very time the United States went to Defense Condition (DEFCON) III. Both situations were atypical. Cuba occurred at a time when the United States had overwhelming strategic superiority and the Middle East crisis, as previously noted, was resolved simultaneously with the American alert. It would be a grave error to take Soviet restraint for granted in a future crisis on the basis of these two incidents.

A superpower crisis involving mutual strategic alerts would be much more difficult to resolve than those of 1962 or 1973. Because there are no observable differences between military preparations initiated for defensive or offensive purposes, it would risk setting in motion a cycle of reaction and counter-reaction. Both sides could seek to protect themselves against preemption, conventional or nuclear, and thereby to reduce whatever incentive their adversary had to do it. But military preparations of this kind would seriously aggravate any crisis by forcing alert levels on both sides to ratchet upwards on a worldwide basis. Soviet or American leaders, like the statesmen of 1914, could find themselves in the position of having endorsed policies that they believed entailed little risk of war only to find out later in the crisis that they had set in motion a chain of events that became increasingly difficult, if not impossible, to halt short of war. In a recent book I have described the process and mechanisms by which this could occur (1987).

Political ignorance of alerts and war plans also threatens to make political leaders captives of pre-packaged military routines just as in 1914. Today, there would be even less chance to circumvent these routines by improvisation because time constraints would be measured in hours instead of days. On this point, General Thomas Power, former commander of the Strategic Air Command, is as adamant as Field Marshal Moltke was before him. "You cannot coordinate a plan," he insists, "after you have been told to go to war. And there is one basic law you must follow. Do not change it at the last minute" (Kaplan, 1983: 298).

To escape from the rigidity of war plans, American defense secretaries since the time of Robert McNamara have ordered the development of a wide range of strategic options. But two decades of SIOP revisions still confront policy-makers with little more than a choice among a small number of possibilities (Ball, 1983). Nor has greater political input resulted in war plans that political leaders would be likely to find any more helpful in a crisis. Henry Kissinger reported that his own doubts about the wisdom of war-fighting strategies, even limited ones, were confirmed in the aftermath of the Arab-Israeli war of 1973. He discovered that the most limited military action envisaged by Pentagon planners in response to a Soviet invasion of Iran entailed pummeling the Soviet Union and its armed forces with more than two hundred nuclear weapons. Kissinger's objection that this would provoke a full-scale nuclear war elicited an alternative suggestion from the Joint Chiefs that they use only two weapons. Kissinger found this unpalatable for the opposite reason (Kaplan, 1983: 370–71; Edwards, 1982: 67–68). The present administration would probably be just as appalled as some of its predecessors by the inappropriateness of its military options, conventional and nuclear, if it made an effort to examine them.

The situation is, if anything, worse in the Soviet Union. Soviet specialists are in general agreement that Soviet consideration of crisis military options would take place in a setting heavily influenced by a military committed to a preemptive doctrine. Stephen Meyer warns: "The lack of alternative military-strategic advice implies that Soviet political leaders would be unprepared for policy innovation under stress and susceptible to professional military influence. These signs all point toward greater dependence on prior planning, with less ability or tendency to reach out for creative alternatives" (Meyer, 1985: 201).

Soviet conventional war plans could also confront Soviet political leaders with the awkward choice of doing too much or too little. In Europe, Soviet conventional forces are geared for an all-out offensive. Jack Snyder warns that this may pose the same problem for Soviet statesmen that the Schlieffen Plan did for Bülow and Bethmann-Hollweg: "Soviet leaders may be self-deterred by the all-or-nothing character of their military options. Alternatively, if the Soviets try to push ahead with a diplomacy based on the 'Bolshevik operational code' principles of controlled pressure, limited probes and controlled, calculated risks, they may find themselves trapped by military options that create risks that cannot be controlled" (Snyder, 1984: 144; Lebow, 1984: 44–78).

Clausewitz was well aware of the problem posed by the ignorance of civilian and political leaders of each other's perspectives and operating environments. His solution was the soldier-statesman who embodied in himself both perspectives and the necessary experience to go with them. Clausewitz recognized, however, that such individuals were rarely to be found. He therefore proposed the less satisfactory expedient of making the military commander-in-chief a member of the cabinet, "so that the cabinet can share in the major aspects of his activities" (1976: 608–09).

Cabinet involvement in the management of war was clearly meant to insure that policy would determine its character. But the commander-in-chief's inclusion in the cabinet was also designed to make his expertise available to the political leadership. Clausewitz recognized that policy ought to take the operational requirements of the military into account; political leaders must be made aware of the variety of constraints and uncertainties likely to affect military performance. Only then could policy be informed by the clashing but equally important perspectives of war in theory and war in the real world. Contemporary American notions of crisis management recognize Clausewitz's first objective, even if they fall short of achieving it in planning and practice. American leaders continue to remain largely oblivious to Clausewitz's second requirement for security policy which is no less critical to crisis than it is to war.

Loss of Control to Emotions

"Savage peoples," Clausewitz wrote, are ruled by passion and "civilized peoples" by the mind. The difference was due to their attendant circumstances and institutions. The Napoleonic Wars had demonstrated that under certain conditions "Even the most civilized of peoples . . . can be fired with passionate hatred for each other." This happens, he argued, when important interests are at stake and when the ensuing conflict endures a long time (1976: 76).

Clausewitz took his contemporaries to task for ignoring the emotional dimension of war. Rid war of passion, he insisted, and states would not have to engage in combat. They could conduct "war by algebra"; paper comparisons of their strength and mobility could be used to determine a war's outcome and results (1976). Clausewitz's scorn was aimed at influential strategists like Jomini who attempted to reduce war to abstract formulae, ignoring entirely the crucial elements of emotions, human performance, and luck. No doubt, Clausewitz would be similarly unimpressed by so much of the contemporary strategic literature that also tries to predict human behavior as complex as risk taking propensity and resolve it in terms of such modern day considerations as hard target kill capability, usable residual forces, and the like.

Clausewitz realized that emotions could affect the judgment of so-phisticated political leaders and military men as well as public opinion. Hostility, hatred, or the heady feeling of victory could lead them to lose sight of the political objectives of a war. When this happened, victory for its own sake became the objective, and "not until [the opponent] was prostrate was it considered possible to pause and try to reconcile the opposing interests" (1976: 593). There are numerous his-torical examples of the phenomenon Clausewitz describes. Cases in point are Bismarck's conflict with Moltke during the German wars of unification and the American decision in the summer of 1950 to invade North Korea (Craig, 1964: 180–216; Pflanze, 1963; Tsou, 1963; Lichterman, 1963: 569–642; George and Smoke, 1974: 188–234; Lebow, 1981: 148–228). The former was the result of generals carried away by the fruits of victory; the latter, the result of public and congressional pressures.

The Cuban missile crisis offers a good example of the influence of public emotions on crisis policy. Critics of Kennedy charge that he risked nuclear war merely to preserve his personal political position. The president's defenders do not deny the influence of domestic political considerations on his behavior but insist that this was merely one of the considerations compelling him to oppose, by force if necessary, Khrushchev's attempt to put missiles in Cuba.[3] First-hand accounts make it apparent that Kennedy's own emotions were engaged from the outset. On 16 October, when McGeorge Bundy informed him of the U-2 photographs that revealed the construction of Soviet missile sites, a furious president exclaimed: "He can't do that to *me!*" The president's "gut" reaction was to treat the missiles as a personal challenge involving personal costs to himself (Neustadt, 1964: 187).

Kennedy remained keenly aware of his broader domestic political problem throughout the crisis. As Theodore Sorensen, one of the pres-ident's most trusted political advisors, put it, Cuba was the "political Achilles heel" of the administration. The prior failure at the Bay of Pigs, followed by Kennedy's well-publicized pledges to keep Soviet missiles out of Cuba, compelled him to remove them by force or the threat of force, or risk electoral defeat if not impeachment (Sorensen, 1965: 675). At the height of the blockade, the president asked his brother why they were risking war with the Soviet Union. "I just don't think there was any choice," Robert Kennedy replied, "and not only that, if you hadn't you would have been impeached." "That's what I think," the senior Kennedy replied. "I would have been impeached" (1969b: 67).

Once again, the Cuban missile crisis may not be the best indicator of future crisis realities. In 1973, the next occasion U.S. strategic forces were put on alert, the public reaction was quite different. The response was mixed, with many Congressmen and media representatives questioning whether an alert was really necessary. One segment of opinion, by no means insignificant, held that Nixon and Kissinger had irresponsibly raised the risk of war in order to deflect attention from Watergate (Kissinger, 1982: 596). Much of this opposition was attributable to the public's loss of faith in the Nixon administration, but it also reflected greater public awareness of the likely consequences of a nuclear war than in 1963.

Today's public is even less likely to push a president in the direction of war with the Soviet Union or to support him so wholeheartedly in a war-threatening confrontation. The American people have not become any more enamored of the Russians but they have become considerably more fearful of nuclear war (Fiske, Pratto and Pavelchak, 1983: 41–65; Kramer, Kalicki and Milburn, 1983: 7–24; Schneider, 1985: 321–64). It is revealing in this regard to go back and look at the newspaper and television coverage of the missile crisis. To be sure, there were critics of the president who feared that his actions could provoke a nuclear war, but most editorials, columns, and "man on the street" interviews, revealed unwavering support for American policy. Nobody expressed a desire for war but the majority of Americans seemed resigned to the prospect if push came to shove. I find it difficult to envisage any circumstance today in which a presidential challenge of the Soviet Union would receive as much unqualified support. Public opinion, I suspect, would be pulling the president back, not pushing him forward.

Cuba is nevertheless illustrative of the kind of process that can provoke a serious superpower confrontation. Kennedy was willing to risk war in Cuba—at the height of the crisis, he estimated the chances to be one out of three—because he felt backed into a corner by Khrushchev (Sorensen, 1965: 705). In addition to the domestic political pressures that I have already described, the president feared that acquiescence to the missiles, or entering into a diplomatic deal to secure their withdrawal, would destroy his bargaining reputation and encourage subsequent Soviet challenges to important American commitments elsewhere in the world (Sorensen, 1965: 677; Kahan and Long, 1972: 570–74; Lebow, 1983: 431–58).

Khrushchev, for his part, may also have felt at the time that he had no choice but to introduce missiles into Cuba. The most widely accepted interpretation of his action is that it was a response to the immediate need to provide the Soviet Union with a second strike capability. This had been made urgent by Kennedy's alerting the Soviets to the fact that the United States knew of the failure of their first generation ICBM, and as a result, of their strategic vulnerability (Horelick and Rush, 1966: 141; Hilsman, 1967: 200–02; Tatu, 1968: 231; Abel, 1966a: 28; Allison, 1971: 52–56, 237–44; Kahan and Long, 1972: 564–90; Lebow, 1981: 64–66, 80–82; Schlesinger, 1965: 18). Kennedy's initiative had in turn been prompted by his perceived need to do something to moderate Khrushchev's bellicosity, alarmingly manifest in his several Berlin ultimata (Hilsman, 1967: 163–64).

If the above analysis is correct, its implications are disturbing. It indicates that a series of avowedly defensive moves had the effect of triggering the most serious superpower confrontation to date. They did so because leaders on both sides had no real grasp of the pressures and constraints acting on their adversary. Unintentionally, they provoked the very behavior they were trying to prevent (Lebow and Stein, forthcoming). Such a chain of events could certainly happen again. In the twenty-five years since Cuba the superpowers give evidence of having developed greater sensitivity to each other's vital interests; this is certainly one reason why we have not had a second crisis of the magnitude of Cuba. However, superpower leaders seem no more able than Kennedy and Khrushchev to see the world through the eyes of their adversary. The Carter administration's reaction to Afghanistan and the Reagan administration's response to the shooting down of KAL 007 give vivid testimony to this continuing inability to empathize (Lebow and Cohen, forthcoming).[4] Soviet and American leaders also appear to be just as ignorant of the internal processes, pressures, and constraints that affect, or sometimes even dictate, their adversary's foreign policy. Herein lie the root causes of another confrontation.

As Clausewitz observed, anger and hostility can also affect the performance of political and military leaders in crisis. In Cuba, Kennedy and Khrushchev appear to have done a good job of keeping their anger under control, although Khrushchev's first cable revealed him to be in a highly charged state. After the Soviet intervention in Afghanistan, Carter, by contrast, not only gave vent to his anger but allowed it to shape his policy (Carter, 1984: 298; Garthoff, 1985: 949). Fortunately, the crisis was not of the magnitude of Cuba; by all accounts the risk of a Soviet-American military encounter was quite remote. Perhaps in more serious circumstances Carter would have behaved differently.

The danger also exists that subordinates will try to escalate a crisis, not because of their political differences with the president, but out of hostility to the adversary. Hotheads could be a real impediment to presidential control over policy, especially in the military where the consequences of irresponsible behavior can be enormous. This problem did not arise during the Cuban crisis; Kennedy and McNamara's problems with the military had quite different causes. Anger, however, is reported to have affected the judgment of some American officers in September 1983 when a Korean Airlines 747 jetliner was downed by a Soviet interceptor.

The belief was widespread throughout the military that the Soviets had shot down an unarmed passenger plane in cold blood. With few exceptions, the military and intelligence officials who knew that an American intelligence plane had also been in the sky that night took it for granted a Soviet pilot could not have mistaken a huge 747 with its distinct silhouette for the smaller RC-135 reconnaissance plane. In the Pacific, senior Navy and Air Force officers are said to have become irate after reading the cable summaries provided by the National Security Agency. They "got emotional," one intelligence officer recalls, and began making plans for retaliation "that could have started World War III." An Air Force general, the same officer relates, asked him to forward a fraudulent intelligence report to the Pentagon that could be used to justify retaliation against the Soviet Union. The general "wanted me to corrupt intelligence" but "I told him to go to hell" (Hersh, 1986: 74).

Shortly after learning of the shootdown, the Air Force dispatched six F-15 fighters and an AWACs surveillance aircraft to Misawa Air Base, 360 miles north of Tokyo. This force was ordered to loiter near the island of Sakhalin, occupied by the Soviet Union at the end of World War II and ever since a bone of contention between Japan and the Soviet Union. Someone at Misawa hoped to provoke an incident. The F-15 pilots, one officer reported, were instructed "to take advantage of the situation" if they were challenged by Soviet interceptors. When alerted to the situation, Fifth Air Force headquarters in Tokyo promptly issued countermanding orders in the hope of preventing an incident. Their intervention was timely because the Soviets, angered by what they initially believed to have been a deliberate American violation of their borders, had intensified air and sea activity throughout the Far East, including in and around Sakhalin. A confrontation could easily have developed (Hersh, 1986: 74).

Anger of the kind that developed in the aftermath of the shooting down of KAL 007 requires an incident that in fact or by virtue of misinterpretation makes the other side appear blood-thirsty and utterly callous. In this instance it was the combined result of ineptitude, which led Soviet air defense to mistake the airliner for an American intelligence plane, and U.S. willingness to believe the worst about their adversary, even after better information became available. The U.S. response in

turn infuriated the Soviets who were convinced that the Reagan administration knew all along that it was a case of mistaken identity but
accused them of deliberate slaughter in order to reap propaganda rewards.

While the KAL 007 episode was idiosyncratic, its structural causes
were not. The concatenation of technical, institutional, and political
factors that were responsible for this escalating spiral of Soviet and
American misjudgments and tensions could occur again and in a more
dangerous setting. Responses based on anger could constitute a serious
impediment to the resolution of such a confrontation.

Political Sabotage

Sabotage is different from our previous categories of loss of control
because of the nature of the motivation involved. To be sure, emotions
may be engaged and institutional perspectives may play a part, but
political sabotage is the result of avowed and pronounced political
differences between subordinates and the national command authority.
These differences may encourage subordinates to disregard orders or to
attempt to change crisis policy by unauthorized initiatives of their own.
Behavior of this kind was an important contributing cause of the outbreak
of war in 1914. In at least two countries, Germany and France, stra-
tegically-placed subordinates pushed their respective allies into more
confrontational policies.

German Chief of Staff Helmuth von Moltke played a particularly
active and independent role throughout the crisis. His goal, from which
he never wavered, was to goad Austria into declaring war on Serbia.
With this end in mind he secretly assured his Austrian counterpart of
German support against Russia if it came to the aid of Serbia. On the
night of 29–30 July, when German Chancellor Bethmann-Hollweg urged
caution on Vienna in response to his belated realization that Austrian
truculence would probably provoke a European war, Moltke sent his
own telegram countermanding the chancellor's request. His intervention
was probably instrumental in forestalling Austrian reconsideration of
their policy (Hoetzendorff, 1921–25, IV: 152; Albertini, 1952, II: 496–
97, 673–77, III: 6–14; Ritter, 1970, II: 239–63).

Maurice Paléologue, the French minister in St. Petersburg, played a
similar role on the Entente side. At the very outset of the crisis, he
committed his country to Russia's support without any instructions from
Paris to do so. He then deliberately misled the French foreign office
about the gravity of the crisis by minimizing the likelihood of Russian
military action in his dispatches. Secure in the knowledge of French
backing, Russian leaders moved toward mobilization. By their own
admission, they would not have done this in the absence of French

support (Albertini, 1952, II: 181–216, 290–328, 528–631; Turner, 1968: 65–88).

Serious political loss of control of the kind that occurred in 1914 seems an unlikely possibility in a future superpower crisis. There are a number of reasons for this. Instantaneous and redundant communication links between capitals deprive diplomats of the independence they once exercised. Washington and Moscow have also implemented a variety of measures to safeguard against the unauthorized use of nuclear weapons. Beyond this, the sheer destructiveness of nuclear war gives it few if any partisans among even the most hawkish elements of either superpower's leadership. However, the possibility of war arising from the willful and unauthorized actions of subordinates cannot entirely be discounted.

The history of post-war American civil-military relations offers several examples of flag officers pursuing policies that were dramatically at variance with presidential directives. The most notorious offender was Douglas MacArthur who made political statements contradicting official policy and conducted military operations in direct violation of his orders from the Joint Chiefs of Staff. MacArthur's actions are believed to have intensified Peking's perception of threat and thus may have been an important contributing cause of Chinese entry into the Korean War (Spanier, 1965; Whiting, 1960: 169–71; Tsou, 1963: 576–80; Lebow, 1981: 148–228).

Curtis LeMay was another notoriously independent general. In the 1950s, he appeared confident that he would not only decide how America would fight a nuclear war, but when it would do so (Rosenberg, 1980–81: 3–38; Kaplan, 1983: 132–134; Herken, 1985: 96–98). Under LeMay's guidance, the Strategic Air Command (SAC) prepared itself to launch a preemptive strike whenever war with the Soviet Union seemed unavoidable. Many SAC officers were dismayed when the Kennedy administration failed to exploit the opportunity provided by the Cuban missile crisis to carry out such an attack. Shortly after the Soviet capitulation, SAC Commander General Thomas S. Power delivered a tirade to a shocked RAND audience about Kennedy's cowardice and his failure to exploit the situation in order to destroy the Soviet Union (Herken, 1985: 168, 364).[5]

The possibility of a serious political-military confrontation in a nuclear crisis is not altogether far-fetched. Imagine a situation in which generals on one side or the other become convinced that they are about to be attacked or are already under attack but cannot persuade a cautious and unconvinced premier or president to respond. In the case of the U.S., it would be possible for one of the unified or specified commanders to order retaliation in the absence of presidential authorization if the crisis had been judged serious enough to disseminate the "go code" part way down the military chain-of-command as a means of guaranteeing retaliation in the aftermath of a decapitating attack (Tate, 1980: 43; Bracken, 1983: 165–69, 199–200). One or more military leaders might be tempted to do this if they believed that the fate of their nation hung in the balance.

This is the stuff that movies are made of; just imagine George C. Scott as the SAC commander strutting across the floor of the White House Situation Room, pleading unsuccessfully with the president to send out the "go code." As a good film would make apparent, the proclivity of a commander to take matters into his own hands would depend at least as much on his personality as it would upon the situation. Governments cannot protect themselves against this danger by technical means alone; they must rely on institutional safeguards that minimize the likelihood of a Curtis LeMay or Douglas MacArthur rising to a sensitive position of authority.

The U.S. is probably more vulnerable than the Soviet Union to the man on horseback because of the nature of the democratic political process. Ambitious generals have from time to time been able to build up enough of an independent power base to make presidents cautious of challenging them. As the fate of Marshal Zhukov testifies, military heroes in the Soviet Union have much less leeway for exercising authority. Soviet political authorities, probably because of their fear of military insubordination, have always gone to greater lengths to control the military more carefully at every level of command. Their efforts seem to have been successful; slavish obedience to civilian authority has been the rule even in circumstances generals saw as certain to lead to disaster (Colton, 1979).

A more likely scenario than military insubordination is the abrogation of presidential authority at the height of a crisis by a cabinet member or civilian advisor. Henry Kissinger's behavior during the 1973 Middle East War gives striking testimony to the extent to which a clever and powerful subordinate can independently shape policy and take it in directions contrary to presidential instructions. The effect, moreover, of Kissinger's independent initiatives was profound; they provoked what was probably an avoidable crisis with the Soviet Union and then needlessly transformed that crisis into the most serious superpower confrontation of the decade.

Kissinger acted without presidential authorization or in direct con-tradiction to it on at least four separate occasions during the crisis. The first occasion was with regard to the military resupply of Israel. Kissinger, along with many other administration officials had been incredulous at first of Israeli reports of their combat losses. They suspected Israel of deliberately exaggerating its military needs in order to extract more aid than it would otherwise receive. When the extent of Israel's setbacks on the ground and in the air were belatedly recognized, and with it, its leaders' growing sense of desperation, Kissinger still dragged his feet. He did so even after the Soviet Union had commenced a major resupply by air and ship of Syria and Egypt on 10 October (Kissinger, 1982: 478–79, 488, 497).

Kissinger and Nixon have propagated the myth that Kissinger favored the massive resupply of Israel but that this was blocked by Defense Secretary James Schlesinger and his department, who were responsible for all kinds of unnecessary delays. Their footdragging was allegedly overcome only when Kissinger went to Nixon and urged him to order an airlift (Kalb and Kalb, 1974: 525–40; Kissinger, 1982: 494–96, 501–02, 512–15; Nixon, 1978: 924–27; Szulc, 1978: 737–39). In reality, it was Kissinger who was responsible for the dilatory response to Israel's increasingly desperate requests for military aid (Luttwak and Laqueur, 1974: 33–40; Zumwalt, 1976: 433–35; Golan, 1976: 45–61; Safran, 1978: 481–83; Szulc, 1978: 735–36; Garthoff, 1985: 369–70). His motive for doing so was to prevent Israel from winning an overwhelming victory which would minimize American influence in Jerusalem, provoke the Soviet Union and the oil producing Arab states, and do nothing to wean Egypt away from Moscow (Kissinger, 1982: 468, 470–71, 476, 487, 493).

Kissinger continued to drag his feet on resupply until 12 October, when an exasperated ambassador Dinitz warned him that Israel was prepared to reassess its relationship with the United States and take extreme measures in its defense. The next day, Nixon summoned the National Security Council and ordered the use of American cargo planes to ferry supplies to Israel. By dawn of 14 October, a massive airlift was underway, but not without a final attempt by Kissinger to strangle it. Tad Szulc reports that Kissinger insisted, without success, on an "absurd and time-wasting condition." American planes were to fly only as far as Lajes Air Force Base on Terceira Island in the Azores where their cargo was to be transferred to a commerical airfield on Santa Maria Island and then offloaded on to El Al 707's (Safran, 1978: 483, 489; Kissinger, 1982: 513–15; Szulc, 1978: 737).

The airlift did not come a moment too soon. Israel's civilian and military leaders were in a mood of mounting despair. Having sustained large casualties, lost a high percentage of their combat aircraft and tanks, and desperately low of critical military stocks, they were prepared to consider extreme measures.[6] Kissinger pushed Israel to the wall because he greatly underestimated the magnitude of Israel's military setbacks and their psychological effect upon Israel's leaders. His policy was a dangerous one under any circumstances because it is very difficult to know just how much bruising is necessary to make one ally compliant but not desperate. Kissinger's miscalculation came close to having tragic consequences for Israel, the Middle East, and international relations in general. Fortunately, Nixon threw his weight behind the airlift which together with subsequent Israeli battlefield successes brought about a reversal of the military situation.

Kissinger's second independent initiative involved an unambiguous violation of presidential orders. On 20 October, at Brezhnev's request and with Nixon's approval, Kissinger flew to Moscow to negotiate a cease-fire. En route, he learned that Nixon had written a letter to Brezhnev informing him that Kissinger was being granted "full authority" and that any commitments he made would have "my complete support." Kissinger was "horrified" because such a grant of authority deprived him of his opportunity to stall a cease-fire until Israel won back the territory captured by Egypt (Kissinger, 1982: 539–548).

In Moscow, Kissinger was handed a copy of the Nixon letter which distressed him further because it implied that he was not only to negotiate a cease-fire but work toward a comprehensive peace settlement. This fundamental change in approach was confirmed in instructions from Nixon that arrived the next day. Nixon's policy was contrary to Kissinger's goal of excluding the Russians from the Middle East. According to Kissinger:

> American strategy so far had been to *separate* the cease-fire from a postwar political settlement and to reduce the Soviet role in the negotations that would follow the cease-fire. What Nixon seemed to envisage now would involve us in an extensive negotiation whose results we would then have to impose on Israel as the last act of a war fought on the Arab side with Soviet weapons. Moscow would receive credit with the Arabs for having forced us into a course we have heretofore avoided. Our leverage on the Arab side would disappear (1982: 547–51).

Kissinger telephoned Alexander Haig in the White House to express his "extreme displeasure" with his instructions. Haig was unsympathetic. "Will you get off my back?" he told Kissinger, "I have troubles of my own." It was then that Kissinger learned of the "Saturday Night Massacre." Unable to reverse his instructions, Kissinger decided to ignore them. "I adhered rigidly," he confides in his memoirs, "to the earlier, more restricted plan approved by Nixon before my departure" (Kissinger, 1982: 552; Garthoff, 1985: 371).

Soon afterwards, in response to a request from Golda Meir, Nixon ordered Kissinger to fly to Jerusalem to confer with Israeli leaders before returning home. He arrived on 22 October and met with prime minister Meir and her cabinet. Not having received any military updates in Moscow, he was surprised to learn just how close Israeli forces were to achieving a stunning victory; he was told that it would take seven days to encircle the Egyptian Second and Third Armies along the Suez Canal, but only three to destroy them from the air. Kissinger suddenly realized why Brezhnev had been so accommodating to all of his conditions and in such haste to arrange a cease-fire (Kissinger, 1982: 559–67; Dayan, 1976: 443–44; Golan, 1976: 82–87).

Kissinger now deviated once again from his instructions. Without any authorization from the White House he tacitly encouraged the Israeli cabinet to postpone implementation of the cease-fire that he had just negotiated. Upon learning how little time the Israelis needed to finish off the Egyptians, he is reported to have exclaimed: "Two or three days? That's all? Well, in Vietnam the cease-fire didn't go into effect at the exact time that was agreed on."[7] As the Israelis had already expressed indignation at the timing of the cease-fire, which would deny them their hard-won victory, Kissinger's comment could only be construed as the green light for a final offensive. Nadav Safran comments:

> The Israelis, who had launched and concluded the entire Syrian campaign in 1967 after the appointed cease-fire time, hardly needed to be instructed about the time difference between agreement and application; consequently, the secretary's remark in their presence and in that context could only be taken by them as an invitation to disregard the cease-fire and go on to try to destroy the Egyptian forces (1978: 492).

Kissinger's motives for encouraging the Israelis to ignore the cease-fire are not altogether clear—it seems contrary to his earlier objective of leaving them vulnerable at the end of the fighting. Whatever the reason, the consequences of his action were undeniably grave. The Soviets, who carefully monitored Israeli military progress, were infuriated. Brezhnev, in a note to Kissinger, called the continuing Israeli offensive "unacceptable" and a "flagrant deceit" (Kissinger, 1982: 570–72). Realizing that his policy was threatening to unravel, Kissinger began to put the screws on Israel. He summoned Dinitz and told him that American aid would be cut off if his country was responsible for more fighting. Together with the Soviet Union he co-sponsored a cease-fire resolution in the United Nations (Kissinger, 1982: 571–75; Nixon, 1978; 938).

Hours after the cease-fire took effect on 24 October, renewed fighting broke out and the Israelis mounted another offensive aimed at severing the Third Army's lifeline to Egypt proper. Kissinger admitted to a "sinking feeling" upon learning the news. He made a renewed effort to coerce Israel into implementing the cease-fire and attempted to mend his fences with the Soviets. A flurry of cables and telephone calls went to Jerusalem, Moscow, and also Cairo, in a frantic effort to head off a Soviet-American confrontation. But Sadat announced that he would call upon the Security Council to send Soviet and American forces to the Middle East to implement the cease-fire. That evening, the famous letter from Brezhnev arrived at the White House with its veiled threat of unilateral Soviet military action unless the United States cooperated in enforcing the Security Council cease-fire resolution (Kissinger, 1982: 575–84).

Brezhnev's "ultimatum," as Kissinger called it, was an indication of Moscow's frustration with the course of Middle Eastern events. Egypt and Syria, two Soviet clients, had been defeated by Israel whose forces now threatened to envelop key Egyptian armies and open the way to a possible advance on Cairo. If Israeli military progress was unchecked, Sadat and Egypt would be humiliated and the value of Soviet backing would be greatly devalued throughout the Third World. The threat of unilateral intervention was designed to save the Egyptian Third Army by goading Washington into taking whatever measures were necessary to restrain Israel. By this means, the Soviet Union sought to salvage some of its lost prestige in the Arab world (Garthoff, 1985: 360–85; Jabber and Kolkowicz, 1981: 438–67; Golan, 1977; Quandt, 1977: 377–89, 578–603; Dawisha, 1980–81: 43–59; Porter, 1984: 113–46).

Brezhnev's letter also reflected exasperation with Henry Kissinger; cease-fires negotiated with the American secretary of state had not been implemented or had quickly broken down as Israel pushed ahead with its offensive. The Soviets were likely to conclude that Israel would only do this with American approval. Upon learning that the Israelis had surrounded the Third Army after the cease-fire deadline, Kissinger himself is reported to have exclaimed: "My God, the Russians will think I double-crossed them. And in their shoes, who wouldn't" (The London Sunday Times Insight Team, 1974: 399). Brezhnev's letter indicated that the Russians did indeed take this possibility quite seriously. Nixon reports that Brezhnev "curtly implied that we might even have colluded in Israel's action." Perhaps the Soviets would have been more restrained if they had not suspected Kissinger of double dealing (Nixon, 1978, II: 495; Garthoff, 1985: 374; Primakov, 1978: 173; Blechman and Hart, 1982: 136).

Kissinger succeeded in putting the most ominous interpretation on the Soviet démarche. He referred to it as "one of the most serious challenges to an American President by a Soviet leader." Brezhnev, Kissinger insisted, had to be rebuffed "in a manner that shocked the Soviets into abandoning the unilateral move they were threatening—

and, from all our information, planning" (Kissinger, 1982: 583–84). Haig thought Nixon "too distraught to participate in the preliminary discussion" and on his recommendation the president was not awakened and told about Brezhnev's letter (Kissinger, 1982: 585). Nor did he attend the National Security Council meeting Kissinger convened for the following morning. That meeting, on 25 October, was restricted to Kissinger, Schlesinger, Haig, CIA director William Colby, Deputy National Security Advisor Brent Scowcroft, Chairman of the Joint Chiefs Admiral Thomas Moorer, and Kissinger's military assistant, Commander Jonathan Howe (Kissinger, 1982: 585–88).

Despite Nixon's claims to the contrary, it is apparent from Kissinger's memoirs and other evidence that he was neither informed beforehand about the substance of the meeting nor asked for his approval of its far-reaching decisions (Kissinger, 1982: 583–85, 592–93; Nixon, 1978: 939–39; Garthoff, 1985: 378–79). At Kissinger's urging, the NSC authorized a DEFCON III military alert of U.S. strategic and conventional forces. In addition, the 82nd Airborne Division was put on an even higher state of readiness, sixty B-52's on Guam were ordered back to the continental United States, naval forces in the Mediterranean were augmented by another carrier, and the *Franklin Delano Roosevelt* and its supporting vessels, already in the western Mediterranean, were moved east to join the two carriers already on station there (Kissinger, 1982: 587–90; Blechman and Hart, 1982: 136–39; Hart, 1984: 214–22). With uncharacteristic modesty, Kissinger admitted that "it was a daunting responsibility to assume" (1982: 585).

American policy during the Middle East war was formulated almost exclusively by Henry Kissinger (Garthoff, 1985: 372). Nixon intervened only to insist on an airlift and to press Kissinger, unsuccessfully, to work for a comprehensive peace settlement instead of just a cease-fire. He was otherwise distracted by Watergate. Vice President Spiro Agnew's resignation, the court battle over the tapes, and the "Saturday Night Massacre" and its repercussions, all of which occurred during the war, confronted Nixon with daily domestic crises. Kissinger's memoirs reveal that he was fully aware of Nixon's preoccupation. He took advantage of it to pursue a policy that was at times quite at odds with that of the president (Kissinger, 1982: 537, 598, 606).

The policy-making context of American policy during the Middle East War was characterized by two extraordinary attributes: a strong and highly respected secretary of state with a policy of his own at times at odds with the president's, and a president who, by virtue of his domestic political problems, was unable to direct or supervise foreign policy on a day-to-day basis. The gravity of Nixon's political problems also went some way toward reversing the usual power relationship between secretary of state and president; Nixon's own legitimacy was increasingly dependent on Kissinger instead of the other way around. This was readily apparent in the president's effort to make political capital from the Middle East war and ensuing Soviet-American confrontation. "He had a need to convince the public that there had been a real crisis," Kissinger reports, and "wanted me to stress his indispensability" (1982: 598–99, 606).

Fortunately, the Soviet-American crisis of 1973 went away almost as quickly as it flared up; it was defused by an effective cease-fire. This outcome should not detract from the gravity of the structural problem that marred American policy during the confrontation. A non-elected official was able to capitalize on his distance from Washington, his standing with the president, and the president's deep involvement in other issues to substitute his judgment and policy for that of the chief executive. His policy led to an unnecessary Soviet-American confrontation and an unnecessary strategic alert. In different circumstances, an abrogation of authority of this kind could have far graver consequences.

Countervailing Forces

According to Clausewitz everything in war is very simple, but the simplest thing is very difficult. The practical problems associated with implementing even the most ordinary commands accumulate to produce a friction beyond the imagination of those who have never witnessed war. For Clausewitz, successful commanders are distinguished primarily by their ability to overcome this friction (Clausewitz, 1976: 113). A similar process affects crisis management. Parochial perspectives, organizational routines, bureaucratic inertia, human lassitude and error, constitute a formidable friction that political leaders must surmount if they are to guide their nation's policies with speed and precision. A great leader, like a great general, is someone who can impose his will on civilian and military institutions and make them responsive to his directives.

Friction makes war a blunt instrument. It does the same to crisis management. Attempts to coordinate the myriad of political and military moves that constitute the substance of crisis management are bound to run into difficulty. In a crisis, even more than war, a small deviation from the envisaged game plan can have profound and detrimental consequences.

Friction, in the form of orders that were never given, received or carried out as planned, plagued John Kennedy's handling of the Cuban crisis (Allison, 1971; Sagan, 1985). Potentially one of the more serious mishaps in this regard was the accidental overflight of the Soviet Union by a U-2 reconnaissance aircraft at the height of the crisis. The president had previously given orders that all air activity in the vicinity of the Soviet Union was to cease. Somehow, word never reached an Alaskan based weather squadron. Khrushchev was inclined to dismiss the incident as an accident but pointedly warned Kennedy that it could also be interpreted as a last minute intelligence mission carried out in preparation for an American nuclear attack (Hilsman, 1964: 17–21; *New York Times*, 12 September 1962: 1; Allison, 1971: 141).

Friction in the Clausewitzian sense ought to play a restraining role in crisis. It should slow down the pace of events by putting obstacles in the way of policy initiatives. In doing so it could deny certain options to policy-makers. This happened in Cuba. Organizational friction and its effects helped to dissuade President Kennedy from ordering an air strike. The air force had added the missile sites and their radars to a long list of targets it had previously identified as critical in any strategic bombardment of Cuba. Because of the size of their target list, they could only devote a small percentage of the available attack aircraft to the missile sites. Largely because of this, they were unwilling to guarantee the destruction of more than ninety percent of the missiles. An improvised plan that held out the prospect of a higher kill ratio might have gained the approval of the president, who was otherwise favorably disposed to the air strike option (Abel, 1966a: 101; Sorensen, 1965: 684, 708–10; Hilsman, 1967: 185; Allison, 1971: 123–26, 200–10). Had the airstrike been implemented, the crisis would have become very much more acute and difficult to resolve (Lebow, 1987b: 135–39).

The Cuban experience indicates that there is no simple relationship between friction and crisis outcome. At the same time, it is apparent that the effect of friction has changed considerably since Clausewitz's day. For Clausewitz, friction could only act to slow things down and keep war from reaching its natural limit. Today, the real danger of friction may be the reverse: failure to coordinate crisis policy with precision could lead to runaway escalation and nuclear war. Cuba gave only a hint of the kinds of problems that can develop in this regard. These problems would be much more likely to retard the resolution of any future superpower crisis of the magnitude of Cuba.

Cuba took place in a much less sophisticated institutional environment. Many communication links were entirely *ad hoc*, the number of players was relatively small, and their roles were often undefined. Strategic weapons, mostly bombers, were slow and recallable. The command and control systems of both superpowers have subsequently grown enormously in size and complexity. They have also become tightly coupled. Strategic weapons put more stress on these systems. They are capable of striking the adversary's political leadership and strategic forces in a matter of minutes instead of hours. They are also less tolerant of error, because missiles, unlike bombers, cannot be recalled. All of these developments would magnify the effect of the kinds of incidents and mishaps that plagued Kennedy's handling of Cuba. There is also reason to believe that the organization complexity of the 1980s makes mishaps more likely (Lebow, 1987b: chapter 3).

Paul Bracken warns that an amplifying feedback loop could develop between the warning and response systems of the superpowers in response to any significant strategic alerting by either one of them (Broad, 1985: A12; Bracken, 1983). This "ratchet effect," I have argued elsewhere, is only one of the dangers of strategic alerts. Their unpredictable organizational consequences, the risk of accident, and the sense of the threat that they convey, make such alerts exceedingly destabilizing. Even if policy-makers recognize this risk—which, on the whole, they do not—the superpowers still have a strong incentive to put their forces on a high state of alert in a war-threatening crisis in order to discourage adversarial preemption. The "logic" of nuclear crisis management therefore dictates the most dangerous of initiatives (Lebow, 1987b).

All of the problems associated with nuclear command and control suggest the need for an additional dimension to the concept of friction. Clausewitz looked to physics for his original metaphor. We might follow his lead because the phenomenon of "superconductivity" seems quite *a propos* to our need. Superconductors are metals that when cooled to very low temperatures offer no resistance to the flow of electricity. They develop no heat from "friction" regardless of the intensity of the current passing through them.

Modern day command and control has similarly transformed the military medium in such a way that it offers increasingly less resistance to efforts by the national command authority to bring the country's strategic forces up to the highest states of readiness. Once set in motion, a strategic alert, like electricity in a superconducting circuit, could assume a life of its own and continue without additional external impulse. Institutional superconductivity could be the cause of runaway escalation that could lead to war in an acute crisis.

Fortunately, the command and control systems of the superpowers do not function as perfect superconductors. There is still a good possibility that mutual alerts, once begun, can be halted short of war, controlled by national leaders, and reversed in the aftermath of a crisis. Nevertheless, there can be little doubt that the last twenty-five years superpower command and control systems have moved steadily in the direction of superconductivity. Nobody knows at what point, how far short of zero degrees Kelvin, to continue the metaphor, a precipitous fall in the possibility of control would make strategic alerts certain harbingers of thermonuclear war. This danger unquestionably exists. It is compounded by the seeming unwillingness of policy-makers to recognize the gravity of the problem (Lebow, 1987b: chapter 4).

Conclusions

This chapter began with a description of the two contrasting forces which, in Clausewitz's view, dominated warfare: emotions, which push war toward its limits, and friction, which works to prevent this. For Clausewitz, the lesson of the Napoleonic Wars was that the balance between these two forces had been permanently altered. The technical, economic, administrative, and political changes associated with the French Revolution had overcome many of the restraints of friction which hitherto had kept war from reaching its extreme expression. My analysis indicates that the relationship between these forces is even more one-sided today; crises and wars are even more difficult to control or keep limited.

My second and related finding is that many of the reasons why contemporary crises and war are difficult to control are different than they were in Clausewitz's day. In superpower confrontations, friction and emotions can work in the opposite sense described by Clausewitz. Friction, to be sure, remains an important limiting force just as it was in the Napoleonic period. However, in the case of strategic alerts, human and institutional factors can also function as superconductors, conceivably carrying escalation up to and beyond the threshold of war despite contrary desires of policy-makers. This would be even more likely in the case of a conventional superpower war in Europe where geographical asymmetries, the co-location of so many important conventional and nuclear assets, and the respective strategies of the two sides—not to mention the effects of the "fog of war"—would make such a conflict exceedingly difficult, if not impossible, to limit (Posen, 1982: 28–54; Mearsheimer, 1986: 3–57).

Emotions can also cut both ways. The Falkland-Malvinas conflict reveals the extent to which emotions, on the part of both leaders and peoples, can act, as Clausewitz warned, to escalate a conflict. According to the foreign minister at the time, Nicanor Costa-Mendez, the original Argentine intention was to occupy the Islands and then to withdraw that evening. This dramatic initiative, it was hoped, would dramatize Argentina's grievances, focus world attention on the conflict, and compel Britain, under pressure from the United States and world opinion, to make a concession on sovereignty. So much for the game plan. The occupation galvanized Argentine opinion in a manner never envisaged by the *junta;* some of them also gave vent to nationalist sentiments and spoke out against the on-going evacuation of Argentine forces. The next day, the *junta* as a whole reversed itself, reinforced the Argentine garrison at Port Stanley, and took the fateful step of appointing a governor general. Similar passions were aroused in Britain by news of the invasion and committed the Thatcher government, whatever its inclination, to a confrontatory response (Costa-Mendez, 21 October, 1986: Interview; Lebow, 1985b: 89–124).

Emotions are likely to have a different and more complex effect on a superpower crisis. At the outset, they may push leaders and public opinion in the United States toward a confrontation. Soviet intervention in Afghanistan and the shooting down of KAL 007 certainly did this. However, the moment any real risk of war is perceived, anger with the adversary will conflict with another powerful emotion: fear of nuclear war and its consequences. Soviet and American behavior in the Cuban missile crisis indicates that fear of nuclear war and the anxiety the very prospect of it provokes is likely to be the dominant emotion. In Cuba, it prompted both sets of leaders to make extraordinary efforts to resolve their confrontation, much to the apparent relief of their respective political constituencies. The 1973 confrontation was a pale shadow of its famous predecessor; even so, the American Congress and public asked a lot of hard questions afterwards about the alleged necessity of a strategic alert. The Korean airline incident was less acute still. Perhaps one reason was the mutual fear of war; the Reagan administration sought to reap all the propaganda value it could while carefully refraining from doing anything that could have provoked a serious confrontation with Moscow.

What are the consequences of a world in which emotions slow down the pace and intensity of conflicts and friction speeds them up? In one sense we are better off. Emotions enter at an earlier stage of a conflict; they are often one of the primary causes of a confrontation, or, if not, are certainly one of its most immediate effects. Friction, by contrast, has its most undesired effects at high levels of escalation involving strategic alerts or actual conventional clashes. To the degree that fear of war is pronounced among policy-makers it should act (and probably has) to moderate superpower truculence, thereby reducing the likelihood of a serious superpower crisis. If such a crisis nevertheless develops, fear of war should help dampen it unless, as is always possible, policy-makers on one or both sides underestimate the seriousness of the situation.

We are worse off in crises that reach high levels of escalation. At this stage of confrontation the accelerating effects of friction are most likely to be apparent. The risk of loss of control due to the other generic causes I have described will also be more pronounced. Loss of control of one kind or another does not automatically make conflicts more difficult to resolve but on the whole it can certainly be expected to have this effect. The various possibilities of loss of control, from causes as diverse as human emotions, clashing political interests, parochial institutional perspectives, and organizational rigidity and complexity, make superpower crisis management a highly dangerous and unpredictable exercise. Wise leaders will do their best to avoid such confrontations.

Nevertheless, caution cannot be taken for granted. The magnitude of interests, national and political, perceived to be at stake, insufficient awareness of the dangers of crisis, and even *hubris*—certainly an important factor in the case of Henry Kissinger—can make leaders more risk-prone than a prudent calculus of cost and gain would warrant. The ignorance, even reluctance, of superpower leaders to face up to the sobering realities of contemporary crisis management, may, in fact, constitute the most important cause of loss of control. In the abstract, leaders are generally reluctant to do anything that creates a serious risk of war. But in practice, they sometimes minimize those risks out of ignorance or convenience. Rarely, in formulating their plans, do leaders seriously consider how they can go wrong and how they will then respond. They would be well-advised to heed Clausewitz's timeless advice: consider the last step before taking the first.

Notes

1. The research and writing of this chapter was supported by a grant from the Carnegie Corporation of New York.

2. Dan Caldwell, "A Research Note on the Quarantine of Cuba, October 1962," *International Studies Quarterly* 22 (December 1978), 625–53, argues convincingly that one of Allison's examples of insubordination, the American navy's alleged failure to implement the president's order to narrow the blockade radius, never occurred.

3. Ronald Steel, "The Kennedys and the Missile Crisis," *New York Review of Books* 12 (13 March 1969), 15–22 *et passim*, argues that Kennedy was willing to risk nuclear war with the Soviet Union solely to safeguard his prospects for re-election. Roger Hilsman disagrees, "An Exchange on the Missile Crisis," *New York Review of Books*, 12 (9 May 1969), 37–38; Graham T. Allison, *Essence of Decision: Explaining the Cuban Missile Crisis* (Boston: Little, Brown, 1971), 187–200, takes a position between these two. He describes domestic considerations as one of several concerns behind Kennedy's decision to force a confrontation over the missiles.

4. In his conclusion to *The Target Is Destroyed: What Really Happened to Flight 007 and What Americans Knew About It* (New York: Random House, 1986), 249–50, Seymour M. Hersh writes that "George Schultz, William Casey, and Ronald Reagan had initially rushed to judgment over Flight 007 in what amounted to good faith—their strong hostility to Communism had led them to misread the

intelligence and then, much more ominously, to look the other way when better information became available. Those who ran the American government did not want to learn that the Soviets had honestly been confused and panic-stricken about the enemy intruder, and so they continued to believe what they wanted."

5. Citing videotape interviews conducted by the Alfred Sloan Foundation with participants in the Cuban missile crisis, Herken reports that LeMay was also unhappy with the Kennedy administration's handling of crisis. He is alleged to have complained that only unnecessary presidential caution had prevented the air force from proceeding with the airstrikes against Cuba *after* the Soviets had capitulated.

. 6. *Time*, 12 April 1976, 39–40; Safran, *Israel*, 483–89, reports that Israel prepared its nuclear option at this time, but these unsubstantiated and undocumented reports seem very dubious.

7. Kissinger, *Years of Upheaval*, 569, claims that he only said that "I would understand if there was a few hours' "slippage" in the cease-fire deadline while I was flying home. . . . " This seems an attempt to explain away his responsibility for the failure of the first cease-fire. The furthest Kissinger is prepared to go in this regard is the suggestion that he may have inadvertently encouraged the Israelis to ignore the cease-fire deadline: "I also had a sinking feeling," he writes, "that I might have emboldened them. . . . " This is a remarkable admission but Israeli sources, Golan, *Secret Conversations*, 86–87, and Safran, *Israel*, 492, indicate that Kissinger was much more direct in his encouragement to them and implied that he was prepared to accept "slippage" of days, not hours. Garthoff, *Détente and Confrontation*, 372, also gives credence to the Israeli version of the conversation.

PART TWO

Superpower Relations

4

U.S.-Soviet Global Rivalry: Norms of Competition

Alexander L. George

We should recognize at the outset that the superpowers have a variety of means at their disposal for avoiding diplomatic crises which, while not war-threatening, inflict serious damage on the overall U.S.-Soviet relationship. Thus, a superpower may employ deterrence strategy to dissuade the other superpower or its allies from encroaching on its interests. Similarly, each superpower may undertake policies aimed at increasing the internal stability and security posture of an ally or neutral state. The superpowers may also rely upon third parties to mediate regional conflicts that might otherwise lead to a superpower confrontation. In the interest of crisis avoidance they may also agree to create neutral or buffer states, or accord each other dominant or exclusive spheres of interest in certain areas. These traditional means of moderating super-power global rivalry are not considered in this article, which addresses, instead, the feasibility of superpower cooperation in developing norms of competition that might help to avoid diplomatic crises arising from their global competition for influence at each other's expense.

On various occasions in the past fifteen years the question has been posed whether the two superpowers might subscribe to a set of general principles—"rules of conduct," "rules of the game," or "norms of competition"—as a means of limiting and regulating their global rivalry. This idea gained currency at the high point of detente in 1972 when Nixon and Brezhnev signed the Basic Principles Agreement. The first few articles of this document suggested that the United States and the Soviet Union had agreed on the need to moderate their global competition so as not to allow themselves to be drawn into dangerous crises. A closer examination of the Basic Principles Agreement in the light of developments in U.S.-Soviet relations in the next few years, however, revealed that it was in fact a pseudo-agreement, one that contained unresolved disagreements and ambiguities that were interpreted differently by the two sides. Nixon and Brezhnev signed a more specific agreement on consultation to deal with situations posing the danger of nuclear war at their second summit in June, 1973. This Agreement on Prevention of Nuclear War was severely tested by the onset of the Egyptian attack on Israel in October, 1973, raising questions in the United States as to whether the Soviet Union had complied with its provisions (George, 1983).

Types of U.S.-Soviet Understandings

Despite the unsatisfactory experience with these two agreements and the gradual demise of detente, interest in the possibility of developing a set of general "ground rules" for limiting involvement of the superpowers in Third Areas persists among some students of U.S.-Soviet relations. As will be emphasized here, it is important to recognize that cooperative arrangements to this end can be quite formal and explicit, or they may be less formal understandings of a tacit or verbalized character.[1] An ambitious proposal for a formal explicit agreement was put forward in 1982 by the American Committee on East-West Accord, based on the ideas of one of its members.[2] The proposal urges that the United States and the Soviet Union negotiate "a precise set of ground rules having to do with specific geography and a specific ban on direct or indirect use of combat forces in those areas." The prohibitions would apply to the Middle East, Southwest Asia, Africa, the Indian subcontinent, and Southeast Asia—presumably also to Latin America and the Caribbean, although these two areas were not explicitly mentioned in the American Committee's statement. It may be noted that the proposal also suggested that the prohibition against introduction of U.S. and Soviet forces into these areas should be extended to include a ban on "covert, paramilitary, or, so-called 'volunteer' combat forces." Also, the Committee proposed, the agreement should stipulate "that neither power would intervene with combat forces *even if* 'invited' to do so by one of the Third World countries"(emphasis added).

While many types of superpower intervention would be excluded by these proposed "ground rules," the prohibition does not extend to the transfer of weapons or the sending of military advisers; nor were proxy forces and those of superpower allies to be explicitly prohibited. Therefore, as is often the case with efforts to define what is not permitted, the result is to make it implicitly legitimate to do everything that is not explicitly forbidden by the agreement.

It should be noted that a superpower's acceptance of general ground rules of this kind would mean that it was willing to accept *any* outcome of a regional conflict, *however harmful to its interest the outcome might turn out to be.* Similarly, unless otherwise specified, adherence to such sweeping ground rules would cancel commitments the United States and the Soviet Union have made to allies in the geographical areas in question to assist in their defense against external attack or armed insurrection. General ground rules of this kind make no allowance for the difference in the relative interests of the superpowers in different areas. The proposed prohibitions would apply across the board to areas in which a superpower had substantial and vital interests as well as to areas in which it had quite limited interests. (The importance of the relative interests of the two sides in a particular area is discussed in the next section of this chapter.)

For these reasons, and perhaps for others as well, it is doubtful whether either superpower would regard ground rules of the kind proposed by the American Committee as acceptable. Both the desirability and the feasibility of such a comprehensive set of prohibitions would be questioned.

The type of cooperation between the superpowers called for in the American Committee's proposal is in the nature of a *formal, explicit agreement* to forego certain kinds of intervention *in many different geographical areas.* It is important to recognize that superpower cooperation to limit competition and involvement in Third Areas can take other forms. Instead of agreeing to a general contractual arrangement that applies equally to many regions, the superpowers can make an explicit agreement that is limited to a specific country or region. Thus, in 1955, they agreed to the Austrian State Treaty conferring neutral status on that country and removing it from the arena of the Cold War. Similarly, in 1962 Kennedy and Khrushchev agreed to the neutralization of Laos. (Both of these agreements took the form of multilateral treaties since the adherence of states other than the U.S. and the Soviet Union was necessary for effective implementation.)

An agreement to limit competition in a particular area can be quite explicit without taking the form of a treaty. Thus, for example, in the winter of 1977–78 the two superpowers made use of traditional diplomatic modalities to reach an understanding regarding the war between Ethiopia and Somalia over the Ogaden. The United States sought and received explicit assurances from the Soviet Union that Ethiopian-Cuban troops would not invade Somalia after expelling Somalian troops from the disputed Ogaden area.[3]

Thus far we have discussed formal, explicit superpower agreements that are either comprehensive in geographical scope or limited to a particular area or country. Superpower rivalry can be limited and regulated also through mutual adjustment and the development of *"norms of competition"*, i.e., less formal and often less explicit understandings. Such norms of a tacit or verbalized character can emerge during the course of superpower competition or reflect *patterns of restraint* that have emerged through past experience which the two sides find useful to observe in new situations. In contrast to the legal or quasi-legal type of formal agreement referred to earlier, norms of competition are analogous to a "common law" which develops through experience and offers useful precedents or benchmarks.

It is important to recognize that the utility of norms and patterns of restraint is often weakened because they contain ambiguities which may tempt one side or the other to probe or to take advantage of the inadequacies of the understanding. While such challenges can weaken or destroy existing norms, nonetheless probes and tests of ambiguous norms sometimes have a beneficial effect by forcing a clarification of ambiguities and closing of loopholes, thereby enhancing the usefulness of the norms for regulating superpower competition.

Tacit and verbalized norms of competition can play an important role, if only because more explicit and formal agreements on "rules" of competition are lacking. But such norms tend to be unstable. Compliance with existing norms or patterns of restraint cannot be taken for granted when new situations arise. It may be necessary for one superpower to take steps to "activate" the norm, to insist upon its relevance in the situation at hand. The other superpower may or may not agree.

Thus, an inherent weakness of norms of competition is that they lack the *institutionalized arrangements and procedures* needed for their clarification and application to new situations. These arrangements are precisely what the superpowers needed to create in order to facilitate implementation of formal negotiated agreements such as the ABM Treaty, SALT I, the Accidents at Sea Agreement of 1972, and the Berlin Quadripartite Agreement of 1971.

Another limitation of many norms of competition is that they are area-specific; that is, they grow out of experience in a particular region where the superpowers have been competing and may not easily transfer to other areas of their competition. This is certainly the case with the norms of competition that have developed in Cuba and the Middle East.

The uses and limitations of norms of competition are well illustrated by the subsequent history of the *quid pro quo* agreement between Kennedy and Khrushchev that helped to bring the Cuban missile crisis to a close. As will be recalled, Kennedy expressed willingness to declare that the United States would not invade Cuba in the future in return for removal of the missiles and an assurance that offensive weapons would not be reintroduced into Cuba in the future. Nonetheless, in the following years ambiguity remained as to whether the understanding was still in force and as to its scope. In early August, 1970, for reasons that remain unclear, the Soviet Union utilized diplomatic channels to inquire whether the Kennedy-Khrushchev understanding remained in force; the Nixon administration responded affirmatively. Shortly there-after, the Nixon administration successfully invoked this understanding as the basis for its objection to the beginnings of the construction of a base in Cuba to service Soviet submarines. Other ambiguities remained, however, and Soviet probing in the form of visits by Soviet submarines to Cuban ports continued, though certain restraints were observed.

A second potential diplomatic crisis over Soviet compliance with the 1962 agreement was more expeditiously and clearly deflected in 1978. This time the question was whether the Kennedy-Khrushchev agreement that banned reintroduction of offensive weapons systems into Cuba extended to fighter aircraft capable of striking targets in the United States. Intelligence indicated that the Soviet Union was possibly replacing Cuban MiG-23 fighter interceptor aircraft designed for air defense with MiG ground-attack planes capable of delivering nuclear weapons against U.S. targets. Diplomatic talks between high-ranking U.S. and Soviet officials resulted in a policy decision by the Carter administration not to make an issue of the matter, given the difficulty of ascertaining whether the new MiG aircraft were capable of carrying nuclear weapons, and to accept Soviet assurances in the matter so long as the number of MiG aircraft remained quite limited.

Within a year, a major U.S.-Soviet diplomatic confrontation erupted in 1979 over the "discovery" of what appeared to be a Soviet combat brigade in Cuba. A State Department review of the 1962 agreement and prior U.S.-Soviet discussions about it failed to turn up evidence that Soviet ground forces had been included in the original Kennedy-Khrushchev agreement or in its 1970 elaboration. But from various past U.S. statements and President Carter's 1978 commitment to oppose Soviet bases in the Western Hemisphere, the State Department concluded that a Soviet combat force in Cuba could be regarded as in conflict at least with unilateral, publicly expressed U.S. policy. However, the Soviet Union refused to accept the U.S. demand for the brigade's withdrawal or to change its equipment to make it more consistent with its stated training mission. On the other hand, the Soviet Union did reaffirm that the brigade's mission was confined to training Cuban forces and promised not to change its function or status. Washington's inept handling of this affair inflicted additional damage on the overall U.S.-Soviet relationship and contributed to the non-ratification of SALT II (Duffy 1983: 285–318).

Types of Competitive U.S.-Soviet "Games":
Implications for Norms of Competition[4]

As noted earlier, proposals of the kind advanced by the American Committee on East-West Accord do not take into account that the balance of interests between the United States and the Soviet Union varies considerably from one geographical area to another. From the standpoint of interests at stake, the global rivalry of the superpowers *is* differentiated. Ground rules that severely limit a superpower's involvement in areas where it has very modest interests may be acceptable to it, but the same severe prohibitions are not likely to be acceptable to that superpower for areas in which it has substantial or vital interests.

As these observations imply, we need to view U.S.-Soviet global rivalry as composed of a *variety* of competitive "games" in different parts of the globe. Furthermore, it is useful to regard the several types of "games" or competitive contests as having *different structures* and somewhat *different logics* (i.e., implications for the task of managing competition in the interest of crisis prevention). As a starting point for further analysis, one may postulate that the fundamental structure of each type of "game" is determined by the balance of interests perceived by the two superpowers to underlie their competition in a given area. By taking into account the *magnitude or strength* of each superpower's perceived interests in each area *and* whether their interests in that area are perceived by them to be *symmetrical or asymmetrical* we can identify six "game" structures of a distinctive kind imbedded in the overall global competition. In presenting this typology of competitive U.S.-Soviet games it is not assumed that the relative balance of interests will necessarily remain the same in each geographical area over a period of time.[5]

The first four of these game structures are the following:

1. *High-interest symmetry:* locales in which both sides recognize that they have very strong, if not vital, interests.
2. *Low-interest symmetry:* locales in which both sides recognize that they have modest interests.
3. *Interest asymmetry favoring the Soviet Union:* locales in which both sides recognize that Soviet interests are clearly and substantially more important than those of the United States.
4. *Interest asymmetry favoring the United States:* locales in which both sides recognize that U.S. interests are clearly and substantially more important than those of the Soviet Union.

It will be noted that each of these game structures rests on the important assumption that the two sides agree on that particular characterization of the balance of interests. This assumption, however, is not in fact always satisfied, and the four game structures thus far identified do not encompass the full range of competitive situations. Our typology must be extended to encompass at least two additional game structures:

5. *Disputed interest symmetry:* locales in which the United States and the Soviet Union do not agree on the relative balance of their interests.
6. *Uncertain interest symmetry:* locales of an ambiguous or fluid nature in which one or both superpowers are not certain of their own or the other's interests and find it difficult to assess how and to what extent their interests will become engaged in a developing, unstable situation.

Such a typology of game structures is useful primarily to remind us of the complexities of the global competition between the superpowers. It would make our task much easier if, in addition, there were implicit in each of these different game structures "logics" of a simple, clear-cut character that could be employed to identify ground rules or norms of competition by means of which the superpowers could regulate their competition. However, while the typology does provide some important guidance as a starting point, additional dimensions of the problem must be addressed.

Thus, in addition to the magnitude of superpower interests and the symmetry-asymmetry between their interests in different geographical areas, other variables and considerations are likely to influence the ground rules or norms each superpower would prefer for each type of "game." And these other variables are likely to make it difficult, though not necessarily impossible, for the superpowers to agree on the rules and norms for competition in each type of "game." These additional variables include, but are not limited to, the *resources* and *strategies* available to the superpowers for use in their competition; the various *domestic and international constraints* on *defining* their interests operationally and in *pursuing* those interests, and the *ideologies, perceptions, and images* that enter into and influence the foreign policy behavior of the superpowers.

Let us consider now what the "logics" of the different U.S.-Soviet competitive games imply as regards norms of competition and how these implications are, or are likely to be, affected by some of these other variables.

Areas of High-Interest Asymmetry Favoring
Either the United States or the Soviet Union

At first glance our model suggests that situations of this type should lend themselves to development and acceptance of rules (or norms) that facilitate crisis prevention. At the extreme, the superpower with dominant interests in a particular area (the Soviets in Eastern Europe, the United States in the Caribbean) may successfully assert a claim to an unchallenged sphere of interest. But the other superpower may be unwilling to withdraw from competition in that area for one or more reasons. While accepting that an asymmetry of interest exists favoring its opponent, it may claim to have certain lesser interests of its own in that area which it is unwilling to forego altogether. Or it may refuse for ideological reasons to forego competing in the other superpower's area of dominant interests. Particularly if it views its global conflict with the other superpower in something approximating zero-sum terms, it may be motivated to try to weaken its adversary's control and influence in its sphere of dominant interests. As the history of the Cold War and the post-detente era teaches us, the superpower with modest interests in the other side's sphere of dominant interests may still choose to compete there *within limits.* These constraints may take the form of a limitation of either the *objectives* it will pursue in that area and/or the *means* it will employ on behalf of those objectives.

When this is the case, it will be difficult for the superpowers to arrive at either a clear-cut understanding on the ground rules or on norms of competition. Nonetheless, *tacit norms* and *patterns of restraint* are likely to emerge which will help to structure and moderate superpower competition in such areas. Indeed, the United States and the Soviet Union have recognized and to a considerable extent have respected each other's areas of dominant interest, though they have done so largely through the medium of tacit norms and *ad hoc* self-imposed restraints.

Thus, for example, since World War II the United States has recognized the important security interests of the Soviet Union in Eastern Europe. But this has not kept Washington from pressing Moscow to settle for an "open" rather than a "closed" sphere of security interest, one in which East European states would enjoy a measure of political freedom and access to the West. The objectives the United States have pursued in Eastern Europe have varied in scope from time to time, being somewhat more ambitious during the height of the Cold War. The means Washington has employed in pursuit of its objectives vis-à-vis Eastern Europe have also varied, but it has observed strict limits in the interest of preventing a dangerous confrontation or war with the Soviet Union. In fact, precisely for this reason Washington has undertaken crisis prevention initiatives on its own on several important occasions. Thus, in Hungary in 1956 and in Czechoslovakia in 1968, the United States found ways of assuring the Soviet Union that it would not seriously exacerbate difficulties Moscow was having in dealing with revolutionary upheavals in these East European countries.[6]

Similar observations might be made about Soviet policy generally towards the Western Hemisphere, a vast geographical area that has been traditionally placed off-limits to European powers by the United States. The hemisphere as a whole has been of relatively low interest to the Soviet Union and therefore not worth either substantial investment of Moscow's resources to compete for influence with the United States or the acceptance of significant risks in so doing. Yet Moscow, for ideological and other reasons, does not forego competing altogether in this sphere of dominant U.S. interest. The most startling and dangerous example of this, of course, was the development of Moscow's close relationship with Castro's Cuba and its abortive effort to place strategic missiles on that island.[7] More recently, in response to opportunities that emerged in the Caribbean and Central America, Moscow has appeared to be probing indirectly and very cautiously via Cuba and Nicaragua to ascertain at what low levels of involvement it can assist the revolutionary process without provoking an American overreaction.

There is uncertainty and disagreement among Americans as to Soviet intentions in Central America; that is, whether the Soviet Union is pursuing ambitious or quite modest objectives. And, as will be noted later in this chapter, when there is ambiguity as to an adversary's *intentions*, policy-makers tend to define the threat in terms of perceived or possible longer-range *consequences* of the adversary's behavior rather than on the basis of its declared or possibly modest objectives. Thus, a superpower's cautious use of quite limited *means* in the policy it adopts towards the other superpower's area of high-interest dominance does not itself provide assurance that the *objectives* it is pursuing are also quite limited, either in the short run or in the long run. This applies not only to the difficulty U.S. policy-makers experience in assessing Soviet policy in Central America but also to Moscow's task in assessing the challenge posed by American policy towards areas such as Eastern Europe that are of high interest for the Soviet Union.

Several provisional conclusions may be advanced regarding the prospects for U.S.-Soviet cooperation in preventing crises in each other's areas of high-interest dominance. In the first place, neither superpower is at all likely to accept ground rules or norms that would handicap its efforts to protect essential interests in its areas of high-interest dominance. While each superpower may be willing to accept some loosening of its hegemonic influence and control in such an area, it can be expected to strongly oppose this development if it appears that the other superpower is attempting to abet or to exploit such changes in order to substantially increase its own influence in that area.

At the same time, the fact that the superpowers are unlikely to agree on ground rules for areas in which either has dominant interests does not mean that they will be unwilling or unable to cooperate, when necessary, in the future as in the past, in order to avoid dangerous crises. Rather, while continuing low-level, restrained competition in each other's spheres of dominant interest, both Washington and Moscow are likely to continue to act with considerable prudence in each other's areas of prime interest. Prudence and self-imposed restraint are likely to be exhibited particularly by limiting the means each will employ in seeking to reduce the adversary's influence in its sphere of dominant interests.

An additional norm of restraint might possibly emerge. Each superpower may be willing to forego efforts to exploit changes that weaken the other superpower's influence in its area of dominant interest. There is some evidence that both superpowers have been prepared to accept some loosening of influence and control in Third Areas generally, including their spheres of dominance. This process of loosening superpower hegemony is likely to be hindered, not helped, if Moscow and Washington attempt to actively hasten and profit from each other's difficulties in this respect.

Areas of Disputed or Uncertain Symmetry

It would appear even more difficult for the two superpowers to agree on ground rules or norms of competition for the parts of the globe which they perceive to be characterized by uncertain and/or disputed asymmetry of interests. The Middle East is a case in point. The Soviet Union, claiming superpower equality with the United States, has tried unsuccessfully for a number of years to get Washington to regard this area as one of high-interest symmetry that requires a joint U.S.-Soviet approach to peace-making in the Arab-Israeli conflict.

While U.S. policy-makers have not denied that the Soviet Union has some legitimate interests in the Middle East, they have not attempted to ascertain what Moscow believes its bedrock interests are in the region and to encourage Soviet leaders to differentiate vital from secondary and tertiary interests. Instead, American policy-makers have tended to ascribe to Moscow an overweening aspiration to substantially increase its influence in the region at the expense of the United States and its allies. In other words, the dominant view in Washington for many years has been that competition with the Soviet Union in the Middle East approximates a zero-sum game. This view has strengthened Washington's disposition to oppose any increase in Soviet influence in the area for fear that it would further destabilize the region and lead to an additional weakening of Western positions.

Under these circumstances it would seem all the more necessary for the two superpowers to address the admittedly difficult task of clarifying what each believes its own and the other superpower's interests to be in the Middle East. Sorting out their respective interests will not be easy, for there are no clear lines between the interests asserted by Soviet and by American leaders in the Middle East as there are in Europe. Rather, because proclaimed U.S. and Soviet interests overlap geographically in this highly unstable region, both sides are aware of the danger that their competition in that region may again draw them, as on several occasions, into tense confrontations, if not also some kind of shooting war.

Although the two superpowers have not succeeded in achieving a clarification or resolution of their conflicting interests in the Middle East, they have at least managed to develop a tacit norm for regulating and limiting their involvement in Arab-Israeli wars. This norm has emerged from experience in dealing with an acute policy dilemma that arises for both superpowers when war breaks out among their regional allies. In this situation both superpowers must back their local allies but, at the same time, they must avoid being dragged into a war with each other.

The United States and the Soviet Union managed to cope with this policy dilemma successfully in the Six Days War in 1967, the War of Attrition in 1970, and the October 1973 War. Their behavior during the course of these three wars evinces a pattern of restraint or perhaps even a tacit understanding of what a superpower is and is not entitled to do in support of its regional ally and what restraints it must observe. Thus, each superpower has learned that it must reckon with the likelihood that the other superpower will intervene militarily in some way to prevent its regional ally from suffering a catastrophic defeat at the hands of other regional actors. To avoid such an intervention, the superpower backing the winning local actor must recognize the necessity to pressure its ally to stop short of inflicting an overwhelming defeat on its opponent.[8]

Variations of this tacit ground rule can be seen in all three Arab-Israeli wars. Towards the end of the Six Day War, Premier Kosygin threatened Soviet intervention if the Israeli army marched against Damascus; he was assured by President Johnson over the Hotline that this would not happen. In early 1970, at a critical juncture of the War of Attrition, when the Israeli air force's deep penetration raids against Egypt were threatening to topple Nasser, Kosygin sent a note to Nixon indirectly warning that the Soviet Union would have to act if the Israelis continued their attacks. Kosygin's warning was not correctly interpreted; Washington did not see the need to exercise its influence with Israel, and the Soviet Union gradually introduced substantial air defense forces into Egypt which brought a halt in Israeli air operations against Egypt. The United States did not attempt to seriously deter or to force a withdrawal of the Soviet military intervention; it implicitly accepted the legitimacy of the Soviet move to save its Egyptian ally from suffering a catastrophic defeat.

Similarly, in October, 1973, when Israel violated the cease-fire worked out by Brezhnev and Kissinger in Moscow and Israeli forces threatened the destruction of the Egyptian Third Army, Brezhnev sent a note to Nixon suggesting joint Soviet-American military intervention to end the war and backed it with a threat of unilateral Soviet intervention. The Brezhnev note was a stern reminder to the United States of its obligation to control its ally. And while Washington responded to the Soviet threat of intervention with an alert of U.S. military forces, it also immediately pressured Israel to stop its efforts to capture the Egyptian Third Army.

The United States, too, on one occasion has invoked this tacit norm. Thus, when Syrian tanks rolled into Jordan in the autumn of 1970, threatening to topple King Hussein, Washington pressed the Soviet Union to pressure the Syrians to get out of Jordan and backed this demand with a threat of military intervention by Israeli forces on Jordan's behalf.

As these four historical cases demonstrate, the tacit norm comes into play only when the regional ally of a superpower is threatened with imminent substantial defeat. Coincidentally, the balance of interests— i.e., what is at stake—clearly shifts in favor of the superpower backing the regional actor that is in serious difficulty, making it both "legitimate" and credible that it would intervene, if necessary, to save it from defeat. At the same time, it should be noted that the tacit norm requiring a superpower to restrain its victorious regional ally does not come into play automatically; rather, it must be activated by a credible threat of intervention by the defending superpower. For various reasons, therefore, this tacit ground rule cannot be regarded as a stable, reliable basis for enabling superpowers to back their regional client states without being drawn into war with each other.

Areas of High-Interest Symmetry

Our model suggests that areas of this kind, in which both superpowers recognizably have very strong, if not vital, interests, ought to lend themselves more readily to developing rules (and, for that matter, tacit norms) for crisis prevention.

A situation of this kind emerged and was recognized as such by both sides during World War II. Roosevelt, Stalin, and Churchill foresaw that once Allied forces crushed Nazi Germany and its allies, a competition for advantage would develop among the victors for filling the vacuum of power in central Europe that might well lead to severe conflict, if not war. Accordingly, the Allied war-time leaders mapped out in advance zones of occupation in Europe for their respective armies and set up procedures and rules for collective decision-making and joint administration of occupied Germany. Recognizing central Europe to be an area that would engage the vital interests of all of the victorious powers, the wartime Allies adopted what may be appropriately regarded as an explicit crisis prevention regime. The cooperative arrangements and institutional structures that were created to implement them, to be sure, did not suffice to cope with the stresses created by subsequent developments. But this historical case illustrates, nonetheless, the possibilities for developing explicit rules and institutional structures in situations of high-interest symmetry.

There are other instances in which mutual recognition of high-interest symmetry has led to explicit agreements, and by no means have all of them collapsed as did the Allied agreement for occupation and administration of Germany. Thus, one may regard the Austrian State Treaty of 1955, the Four Power Agreement on the status of West Berlin in 1971, and the Helsinki Accord of 1975 (whatever its imperfections) as successful or partly successful efforts to make cooperative arrangements to limit competition in a region, like Europe, of high-interest symmetry.

Areas of Low-Interest Symmetry

At first glance it would appear that geographical areas in which both superpowers have only modest interests should lend themselves to rule-making in the interest of crisis prevention. Underlying this 'logic' is the presumption that since what is at stake for the two superpowers in such areas falls well short of engaging vital interests, it would be highly rational and hence relatively simple to agree on ground rules strictly limiting both the levels of investment in their competition and the risk that such competition might escalate to mutually undesired levels of conflict.

As experience demonstrates, however, such a presumption is not always justified. In the first place, it has often been noted, great powers that have global interests tend to gradually expand the concept of their security requirements. The defense of critical outposts or lines of communication tends to lead to an inflated conception of security requirements. Robert Jervis cites Balfour's complaint to illustrate the tendency of security requirements to snow-ball and to take on an open-ended character: "Every time I come to a discussion—at intervals of, say, five years—I find there is a new sphere which we have got to guard, which is supposed to protect the gateways of India.Those gateways are getting further and further away from India, and I do not know how far west they are going to be brought by the General Staff" (Jervis 1978: 169).

In the second place, the simple logical premise that the superpowers should find it relatively easy to agree upon rule-making that strictly limits competition in areas of low-interest symmetry overlooks incentives and complications that can and do emerge. In fact, the superpowers may find a contrary "logic" more appealing: it is precisely in areas where one's opponent has quite modest interests that assertive policies to increase one's influence, even at the expense of the opponent's interests, can be safely pursued. In other words, areas of low-interest symmetry may be perceived as offering *opportunities*—not dangers—for *marginal gains*, and such policies are not judged to carry with them any appreciable risk of uncontrollable escalation to a war-threatening confrontation with the superpower adversary.

Competing with the rival in areas of low-interest symmetry may also be viewed as offering tempting opportunities for pursuing a longer-range strategy for weakening the other superpower's global influence. Thus, one superpower may attempt over time to gain a series of marginal gains in a number of areas, each of which is of limited value but which cumulatively would substantially weaken the other superpower. This strategy may be regarded as an attractive, low-cost and low-risk way of enhancing one's own global security position: thus any weakening of the opponent's influence and control, even in peripheral areas, puts him on the defensive, distracts him, and reduces his capabilities for threatening and damaging one's own interests. In other words, an "offense" of this kind is really a good indirect "defense."

The mere possibility that the adversary is pursuing a long-range "offensive-defensive" strategy of this kind creates the basis for distrust and misperception of intentions underlying some of the specific, more limited actions it undertakes in Third Areas. Since an adversary's intentions, particulary its longer-range aims, are often difficult to as-certain, one is inclined to judge those intentions not by what the opponent says but rather on the basis of one's perception of the possible long-run *consequences* of the adversary's behavior. The ambiguity of the adversary's "intentions" and the greater significance in many instances of the "perceived consequences" of its behavior is the source of much difficulty generally in superpower relations.

We have noted the marked tendency for the abstract "logic" of restrained competition in areas of low-interest symmetry to be displaced by the quite different "meta-logic" of global superpower competition. What ought to remain a low-stakes "game" in areas in which Moscow and Washington have only modest interests assumes inflated importance from time to time because such contests *cannot be easily or reliably decoupled* from the higher-stake "games" in which they are engaged in other geographical areas. As is well known from the experience of the Cold War, "gray areas" of little importance in and of themselves are often perceived by one and/or the other superpower to have considerable actual or potential *strategic significance*. In addition, the loss of influence in these areas is sometimes expected to have adverse *political consequences* in the domestic arena or on the international scene.

Devising "rules" or understandings to prevent escalation of low-level competition is further complicated by the fact that different gray areas are perceived to have different strategic and political significance. Such judgments tend to be highly context-dependent and subject to change, and the two superpowers may operate with different estimates regarding the significance of a particular area to each other.

As a result, superpower competition in gray areas is riddled with numerous complexities and uncertainties that cannot be easily anticipated. This increases the likelihood of misperceptions and actions that contribute to escalation of the stakes and additional superpower involvement. In addition, one or both superpowers may experience the dilemma of "sunk costs" in an area in which its efforts to compete have not gone well. When an initially low-level, low-risk involvement on behalf of limited objectives unexpectedly fails, it is difficult to avoid the temptation to increase one's involvement somewhat in order to avoid a setback and in the hope of securing a better outcome. Thus, the mere expenditure of resources by a superpower in a Third Area competition increases its stakes in that competition and, in this sense, "sacrifice creates value."

Not merely the expenditure of resources but the commitment of prestige can also increase the stakes and encourage escalation. Prestige is often put on the line in the course of public statements and military maneuvers that are intended to convey resolution in order to impress the opponent. But the rhetorical inflation of the importance of what is at stake that often accompanies efforts to signal strong and credible resolution is not without its own kind of costs and risks since, if it does not have the desired impact, it leaves the dissatisfied superpower in the unsatisfactory position of having either to back down, to make concessions to secure a compromise solution, or to escalate its involvement.

In principle, to be sure, if the superpowers do not agree beforehand upon the ceiling to place on their involvement in a Third Area, they can presumably cooperate to establish *ad hoc* "ground rules" to limit the danger of escalation after they begin to compete. Acceptance of ground rules, however, implies a mutual willingness to accept whatever outcome, however disadvantageous, of the competition conducted within those ground rules. Otherwise, the only alternative to further escalation by the disadvantaged side as the competition evolves is the willingness of its adversary to offer an acceptable compromise settlement. But the side that holds the advantage in a local contest—as the Soviets did in Angola in late 1975—may be unwilling to forego the full measure of its prospective success for various reasons. It may feel that its objectives are "legitimate" whereas those of its opponent are not, that it has earned its success, that the opponent must be taught a lesson, that there would be a serious domestic backlash if it granted its opponent a generous compromise settlement, etc.

We have discussed a variety of factors that constrain and complicate the ability or willingness of the superpowers to cooperate in developing ground rules or norms for keeping their competition in areas of mutual low-interest at safe levels. One should not conclude from this that superpower cooperation for this purpose is wholly infeasible but, rather, that further efforts to arrive at such "rules" must take improved account of complexities better known now than in the early 1970s, when Nixon and Brezhnev took the first steps toward developing such understandings. It is clear from their abortive effort, as events later in the decade were to make plain, that Moscow and Washington had not really agreed on whether, to what extent, and how to de-couple their competition in so-called "gray areas" from their global competition. The "lessons" of this experience need to be clearly understood if the superpowers are to be more successful in preventing competition in Third Areas from undermining any new efforts they may make to improve and stabilize their over-all political and strategic relationship.

Underlying much of the preceding discussion of the various "logics" for regulating U.S.-Soviet competition that might be implicit in the particular configuration of their relative interests in different parts of the globe is *the assumption that each superpower is capable of determining what those interests are and of successfully communicating this to its adversary.* We need to examine this important assumption more closely now.

Superpower Interests: Difficulties of Determination and Communication

It is often said, with considerable justification, that the United States and the Soviet Union can reduce the risk of confrontations by timely clarification and communication of their interests in particular areas and situations. If we were to systematically examine the history of U.S.-Soviet relations from this standpoint, however, we would find many episodes in which they failed to do so. Some of these failures might be attributed to oversight, human error, technical communication difficulties of a kind that could be rather easily avoided or improved upon in the future.

Other failures to define and communicate one's interests effectively and successfully cannot be so easily explained and are rooted in causes that cannot be so readily eliminated. One root cause has to do with *difficulties of diplomatic signaling and communication*—e.g., a failure to convey what one's interests and intentions are in a timely, clear manner that is comprehensible and credible to the opponent, and a failure of the recipient to attend properly to serious communications directed towards him and to interpret them correctly. There are various constraints on the ability of the superpowers to communicate effectively with each other that deserve the most careful study. Indeed, this is a common problem that could greatly benefit from joint U.S.-Soviet analysis of past failures. It is passed over quickly here to turn to another root cause of failures to convey one's interests on a timely basis—namely, *the difficulty superpowers often experience in deciding what their interests are in a timely and reliable way.*

Why do such difficulties arise? It is useful to begin by recognizing that not all of a superpower's interests extending over the globe are equally important; each superpower has to *differentiate* its interests. But it is much easier for an investigator to devise a typology of interests—high, moderate, low or non-existent—than it is for Moscow or Washington to make differentiated assessments adequate for the purposes of conducting foreign policy.

It is relatively easy for a state to recognize that it has interests in a particular area that are as yet not achieved or are being threatened by another state. It is a far more difficult, yet necessary, task to assess the *value* one should place on the achievement or protection of those interests. Judgments of the value of one's interests are often difficult to make in the abstract and in advance of actual decisions to expend resources to enhance those interests. Thus, *the real value of one's interests often can be determined only by deciding what price one is prepared to pay in order to realize or protect those interests.* But the price one is willing to pay may be difficult to anticipate in advance of circumstances which require expenditure of resources for that purpose. As a result, *prior* evaluations of one's interests may prove to be grossly unreliable; a superpower may embark on a course of action to protect or advance certain ostensibly modest interests on the basis of what proves in due course to have been a gross *underestimate* of the price tag it is now willing or is forced to accept. Similarly, the advance valuation of interests may turn out to be a substantial *overestimate* of the level of costs and risks one is willing to accept when action is required.

Miscalculations by policy-makers of the value of state interests arise from a number of different sources. Fundamental is the fact that the concept of "national interest" has the characteristics of what decision theorists refer to as a "non-operational goal"—i.e., one that does not provide a measuring rod for comparing and choosing among alternative policies. National interest is similar in this respect to concepts such as "the general welfare" and "the public interest." Such concepts cannot be employed as a utility function in rigorous policy analysis; they can be related to specific choices of action only through various subgoals which they presumably encompass. "National interest" includes a variety of subgoals that usually *compete* for influence in the conduct of foreign policy. But there is lacking an operational common denominator for weighing the relative importance of subgoals. Hence, the relative weight to be given to various subgoals is a matter left to the authoritative (but subjective) judgment of one or more top-level officials. Their judgment in turn is subject to the play of political forces and the requirement for some degree of consensus on the level of costs and risks to accept in pursuing the national interests in the particular situation at hand and as that situation evolves. (For further discussion, see George, 1980: 217–237.)

The tasks of differentiating one's interests in various parts of the globe and operationalizing the value to be accorded them do not account for all the difficulties foreign policy-makers experience in deciding what their state's interests are and conveying this reliably to others. In addition, we must recognize that a superpower's interests in some Third Areas are often *complex, contingent,* and *context-dependent* in ways that neither the superpower itself nor its opponent can foresee. A superpower may have diverse, competing interests in a particular area that are not easily sorted out and balanced in order to decide what actions to undertake on its behalf. To this complexity of interests is often added the fact that the value of some of these interests may be highly contingent upon the circumstances under which it becomes necessary to decide by what means and how far to go in support of those interests. Thus, for example, in 1949 U.S. policy-makers placed modest value on *the strategic importance* of South Korea in the event of a general war with the Soviet Union, but then in late June, 1950 they suddenly placed much higher value on *the Cold War importance* of South Korea's defense when it was attacked by North Korea. As this example illustrates, the definition and valuation of interests is often highly context-dependent and the context in which such judgments have to be made often changes unexpectedly and dramatically.

Similarly, the value of a superpower's perceived interests in a particular area may escalate simply in consequence of competitive interaction with the other superpower or its clients. And *domestic* and *allied* constraints, as is well known, are often unpredictable factors complicating a superpower's ability to make a reliable determination of its interests in a particular area or to pursue those interests in ways policy-makers, freed from such constraints, would think appropriate. It should be recognized that constraints of domestic or allied opinion may work in either direction, either to magnify or to reduce the level of resource expenditures policy-makers believe to be consistent with the true value of the interests at stake.

The willingness and ability of the superpowers to clarify their interests and intentions are, perhaps paradoxically, more problematic in their competition in "gray areas" of relatively low interest. One reason why Soviet and U.S. leaders seem reluctant in many situations to define and delimit their interests is that by doing so they might appear to "give away" such areas or encourage the other side to proceed to enhance its influence. Additionally, U.S. policy-makers are constrained from clarifying or delimiting their interests in certain Third Areas by domestic politics or by sensitive allies. There is the ever-present likelihood that someone in the foreign policy bureaucracy, Congress, or vocal interest groups will be quick to charge the administration with being insufficiently attentive to protecting American interests abroad.

Sometimes responsible policy-makers are not able to judge the full weight of U.S. interests in a gray area until competition with the Soviet Union or its proxies has escalated and is approaching a crisis stage. Often only when a situation has deteriorated to a certain point do its broader ramifications for U.S. interests become evident in Washington, forcing consideration of a strong response.

Such dilemmas cannot be avoided merely by enjoining American policy-makers to define their interests in advance and to "draw a line," for in many situations what is at stake for the United States does increase substantially and somewhat unpredictably as a result of actions by the Soviet Union or its proxies, or through internal developments in the area in question.

Thus far we have emphasized and tried to explain why superpowers often find it difficult to decide what their interests are in certain areas and, in particular, the value to be accorded those interests. The other side of the coin, not surprisingly, is that each superpower also often finds it difficult to ascertain its opponent's interests and valuation of those interests in a particular area. In recent years American policy-makers have frequently experienced this difficulty. Moscow's concept of its "security requirements" appears to U.S. observers to be increasingly opaque and elastic. It is not always clear how Soviet foreign policy-makers differentiate bedrock security requirements from other interests and incentives. The question arises whether acquisition of an enhanced global military reach has encouraged Moscow to expand its conception of Soviet foreign policy interests. If so, is this simply because enhanced capabilities now bring within reach more opportunities for increasing influence or because increased Soviet military power has led to a less cautious way of calculating risks or a willingness to accept greater risks than in the past? Similarly, American observers wonder whether and to what extent Moscow's claim to the status of superpower "equality" with the United States influences Soviet leaders' conception of their foreign policy interests.

Given the difficulties American and Soviet leaders experience from time to time in determining their own and each other's interests in various areas of their global competition, it is all the more useful that serious efforts be made to discuss these matters in appropriate diplomatic channels. Informal working groups, such as the Dartmouth Conference Task Force on Regional Conflicts and the Harvard-Soviet group on Prevention of International Political Crises, can also play a useful role in this respect.

Prospects

The preceding discussion of the abortive Nixon-Brezhnev experiment with "general principles" and our analysis of subsequent efforts to devise general "codes of conduct" to regulate U.S.-Soviet competition suggests that such approaches are not very promising. In their place our analysis suggests that more attention be given to what may be called a *case-by-case* approach that focuses upon the relative interests of the two superpowers in each specific area. And, in fact, it is in this direction that informal U.S.-Soviet discussion groups such as the Dartmouth Conference Task Force on Regional Conflicts and the U.S. and Soviet governments have been proceeding in recent years.

To be sure, President Carter and Chairman Brezhnev did reaffirm their commitment to the Basic Principles Agreement of 1972 in a formal communique following their signing of the SALT II treaty in Vienna on June 18, 1979. However, when President Reagan entered office in 1981 the question arose whether he would consider the Agreement as still operative. During the course of his first term and into the first year of his second administration, although he did not explicitly reject the Basic Principles Agreement, President Reagan gave no indication that he favored continued adherence by the United States. Indeed, the general thrust of his policies and pronouncements virtually excluded this possibility. Soviet leaders themselves could hardly have entertained such an expectation. Public accounts of preparations for the Geneva summit meeting of Reagan and Gorbachev, and of what transpired there, suggest that the status of the Basic Principles Agreement was not even discussed. Nor is there any reason to believe that either side proposed a new set of general principles for regulating competition in third world areas.

Instead, as was expected, the two leaders at the summit agreed in their joint statement of 21 November to continue the practice they had instituted early in 1985 for frequent diplomatic discussion of regional issues at the expert level. It will be recalled that the first step in this direction was taken by President Reagan in his address to the United Nations on September 24, 1984, in which he proposed a series of Soviet-American regional discussions to alleviate tensions. Shortly thereafter President Reagan proposed the idea of discussing the Middle East in detail to Foreign Minister Andrei Gromyko when they met in Washington. Later, Secretary of State Shultz discussed the idea with Gromyko. Subsequently, U.S. and Soviet delegations met for two days in Vienna on February 19 and 20, 1985 to discuss Middle East issues. The talks were restricted to an exchange of already familiar views and were primarily of symbolic importance. Evidently no effort was made to develop a more ambitious agenda for a subsequent meeting or indeed to schedule a second meeting.[9] Subsequent meetings were held to discuss southern Africa issues and Afghanistan, and a similar meeting was agreed to for discussion of Far East issues.[10]

While these meetings constitute the first steps toward creating a procedural mechanism for serious bilateral discussions of regional problems on a frequent and timely basis, it remains to be seen whether such talks can move from a symbolic level to negotiation aimed at clarifying, narrowing, and possibly resolving substantive disagreements. For this development to take place, each side will have to prepare thoroughly for serious and constructive negotiation rather than a mere restatement of already familiar positions. At such meetings representatives of the two sides should attempt to achieve mutual clarification of the specific configuration of the case at hand—that is, what is at stake for each side in the area in question; what actions by each side would be regarded as threatening by the other side and as requiring some response; what is the danger of unwanted escalation; whether other external actors already are or may become involved and how this development can be controlled; what development and outcome of the local situation will and will not be acceptable to each of the superpowers; and whether diplomatic solutions can be worked out.

An important advantage of the case-by-case approach proposed here is that it would bring the two superpowers together in the most serious kind of diplomatic conversations at an early stage in the development of a local situation, before it gets out of hand. Even if the efforts of the United States and the Soviet Union to devise an *ad hoc* understanding covering a specific situation proved abortive or only partly successful, the timely diplomatic exchange between them could have the useful result of mutual clarification of interests engaged by that situation. It would offer the possibility of correcting misperceptions of each other's intentions and activities that might otherwise result in escalation of mutual involvement. It could lead to encouragement by the superpowers of efforts by third parties or the United Nations to deal with the local situation before the Soviet Union and the United States were drawn in more actively.

Acknowledgments

The author is pleased to acknowledge support for the research on which this paper is based from The Carnegie Corporation of New York and the Center for International Security and Arms Control, Stanford University. The ideas presented in this chapter benefited from the opportunity to participate in several dialogues of American groups with Soviet academicians: the meeting in Moscow, November 28-December 3, 1983, of the Dartmouth Conference Task Force on Regional Conflicts and the meetings at Harvard (May 11–13, 1984) and in Moscow (February 25–28, 1985) of the Harvard-Soviet group on Prevention of International Political Crises sponsored by the International Research and Exchanges Board (IREX). An earlier version of this paper was presented at the XIIIth World Congress of the International Political Science Association, and was published in the *Journal of Peace Research* 23 (1986).

Notes

1. For useful discussions of the variety of "norms" and "rules," other than those encompassed by international law, that serve to regulate international politics, see Bull (1977), Cohen (1981), Gowa and Wessell (1982), Goldmann (1969), Kael (1983), Matheson (1982), McWhinney (1964).

2. The proposal was briefly described in a newsletter, *Basic Positions*, issued by the American Committee on East-West Accord (1982). It was described in more detail by a member of the Committee (Cox, 1982: 156–164).

3. See Napper, 1983: 225–254.

4. This section draws upon and elaborates the discussion in George, 1983: 365–398.

5. The author is indebted to John Stremlau for clarification of this point.

6. For an analysis of U.S. responses to crises in Eastern Europe see Valenta, 1982.

7. Dinerstein (1976) provides an interesting, plausible account of how Khrushchev, beginning in July 1960, moved step-by-step to draw Cuba away from the United States' sphere of influence into its special relationship with the Soviet Union and takes note of U.S. responses which had the effect of facilitating Khrushchev's strategy. An insightful commentary on this case as an example of how states "make rules" is provided by Cohen, 1981: 108–113.

8. Other analysts of Middle East conflicts have also noted the emergence of this tacit norm. See Dismukes and McConnell, 1979: 276–278; Jonsson, 1984: ch. 5; and Evron, 1979: 17–45.

9. *New York Times*, February 13, 20 and 21, 1985.

10. *New York Times*, June 19 and September 7, 1985.

5

Arms Control Negotiations and the Stability of Crisis Management

Karen Patrick MacGillivray and Gilbert R. Winham

Introduction

Since the early 1960s arms control negotiations have occupied a large and growing proportion of the political relations between the United States and the Soviet Union. In recent years these negotiations have become the main component of superpower diplomacy, and more specifically, they have become a litmus test of the capacity of these governments to deal effectively with each other. This is a test that by most measures these governments are failing (Vogele, 1986: 1).

There are undoubtedly good reasons why the superpowers should negotiate arms control. If the two countries could reach effective arms control agreements, it would likely lead to greater stability in their political relationship. It could as well reduce the number of nuclear weapons in the world, with corresponding lower costs for defense, and the result might arguably be a reduced overall risk of nuclear war. On the other hand, failure to reach arms control agreements is itself a stimulant to superpower competition, and it also acts as an incentive to nuclear proliferation in non-Western countries. Furthermore, since both international and domestic public opinion place a high priority on the arms control process, failure to negotiate and conclude agreements creates a public climate of fear and uncertainty. This is a problem in its own right, but in democratic countries it can further lead to unstable policies as electorates and legislatures seek to force the disarmament issue on reluctant governments.

While there are many benefits from arms control agreements, the possibility that there might be costs associated with negotiating arms control is less evident, particularly to those who in principle seek to slow the arms race. Negotiations are nothing more than formal communication, and it is not usual to think in terms of the opportunity costs of communication. However, negotiations are a particular type of communication that mixes cooperative and conflictual motivations. This mix is inherently frustrating, and the frustration mounts to intense levels and infiltrates public policy when agreements seem perpetually out of reach.

Negotiations are intended to produce a search for reciprocal concession, but when this search is conducted between intense rivals, it can paradoxically produce a movement away from reciprocal concession as parties attempt to establish bargaining chips to insure maximum maneuvering room in future negotiation. Furthermore, negotiations structure political decisions in terms of the bilateral relationship at the expense of unilateral policy-making, with the result that policy is made to suit the negotiation process rather than the reverse. By comparison, a more unilateral policy process might better serve the security needs of both countries. While such a process would clearly be self-interested, it might arguably be more accommodating than a security policy motivated by the need to protect a strong negotiating position.

One possible cost of the arms control process is that it does not prepare the superpowers to manage future nuclear crises, and instead may even reduce the capacity of these governments for crisis management. Crisis management is generally thought to mean the capacity of top leadership to maintain control (Lebow, 1981: 292) in a situation which involves a threat to important national values, a belief that time for action is short, and an expectation that military hostilities may result from the situation (Hermann, 1987). The goals of crisis management are generally to ensure that on the one hand a crisis does not spin out of control and lead to war, while on the other hand the crisis is resolved in a manner that protects important national values (Williams, 1976: 30).

The concept of stability is crucial in the management of crisis. One dimension of stability is crisis stability, which is a matter of whether weapons systems themselves and their associated technologies create pressures on the parties to initiate hostilities, or whether these systems exert pressures in the opposite direction. Normally crisis stability is a function of the deterrent capability of nuclear weapons, and weapons that provide assured second strike capability usually also increase crisis stability (Frei, 1983: 10). Political stability, on the other hand, refers to the ability of protagonists to maintain communication with each other, and to ensure that points of conflict do not overwhelm the parties' mutual interest of avoiding war. In terms of the classic tools whereby strategists assess their adversaries, crisis stability refers to the military *capabilities* of the protagonists in a crisis, while political stability is a matter of their *intentions*.

In assessing the contribution of arms control to crisis management, it is obvious that crisis management is influenced by a number of factors, some of which are wholly beyond rational planning, and that arms control may only have a small influence in future crisis behavior. Yet the arms control process constitutes the main element of superpower diplomacy, and it plausibly has a structuring effect on future crises between these parties. Therefore, from the perspective of crisis stability, one can ask whether the arms control process motivates the parties to produce (or retain) weapons that increase rather than decrease the ability of the parties to manage crises. And, from the perspective of political stability, one can query whether arms control promotes a reciprocal understanding of the important political and strategic interests of the superpowers, or whether it promotes disagreement between the adversaries that might be unhelpful or misleading during a future crisis.

To assess these questions, this paper will review three arms control negotiations: SALT I, SALT II, and the negotiations on nuclear and space-based weapons conducted during the Reagan Administration. Included in this review will be the incentives leading the parties to negotiate their foreign and defense policy objectives, and the results of the negotiations. The final sections of the paper will examine in greater detail the impact of these arms control negotiations on the capacity for crisis management between the United States and the Soviet Union.

Strategic Arms Limitation Talks I (SALT I)

Incentives to Negotiate

After more than two decades of rivalry following World War II, American and Soviet leaders recognized a need to accommodate their military/strategic interests in a manner that would reduce the threat of accidental or deliberate nuclear war. Advances were continuing in weapons technology and increasing numbers of strategic weapons were deployed by both the United States and the Soviet Union, which created an incipient threat to deterrent stability. Furthermore, scarce resources were being consumed by the defense requirements of the two rivals. Confronted with these realities and encouraged by the success of other arms control agreements (in particular, Article VI of the Non-Proliferation Treaty of 1968), American and Soviet leaders sought an agreement to restrain the design, production, deployment and control of strategic weapons.

Internal factors also motivated each government to negotiate. American participation in SALT was important to the Nixon Administration. The Administration considered it impossible, for financial reasons, to regain strategic superiority over the Soviet Union, while at home it came under increasing pressure to divert resources from the military to the civilian sectors of the economy. As the Kalbs (1974: 100) noted: "[Americans were] . . . weary of a quarter century of Cold War and Iron Curtain policies, of confrontation and conflict, [and] of billions going into a nuclear technology that kept turning out more and more terrible weapons for mass death." The prospect that the Soviet Union might deploy a nation-wide anti-ballistic missile (ABM) system to neutralize American retaliatory missiles further motivated the Nixon Administration, as did the possibility that first line inter-continental ballistic missiles (ICBMs) would become vulnerable to the threat of a strike by Soviet offensive missiles. Finally, the evolution of surveillance technology and its potential application to arms control verification made negotiation of a strategic arms limitation agreement practicable.

The Brezhnev-Kosygin Administration in the Soviet Union was also interested in negotiation. By 1968, the Soviet Union had attained a position of numerical parity with the U.S. strategic arsenal consisting of ICBMs, submarine-launched ballistic missiles (SLBMs), and bomber forces (including those under construction). Its leadership was anxious to protect against qualitative advances that might be made by the American scientific community in ABM and multiple independently-targeted re-entry vehicle (MIRV) technology. Relations between the Soviet Union and China were less strained as a result of a series of border talks; nevertheless, the effect of a cooperative Soviet-American approach to strategic arms limitation would support Soviet diplomacy with the Chinese. And finally, the Soviet Union had an economic interest in avoiding an unbridled arms race with the United States.

Foreign and Defense Policy Initiatives

According to a knowledgeable figure in the American delegation (Garthoff, 1978: 3), the United States and the Soviet Union quickly reached agreement on the principal objectives to be sought in the course of the negotiations. In a series of prior confidential exchanges, the parties agreed explicitly that a main objective of SALT would be to maintain a stable deterrent relationship between the United States and the Soviet Union through negotiated limits on offensive and defensive strategic arms. Implicitly, they also agreed to acknowledge and maintain strategic parity, and to balance arms limitations in order to assure equal security for both parties.

Despite this common ground, each delegation had individual objectives. On the U.S. side, Presidential candidate Richard Nixon had previously underlined the necessity for clear-cut military superiority over the Soviet Union. However, on the advice of Henry Kissinger, the U.S. Government substituted sufficiency for superiority as the objective of American defence policy, in part because of a belief that " . . . against the background of an unpopular Vietnam War, the American public would not support additional expenditures for new strategic weapons" (Zumwalt, 1976: 304). To ensure the United States had sufficient military strength to defend U.S. commitments, the American delegates sought an agreement which would (i) prohibit the deployment of a Soviet ABM system capable of neutralizing American retaliatory missiles; (ii) arrest the Soviet ICBM and SLBM deployment programs, in order to address the problem of the increased vulnerability of American Minuteman ICBMs to growing numbers of Soviet heavy SS-9 ICBMs; and (iii) reduce or limit the throw-weight of existing or replacement Soviet ICBMs. In effect, the U.S. delegates sought to forestall the emergence of a changed configuration of strategic power that might favor the Soviet Union.

Although limits on strategic arms were important, the Nixon Administration did not regard such limits as an isolated issue in Soviet-American relations. American foreign policy was instead based on the concept of "linkage," with progress on one issue seen as affecting progress on all issues. Progress in SALT was therefore linked to the positive resolution of other divisive political conflicts. Arms control thus became a means to gain leverage over Soviet foreign policy-making. In this manner, the American leadership hoped to improve Soviet-American relations by dissuading the Soviet Union from activities which conflicted with U.S. interests.

On the Soviet side, the fundamental political objective was American acknowledgement of strategic parity with the Soviet Union. Secretary General Brezhnev and Premier Kosygin sought to use SALT to gain international recognition for a shift in the balance of power by codifying Soviet status in an international agreement with the United States. An agreement was thus viewed as enhancing the superpower status of the Soviet Union within the international community. SALT provided a second political objective for the Soviets, namely to maneuver West European anxieties over the outcome of the talks into open splits between the United States and its allies.

The Soviets also sought military objectives in the negotiations. Their delegation hoped to forestall an extensive American deployment of ABM systems, even if such an objective required the Soviet Union to set aside its own plans to deploy comparable systems. Soviet ICBM and SLBM deployment programs were to be left unrestrained; but MIRVed ICBM and SLBM deployments by the United States were to be delayed or, if possible, prevented. The Soviets sought to conclude an arms control agreement which relied on national technical means of verification and to decline any American offers to undertake on-site inspection. Finally, they made every effort to limit American forward-based nuclear delivery systems capable of striking the Soviet Union, which for the most part included tactical aircraft stationed in Western Europe and aircraft carriers situated near the Soviet Union.

Results

The first phase of the strategic arms limitation talks produced two agreements which were signed by the U.S. and the Soviet Union in Moscow on May 26, 1972: the Anti-Ballistic Missile Treaty (ABM Treaty) and an Interim Agreement.

The heart of the ABM Treaty was Article III. It spelled out provisions under which each of the contracting parties may deploy two limited ABM systems, one at the national capital and one at an ICBM deployment area. The Treaty limited each party to no more than 100 launchers and 100 associated interceptor missiles at each launch site. Both ABM and non-ABM radars were subject to a number of further restrictions.

The Treaty provided other important qualitative limitations. In Article V (1), the contracting parties undertook not to develop, test, or deploy ABM systems or components which are sea-based, air-based, space-based or mobile land-based. They also accepted severe restrictions on ABM launchers; specifically, they agreed not to build ABM launchers capable of rapid reloading, or of launching more than one ABM interceptor missile at a time. Additionally, in an ancillary Statement, they agreed not to develop, test, or deploy ABM interceptor missiles with more than one independently-guided warhead.

One important qualitative limitation was that imposed on future exotic and revolutionary types of ABM systems, a limitation that became problematic for the Strategic Defense Initiative of the Reagan Administration. The parties prohibited deployment of any ABM system consisting of devices other than ABM interceptor missiles, ABM launchers, or ABM radars. A corollary provision prohibited the conversion or testing of other systems to perform an ABM role. This latter prohibition applied to anti-aircraft or air defense systems, and was invoked as part of a common understanding in Article VI not to provide an ABM capability to non-ABM systems.

The Treaty also dealt with the contentious issue of verification. The contracting parties agreed in Article XII not to interfere with each other's national technical means of verification, and not to use deliberate concealment measures to evade the other's technical monitoring capabilities.

The parties established a Standing Consultative Commission to promote the objectives embodied in the ABM Treaty and the Interim Agreement, and to facilitate the implementation of the provisions of these agreements. A key function of the Commission was to monitor parties' compliance with the obligations of the SALT I Agreements; however, it was further charged with the responsibility of addressing general issues related to the agreements.

The duration of the ABM Treaty was to be unlimited. However, a formal review of the agreement was provided every five years. In addition, Article XV of the Treaty contained a "safeguard clause" allowing each party the right to withdraw upon six months notice in the event its national interests were jeopardized by extraordinary events related to the Treaty.

The Interim Agreement was signed on May 26, 1972, after the parties failed to reach a more complete agreement.[1] The agreement provided for the limitation of offensive strategic arms for a period of five years. It prohibited both the construction of additional land-based ICBM launchers and the conversion of older launchers for use on modern, heavy ICBMs. The Agreement placed conditions on the modernization and replacement of land-based ICBM launchers, limiting increases in their size, and increases in the numbers of test and training launchers for ICBMs and SLBMs. Limits were also placed on ballistic missile submarine and SLBM launchers. The number of SLBM launchers could be increased only if certain other ICBM or SLBM launchers were destroyed.

The Agreement reiterated the commitment on verification contained in the ABM Treaty. Verification was to be carried out by national technical means and in accordance with the principles of international law. Interference with, or deliberate concealment from, such means of verification was prohibited. Finally, as in the ABM Treaty, the Interim Agreement contained a safeguard clause, and the parties agreed to use the Standing Consultative Commission to resolve conflicts related to the Agreement.

Despite their adversarial relationship, the United States and the Soviet Union took a first step toward limiting strategic arms in the SALT I Agreements. A by-product, and perhaps necessary condition for the Agreements was the considerable improvement in relations between the superpowers. The Agreements did not halt the Soviet-American strategic arms race, but the ABM Treaty did impose sharp limits on ABM systems, and the Interim Agreement did establish a ceiling on the aggregate number of ICBM and SLBM launchers operational or under active construction. Defense costs were undoubtedly reduced by avoiding competition on the development of increasingly sophisticated ABM systems.

The ABM Treaty was well received in the United States. It reinforced the assumption of mutual assured destruction, which was essential to the stability of nuclear deterrence. From the American perspective, a key objective was attained by heading off a large-scale Soviet ABM system which could have blunted the retaliatory capacity of the United States. With regard to the Interim Agreement, American reaction was more ambivalent. Arms control proponents criticized the Agreement on the grounds that it was a far cry from being a comprehensive limitation of offensive strategic arms. The levels at which ICBM and SLBM launchers had been frozen were seen as unnecessarily high, and there were objections that agreement was made only on limitation, and not reduction, of offensive strategic arms. Others charged that the Agreement favored the Soviet Union by providing inferior levels of land-based ICBMs and ocean-based SLBMs for the United States, thereby conceding to the Soviets a substantial advantage in missile throw-weight.

In the internal debate, the Administration and the Congressional leadership largely succeeded in deflecting criticism of the Interim Agreement. The ABM Treaty was ratified by an overwhelming vote of 88-2 in the Senate. The Agreement was approved by the same margin in the Senate and 307-4 in the House of Representatives. However, the Senate resolution approving the Interim Agreement included an amendment (the Jackson amendment) urging adherence to the principle of equality of intercontinental strategic forces in future strategic arms negotiations.

The Soviet Union strongly endorsed the SALT I Agreements. Its political objectives were achieved with the recognition that parity would be the basis of strategic arms control agreements negotiated between the superpowers. An extensive American deployment of ABM systems was forestalled by the ABM Treaty, which reduced the risk of a new round of competition between offensive and defensive arms. Finally, the levels of submarine delivery vehicles set in the Interim Agreement were sufficient to establish a Soviet deterrent capability against vital American targets.

Strategic Arms Limitation Talks II (SALT II)

Incentives to Negotiate

The 1972 Interim Agreement required the United States and the Soviet Union to continue active negotiations on strategic arms. However, this obligation was not the only factor in the move toward a second negotiation. American and Soviet leaders both expressed a common desire to capitalize on the momentum toward better U.S.-USSR relations, and to avoid intensifying a strategic arms race. Furthermore, economic pressures undoubtedly convinced the leaders to begin SALT II.

In addition to these incentives held in common, additional factors motivated the American side. Public opinion pressed the Nixon Administration for a new agreement that would establish "equal aggregates" or equality in the various categories of strategic weaponry. It therefore committed itself to negotiate a long term replacement for the Interim Agreement which would establish parity between the rivals.

Foreign and Defense Policy Initiatives

Both parties to the second phase of strategic arms negotiations agreed on the goal of replacing the five year Interim Agreement with a comprehensive treaty of indefinite duration. Within this general framework, American objectives were, first, to draft a formula for "essential equivalence" based on both quantitative and qualitative considerations. To this end, the United States sought substantial reductions in ballistic missile throw-weights, in order to decrease the Soviet advantage in the major aggregate of strategic nuclear capability. Second, U.S. negotiators hoped to use a SALT II Treaty to enhance deterrent stability by reducing the attractiveness of a first strike option. This would be accomplished through a reduction (especially on the Soviet side) of heavy missiles and other delivery vehicles armed with multiple, independent warheads. The U.S. delegation also sought to slow the rate of modernization and replacement of the Soviet SS-II ICBM missiles. The U.S. proposals left open an option to develop a new mobile ICBM (i.e., the MX), in order to reduce the vulnerability of the American ICBM force to surprise attack. Third, the United States expected that any agreement reached had to be adequately verifiable by national technical means, and furthermore, that the interests of U.S. allies were to be protected. To this end, the American delegates wanted to exclude forward-based systems in Western Europe from the talks, and to impose limits on the deployment of Soviet Backfire bombers. However, the development and deployment of a full range of cruise missiles was to be permitted.

The objectives of the Soviet Union in the negotiations appeared less sweeping. First, the Soviet Union again expected to use the negotiations to confirm its superpower status in the international community, and therefore insisted on parity as the basis of any agreements negotiated with the United States. Second, the Soviet delegates sought to capitalize on the advantages gained in SALT I by avoiding concessions in ballistic missiles where they held a numerical advantage. Finally, the forward-based systems issue was to be revived. The Soviet leadership was determined to use arms control negotiations between the superpowers as a means to loosen ties between the United States and its European allies.

Results

The SALT II Agreements reached between the superpowers consisted of two documents: a 19 article *Treaty*, to remain in force until December 31, 1985, and a four article *Protocol*, to remain in force until December 31, 1981. Article III of the Treaty established equal ceilings on the total number of strategic nuclear delivery vehicles (SNDVs), with each contracting party agreeing to limit its SNDVs to 2250. It also established equal sub-ceilings within the above limits on different categories of SNDVs. As one example, a limit of 820 was imposed on the number of MIRVed ICBM launchers.

The Treaty and the Protocol imposed various other limitations on SNDVs. For example, Article IV of the Treaty placed restrictions on missile conversions and modification, on numbers of warheads, and on numbers of long range cruise missiles to be deployed abroad aircraft. Elsewhere, the Protocol prohibited the deployment of mobile ICBM launchers or the flight testing of ICBMs from such launchers, the deployment of land-based or sea-based cruise missiles capable of a range in excess of 600 kilometres, and the flight testing or deployment of ASBMs. Finally, Article IX of the Treaty prohibited the development, testing and deployment of several types of offensive strategic arms such as ballistic or cruise missile launchers placed on the ocean floor.

The Treaty set forth verbal definitions and rules for counting offensive strategic arms. It also included provisions prohibiting interference with national technical means of verification, and it established a mechanism for resolving conflicts related to the SALT II Agreements.

In addition to the two basic documents, there were a series of 98 Agreed Statements and Common Understandings which further elaborated the obligations of the two parties under the Treaty. An example might be the statements made by Secretary General Brezhnev and President Carter on the Backfire bomber. A *Joint Statement of Principles and Basic Guidelines* outlined the intent of the U.S. and the Soviet Union to continue negotiations on the limitation of strategic arms, and finally a *Memorandum of Understanding* established numerical data on certain categories of offensive strategic arms.

The SALT II Agreements constituted a serious attempt by the U.S. and the Soviet Union to limit strategic arms. The Agreements imposed quantitative limitations and modest but significant qualitative limitations on various categories of offensive strategic arms. As a result, they reduced uncertainty about future force levels. Such uncertainty encourages parties to make "worst case" projections and therefore tends to fuel the deployment programs on both sides. The Treaty protected national means of verification; in most cases it appeared to be adequate to detect cheating on any scale that could threaten the national security of the parties. The agreements also established a data base of offensive weapons, the maintenance of which further reduces uncertainty regarding the composition of strategic forces.

The SALT II Agreements were not without flaws. The Agreements did not reduce the predominant role of nuclear weapons in superpower relations. As arms control agreements, the SALT II Accords required only a slight reduction from then-existing levels of strategic weapons. Within an overall aggregate, the Treaty set sub-limits on various categories of weapons, which effectively encouraged parties to build up to the sub-limits and to modernize and develop new weapons outside the sub-limits. The parties' adherence to the Agreements will not result in a reduction in offensive strategic arms but in larger numbers of arms which are faster, more accurate, and more difficult to detect and defend against. The Agreements did little to slow the arms race, or to reduce its economic costs.

In the United States, those who supported the SALT Agreements argued they had preserved "essential equivalence" between asymmetrical strategic forces, and that this had required a greater sacrifice from the Soviet Union than from the United States. They pointed out that the Agreements assured both parties a survivable nuclear deterrent, imposed predictable limits on future force postures, and established a workable framework for future reductions in force levels. It was also claimed that the Treaty was carefully drafted to take maximum advantage of the existing intelligence monitoring capabilities of the United States.

However, support had diminished even before the Agreements were completed, and the documents were heavily criticised in U.S. domestic politics. The major objection was that the Agreements left intact the asymmetries in the force structures of the parties, which included a large Soviet advantage in heavy missiles with superior throw-weights and higher deliverable megatonnage. This reinforced American fears of a "window of vulnerability" from a hypothetical Soviet first strike with heavy ICBMs. A further criticism was that verification of Soviet compliance with the provisions of the SALT II Agreements was beyond the national technical means of the United States. The arms control community further objected that the agreements did not provide significant reductions in offensive nuclear arms and therefore merely "institutionalized" the arms race.

On the Soviet side, the Agreements were attractive despite the fact that they imposed both quantitative and qualitative limitations on Soviet offensive strategic arms. First, the Agreements achieved a psychological (and political) equality with the United States which appeared to outweigh a concern over technical equality in weapons systems. Second, the documents codified certain advantages previously gained by the Soviets in throw-weight, ICBM counter-force potential, and deliverable mega-tonnage. Finally, the Agreements included limits on ground-launched and submarine-launched cruise missiles (GLCMs and SLCMs) while avoiding commitments on Soviet Backfire bombers and SS-20 medium-range ballistic missiles. This arguably left the Soviets in a better strategic position in the European theatre.

The debate on the SALT II Agreements in the United States was prolonged, during which it became increasingly unlikely that the accords would be ratified by the Senate. Late in 1979 Soviet forces entered Afghanistan, which led President Carter to withdraw the Agreements from the Senate. Subsequently, the Reagan Administration took the position that the Agreements were "fatally flawed" and treated the matter as a dead issue, although in 1982 both parties issued public statements of their willingness to abide by the Agreements if the other side did likewise. From the perspective of the negotiation process, the SALT II Agreements remain in an uneasy equilibrium between success and failure.

Negotiations on Nuclear and Space Arms

Incentives to Negotiate

Talks on the limitation of strategic arms (START) and on the reduction of intermediate range nuclear weapons in Europe were begun in 1981 by the Reagan Administration. These talks were broken off in 1983 by the Soviet Union when the United States and its NATO allies carried through an earlier NATO decision to deploy cruise and Pershing II missiles in Europe to counter the Soviet Union's SS-20 medium range missiles. However, by 1985 a combination of military, political, and economic factors motivated the superpowers to convene negotiations on nuclear and space arms.

Initiatives by both parties to modernize their strategic forces figured prominently in the decision to negotiate. On the U.S. side these initiatives consisted of:

1) the modernization of the American ICBM force with the deployment of 100 MX Peacekeeper missiles;

2) the modernization of the American bomber force with the deployment of 100 B-1B strategic bombers, the development of the Advanced Technology Bomber, and the deployment of air-launched cruise missiles;

3) the modernization of the American SLBM force with the production of Trident submarines, the development of the Trident II missile, and the deployment of SLCMs;

4) the upgrading of strategic weapons command, control, and communications; and

5) the stepping-up of efforts to develop a space-based defense against nuclear weapons, known as the Strategic Defense Initiative (SDI).

Of these various modernization initiatives, the Soviets were particularly concerned about SDI. For one thing, strategic defense had the capacity to overturn the concept of deterrence as it had been applied since the ABM Treaty of 1972. Furthermore, the Soviets had a long-standing concern for American technological superiority, and they feared that the development of a defense system by the Americans, in conjunction with larger numbers of offensive arms, would deprive the Soviet Union of its existing strategic advantages and give the United States a first strike capability. In addition, the deployment of American Pershing IIs and cruise missiles in Europe and the testing of the American F-15 anti-satellite (ASAT) system provided further incentive to negotiate.

American leaders were also concerned about strategic force modernization on the Soviet side. The Soviet Union had announced successful tests of its own GLCMs. It further announced that its unilateral moratorium on base construction for new SS-20s aimed at Western Europe would be lifted in the event of the deployment of American intermediate range nuclear forces. It was later confirmed that about a dozen new SS-20 bases were under construction. Finally, reports said the Soviet Union had tested a boost vehicle that might represent the first step toward the development of an ASAT system capable of destroying American satellites at high altitudes.

Political concerns were another reason the superpowers reestablished negotiations. The Soviet Union resumed bargaining without losing face by referring to the talks as "new" and by reiterating their position that negotiated reductions of intermediate weapons could not be carried out without the withdrawal of American intermediate-range nuclear forces (INF) from Europe. With the accession of Gorbachev to the Soviet leadership, a dramatic new flexibility was introduced into the Soviet negotiating posture. For their part, the Americans supported negotiations in order to allay the anxieties of allies about SDI, and to improve strained East-West relations. As well, President Reagan responded to internal political pressure in reestablishing negotiations, in order to demonstrate his Administration's capacity to contribute to better super-power relations.

Economic factors also played a role in the resumption of negotiation. The economy of the USSR was severely depressed; large expenditures on arms reduced the capacity of the Soviet government to deal with this problem. On the U.S. side, the Administration recognized that continued Congressional support for defence expenditures, including such key programs as the MX, the F-15 ASAT, and SDI, was linked to a willingness to negotiate arms control with the Soviet Union. Hence for both superpowers internal priorities gave the negotiation new importance.

Foreign and Defence Policy Objectives

In a meeting on January 7, 1985 between American Secretary of State George Shultz and Soviet Foreign Minister Andrei Gromyko, it was agreed to take up matters of nuclear and space arms under one negotiation; specifically, to include strategic and medium-range nuclear weapons, and strategic defense systems. Within this general framework the parties had several objectives (Nitze, 1985). The Americans again sought to reduce Soviet advantages in land-based ballistic missiles. Due to their large number and accuracy, these were assumed to create a first strike potential against American land-based ballistic missiles. The Soviets resisted this demand because it would limit the most effective strategic forces of the USSR, and because it was an incentive to the Americans to negotiate SDI. Second, the Americans made clear that any agreement on intermediate forces should be based on the principle of equality of force levels, including those stationed outside the European theatre of conflict in Asia and the Far East. At the same time, they sought to establish that British and French nuclear weapons were independent of those of the United States, and were not to be included in any INF agreement between the superpowers.

Third, U.S. representatives hoped to secure Soviet approval for an American plan to shift from reliance on offensive nuclear arms towards reliance on defensive, preferably non-nuclear systems. This was consistent with President Reagan's rhetoric that "mutually assured survival" would be more stable than mutually assured destruction. As part of this plan the negotiations were to be directed away from limitations on outer space weaponry, particularly on research and development of defense systems. For example, existing ASAT weapons could be limited, but the United States was reluctant to limit future development of such weapons since they might involve technologies similar to ballistic missile defense systems. The U.S. position on missile defense created problems with the ABM Treaty. President Reagan's Strategic Defense Initiative appeared to violate the Treaty, and the United States either had to defend SDI as consistent with the Treaty or else risk widespread criticism by apparently ignoring one of the more effective arms control agreements between the superpowers. To deflect this criticism, the United States itself made sharp allegations about Soviet non-compliance with the Treaty, and used this issue to question how far the Soviets could be trusted to carry out arms control agreements.

Soviet objectives at the negotiation were, first, to prevent the militarization of outer space. American research on new defensive technologies would oblige the Soviet government to step up its own research at tremendous costs, and the possibility of a breakthrough on defense technology created a threat that offensive strategic forces could be neutralized. Consequently the Soviets initially insisted on a comprehensive ban on research and development, as well as testing and deployment, of space-based arms. The Soviet government attached considerable importance to this objective; it appeared willing to make substantial concessions in the area of nuclear arms limitation, if such concessions were reciprocated in limitations of space arms. A second Soviet objective, should the Reagan Administration agree to negotiate on SDI, was to achieve reductions of both strategic arms and intermediate range nuclear weapons.The Soviets proposed a freeze on both American and Soviet nuclear arms and an end to further missile deployments. This had the advantage of maintaining their land-based ICBM forces while limiting U.S. strategic force modernization efforts. Finally, the Soviets hoped to secure withdrawal of cruise and Pershing II missiles stationed in NATO countries, and to include British and French weapons in any INF accord.

Results

By the end of 1986, Soviet-American negotiations on nuclear and space arms had consisted of six rounds of negotiations in Geneva, various meetings between American Secretary of State George Shultz and Soviet Foreign Ministers Andrei Gromyko and Eduard Shevardnadze, encounters between arms control experts, and finally a summit meeting in Reykjavik, Iceland between President Reagan and Secretary-General Gorbachev. All this activity failed to produce an arms control agreement.

The Reykjavik Summit, held on October 11–12, 1986, developed, perhaps unintentionally, into a full-blown bargaining session. The Soviets tabled a number of far-reaching proposals which included substantial concessions from their previous positions. While a package could not be concluded at the Summit, it was clear the meeting would provide direction for future negotiations.

The leaders completed verbal agreements in two areas. On medium-range missiles, the parties accepted a version of an earlier proposal by the United States banning all medium-range missiles from Europe (known as the zero-zero option). Each side was allowed to retain 100 missiles, with the American missiles being stationed in the United States, and the Soviet missiles in Soviet Asia. On testing, the Soviets dropped their long insistence on a complete moratorium on nuclear weapons testing. The two sides agreed to a U.S. plan for a staged agreement on testing, first emphasizing verification of existing agreements and then moving toward a reduction in the number and yield of tests, with the ultimate goal a complete cessation of testing.

On strategic nuclear weapons the agreement was less complete. Both sides agreed to reduce nuclear launchers, missiles and bombers to 1600 and the number of warheads to 6000 which was described as a 50 per cent cut in nuclear forces over a 5-year period.[2] In addition, the Americans proposed to eliminate all ballistic missiles in a ten-year period, although the Soviet Union appeared to insist such a ban should include the entire nuclear arsenal on both sides. At this point, however, the negotiation turned more on the ABM Treaty and the Strategic Defense Initiative, which became linked to the issue of strategic offensive weapons. The parties had agreed to extend the ABM Treaty for 10 years and the United States had agreed to some limitations on a proposed missile defense system. However, the parties disagreed on the extent of allowable SDI research during the 10 year period, and on missile defenses that might be permitted after that period. The Americans insisted that research, testing and development of SDI should continue during the 10 year period, with deployment possible thereafter, which amounted to no effective restraint on the momentum of the program. The Soviet position was to limit permissible research on SDI to the laboratory, which arguably would go beyond a minimal interpretation of the limits of the ABM Treaty. The talks broke down on this issue.

It is clear the Soviet strategy was to strengthen the ABM Treaty in order to slow SDI, and they offered a large package of concessions to make their position attractive. While President Reagan was willing to agree to delay deployment of defensive weapons for ten years (a delay which was technologically unavoidable in any case), he was unwilling to give up the right to develop and test them as well. In explaining to the nation his refusal to accept the Soviet package, the President stated:

> SDI is America's insurance policy that the Soviet Union would keep the commitments made at Reykjavik. SDI is America's security guarantee—if

the Soviets should—as they have done too often in the past—fail to comply with their solemn commitments. SDI is what brought the Soviets back to arms control talks at Geneva and Iceland. SDI is the key to a world without nuclear weapons. (Reagan, 1986)

The President's statement makes it clear that the United States simply did not trust the USSR to live up to its agreements and wanted to retain SDI as insurance against Soviet cheating. Similarly the insistence by the Soviet Union that the development of new defensive technologies be confined to the laboratory was part of an effort to acquire "insurance" on its own part. Moscow sought to insure that at the same time it was dismantling nuclear weapons the United States would not be developing a defense system that could neutralize the retaliatory capability of a reduced Soviet nuclear arsenal. Indeed, the Soviets carried this argument one step further by claiming that once offensive arms were eliminated, there would be no need of ballistic missile defense at all.

No agreement on nuclear and space arms was reached at Reykjavik. However, the outcome should not obscure the fact that for the first time in Soviet-American arms control negotiations significant proposals were exchanged to reduce and not merely limit nuclear arms. The outcome did not preclude future progress on nuclear arms control, as the proposals were not withdrawn but were left on the bargaining table for diplomats to reconsider in Geneva.

However, problems remain that will make agreement on the reduction of nuclear arms difficult. NATO allies fear that withdrawing American medium range missiles from Europe would leave Western Europe in an inferior position relative to Eastern Europe, given the Warsaw Pact's overwhelming superiority in conventional forces and short-range nuclear weapons. These fears insure that any reductions involving the European theatre will be a delicate matter. More important, any future agreement appears to be contingent on de-linking arms reductions from SDI, and/ or a change of positions on the latter issue. In the United States, the Reagan Administration saw SDI not only as a bargaining chip to obtain substantial reductions in Soviet offensive nuclear weapons, but also as a plan to which the President was deeply committed personally. The Administration could not be expected to abandon an initiative that it had promoted with such conviction. On the Soviet side positions were equally tightly drawn. For the Soviet Union, an improvement in defensive systems would be a threat to the stability of nuclear deterrence. The U.S. pursuit of SDI was viewed simply as another step in the arms race, as the following statement from a speech by Secretary General Gorbachev made clear:

> After Reykjavik . . . it is clear to everyone that SDI is a symbol of obstruction to the cause of peace, the epitome of militarist schemes and of the unwillingness to remove the nuclear menace to mankind. There can be no other interpretation of it, and this is the most important lesson from the meeting in Rejkjavik (Schmemann, 1986).

It is clear that Secretary General Gorbachev was eager to conclude an arms control agreement at Reykjavik. His proposals were far-reaching, and they included initiatives that were particularly attractive to the West. For example, the Soviets dropped an earlier demand that limitations on independent British and French forces be included in any INF agreement. This meant the Soviets were prepared to accept *de facto* equality between the United States and the Soviet Union for the purpose of INF reductions. However, for the Soviets at Reykjavik, concluding an agreement on nuclear weapons was clearly secondary to gaining control of the development of new defensive technologies. The Reykjavik Summit only served to demonstrate how far apart the parties were on this fundamental issue.

Arms Control Negotiation: An Assessment

The record on nuclear arms control is disappointing, as evidenced by the previous survey. Of the various agreements or attempted agreements, only the ABM Treaty was an unambiguous success. The ABM Treaty was based on a shared strategic concept that defense is pointless and even destabilizing in an age of offensive nuclear weapons, and it provided an acceptable mechanism to put this concept into practice. The Treaty effectively limited the arms race in defense weapons. On other agreements, such as SALT II, weapon limitations were set sufficiently high as to constitute no real deterrent to the increase of nuclear weapons by the parties. In other cases where negotiations resulted in non-agreement, the failure of arms control was both procedural as well as substantive. On balance, the diplomatic record on arms control is one of failure, and the failure is all the more evident when compared to the fact that since the early 1970s when SALT II was being negotiated the nuclear arsenals of both parties have nearly doubled (Russett and Chernoff, 1985: 84).

Analyses of arms control negotiations often assume that failure is a result of the poor political climate between the United States and the Soviet Union. For example, Fallows (1984: 141) has argued: "The failure of arms-control negotiations is a symptom, not the cause, of the worsening relations between the superpowers." This argument assumes negotiations are wholly derivative of the political climate in which they are situated.

However, this is not always the case. For example, multilateral trade talks in the GATT are explicitly pursued as a means to forestall protectionist actions and improve the political climate among the parties. Similarly, arms control negotiations may not be wholly derivative of the political climate, but may instead have an independent capacity to structure superpower relations. If this is so, the recent record suggests that arms control negotiations may in fact undercut the goals of arms control, which are mainly to forestall an arms race.[3]

A major task of arms control is to contain the rivalry in weapons procurement. When arms control is successful, as in the ABM Treaty or the Seabeds Arms Control Treaty of 1971, it has the effect of closing off an area of competition to the parties. In fact there are few areas of technological or military significance that the parties have closed in this manner. With the exception of the ABM Treaty, successful arms control agreements have tended to occur at the margins of the strategic competition, involving weapons on which major technological advances have already occurred. Conversely, arms control agreements rarely touched those weapons on which the potential for technical advance was the greatest. For example, SALT I did not include limitations on MIRV technology, where the United States had a lead in the early 1970s. The Soviet Union subsequently caught the United States, and in 1975 began to MIRV its missiles. The SALT II Treaty addressed the problem presented by MIRVed missiles, but by this time the momentum of technology had shifted to cruise missiles and increased ICBM accuracy. These latter problems were not effectively controlled in SALT II. Finally, negotiations during the Reagan Administrative have been characterized by the unwillingness of the United States to accept controls on SDI, the latest technological development in strategic weapons.

The fact that arms control lags behind weapons technology substantially reduces its capacity to restrict the competition in arms. Furthermore, by achieving some limits on less modern weapons, arms control arguably channels arms competition into newer and more modern weapons technologies. Arms control likely enhances the pressure to make technological improvements in weapons by creating an incentive to establish a dominant position in new technologies before they risk the possibility of being restrained by the arms control process.

Arms control is accomplished through negotiation, and this process itself reduces the effectiveness of arms control to restrain the arms race. One problem is the internal politicking that accompanies arms control negotiations. Arms control proposals are highly politicized and negotiating them generates extensive debates within parties, particularly in Western democractic countries. For example, U.S. negotiator John Dean (Sloss and Davis, 1986) has remarked of his experience in the Mutual and Balanced Force Reductions talks in Vienna that his time was apportioned roughly as follows: 30 percent consulting with Washington, 25 percent coordinating his delegations, 40 percent consulting with allied delegations and only 5 percent for negotiating with the other side. The diverse interests that must be satisfied in the internal process leave arms control vulnerable to counter-pressures. Some of the constituents needed to support arms control proposals set demands inconsistent with arms control objectives as the price of their support. For example, in the United States it is difficult to achieve a consensus for arms control without the support of the military. This gives the military a means to bargain for new weapons. One such case occurred with the MX missile, which was offered to the U.S. Air Force by the Carter Administration as compensation for the President's decision to scrap the B-1 Bomber and for their support of SALT II.

The interagency process reduces the capacity to accomplish arms control objectives because the military and defense bureaucracies of both superpowers are geared more to procuring weapons and providing defense than to controlling or reducing arms. These actors have a necessary role in interagency debates over arms control, but their collective influence runs counter to the objectives of arms control, especially when they act to defend their internal interests against other domestic constituents. The result is that agreements between the parties that might achieve arms control risk being overturned by internal pressures, while positions that might be successful internally have little effect in controlling arms.

A second problem produced by the negotiation process is that it encourages the parties to develop a strong bargaining position toward each other, and to evaluate the negotiation in terms of its usefulness in extracting concessions from the other side. The bargaining process therefore creates values that might not exist independent of the bargaining. In trade negotiations, this phenomenon is observed when nations retain small duties that have no meaning in terms of trade policy, but are useful to induce concessions in future negotiations. In the same manner arms control negotiations encourage the parties to retain weapons that have little military value as bargaining chips in later negotiations. The result is to skew force structures toward the needs of the negotiating process rather than the needs of defense or national security. The impact of this on the military has been noted by a former naval officer: "The (deterrence) targeteer is particularly affected. He is saddled with unwanted junk. For example, we would have abandoned the Titan years ago, had it not been a "bargaining chip" for arms control negotiations. The targeteer and the operational commander begin to see nuclear weapons as bargaining chips in the game of arms control, not military weapons for defeating or even deterring the enemy" (Miller, 1986: 42).

The negotiation process, and the search for a secure bargaining position, also lead to the development and procurement of new weapons. For example, the MX missile is often cited as a weapon that was inspired less by U.S. military requirements than by the need to demonstrate that the United States had the will to counter Soviet strengths in the category of heavy missiles. A better example of negotiating imperatives leading to weapons development is President Reagan's aforementioned defense of the SDI program. SDI, claimed the President, was what brought the Soviets back to arms control talks, and was the mechanism to ensure they would keep their commitments in future negotiations. The President's rationale for this dramatic new departure in U.S. defense policy places greater emphasis on what it means for the bargaining process than for the security of the United States. This creates the appearance of the means overtaking the ends of defense policy.

A third problem with arms control negotiations is that they focus on the quantitative aspects of security at the expense of the qualitative. It is natural for the bargaining process to emphasize numbers and counting. The use of quantitative variables increases precision in negotiation, and often helps the parties to evaluate and exchange concessions. The problem, however, is that the number of nuclear weapons bears little relation to the importance of weapons, either from the perspective of the arms controller or the defense planner. Characteristics such as accuracy, speed, penetration capability and survivability are far more important in military terms than are gross numbers of weapons, and they are not dealt with adequately in negotiations that focus excessively on numbers. Then too, other matters of political or symbolic significance often figure in arms negotiations, such as the presence of American nuclear forces on European soil. These issues are unlikely to be dealt with adequately in a missile-counting approach to arms control.

When negotiations are deeply adversarial or distrustful, it is likely that a quantitative approach to bargaining lessens the prospect for reaching agreement. Numbers create a semblance of precision and encourage parties to negotiate on the basis of numerical parity, but the inherent uncertainty of the data makes it difficult to conclude agreements on this basis. The force structures of the United States and the Soviet Union are very different; U.S. strategic capabilities are diversified into intercontinental missiles, aircraft and submarines, whereas Soviet capabilities are highly concentrated in strategic missiles. In this situation the search for numerical parity, especially within subcategories of weapons, has proved to be an impossible task for negotiators. As a way around this problem negotiators have adopted the goal of "essential equivalence" in arms talks, but the tendency to count and compare numbers of weapons has made this concept unworkable. By analogy, quantitative issues (such as wages) in labor negotiations are recognized as the most difficult issues to settle, and parties often try to get agreement by bringing qualitative issues like working conditions into the negotiation. In strategic arms talks, the parties have become locked into negotiations over weapons that are as precise and quantitative as wage negotiations, but without the advantage of a common currency that structures wage negotiations and renders them less uncertain.

In the last analysis the purpose of superpower diplomacy, as in any diplomacy between intensely hostile parties, is to establish an understanding of mutual limits. Diplomacy should communicate interests and commitments, the range of permissible activities and the acceptable policy mechanisms for carrying out those activities. Negotiations over weapons are a normal part of this diplomacy. However, in the past two decades arms control negotiations have become the mainstay of superpower diplomacy. The result is to focus superpower diplomacy on the capabilities of the parties rather than on their intentions, and on the elements (such as weapons technologies) in their relationship that change most rapidly rather than the elements (such as political interests) that tend to remain constant. Perceptual and political concerns thus become less important, with the result that strategic consensus, such as existed in the 1960s on missile defense, is less attainable.

An example of the tendency of arms control negotiations to focus debate on capabilities is seen in the issue of verification. Despite enormous strides in national technical means of verification, verification remains a key Western demand in arms control. This is a plausible demand in the context of negotiating limits on weapons; nevertheless, it inevitably exacerbates political relations between the superpowers. Verification focuses debate on specific numbers and characteristics of weapons, rather than on the generalities of their strategic uses, and it is on the specifics where the parties—either wittingly or unwittingly—are most likely to mislead each other. Verification forces the issue of trust into Soviet-American relations at precisely the point where the parties are least likely to prove trustworthy. As pursued in arms control, verification is a sophisticated concept applied to a primitive relationship. The goals of U.S.-USSR strategic diplomacy are mainly to keep the parties from initiating a mutually suicidal nuclear war; these are not complex goals, compared to other endeavors nations make in international relations. By allowing arms control, along with issues like verification, to dominate the superpower agenda, the United States and USSR have chosen the most difficult terrain on which to pursue what few common interests they do have.

Arms Control Negotiations and Crisis Management

The most important requirement for crisis management between superpowers armed with nuclear weapons is crisis stability, defined as the capacity of strategic forces to resist surprise attack. Stability is assured if strategic forces are invulnerable. This gives an attacked party the capacity to retaliate, removing any advantage in striking first. Crisis stability is the foundation of deterrence, and it is largely a function of the characteristics of weapons deployed by the parties. In the early development of nuclear arsenals, crisis stability came to be identified as the crucial issue of strategic planning, and early analyses of this problem pointed out the danger of relying on vulnerable, forward-based bomber fleets for nuclear deterrence. These analyses led to the development of more secure weapons with second strike capabilities, notably ICBMs in hardened silos, and especially nuclear missile submarines (Polaris). Armed with these weapons, leaders on both sides could confront a crisis relatively confident that the weapons themselves deterred, and did not encourage, a surprise attack.

The technical developments that enhanced crisis stability in the early 1960s came to threaten it later in that decade. One destabilizing weapon was ABM which, if deployed around population centers, provided the possibility of defense, reducing the deterrent value of an adversary's offensive weapons. Fortunately from the perspective of crisis stability, ABM had great liabilities in that it was uncertain, costly and alarming to the public, and as a result the superpowers were able to side-track it through an international agreement.

A more serious threat to crisis stability was the multiple independently targetable reentry vehicle, which increased the number of warheads per missile. Unlike ABM, MIRV was consistent with an offensive strategic posture, and could be seen merely as a technical upgrading of existing forces. However, MIRV so increased offensive capabilities that it raised again the spector of preemptive first strike. Nuclear missiles have some capability to destroy other missiles in their silos prior to the latter being launched. If the probability of destruction is less than unity, then missiles armed with single warheads on one side could never completely destroy an equivalent number of missiles on the other side. However, once missiles are MIRVed the situation is reversed, and the probability exists that a given number of missiles equipped with multiple warheads could completely destroy an equivalent number of an adversary's missiles. Crisis stability is thus lost, and there is no straightforward way to recover it.

The Soviet deployment of MIRV, combined with the traditional large throw-weights of Soviet missile forces, created by the late 1970s a credible first strike capability against U.S. land-based missiles. This alarmed opinion in the United States over a potential "window of vulnerability," and it led to increased pressure by the Reagan administration to upgrade strategic forces. The Administration moved ahead with the MX missile, a large land-based missile with multiple warheads, in an effort to correct the perceived gap in U.S. strategic forces. Two observations can be made about this U.S. action. One is that a tendency exists on both sides to match weapons systems of the other, which is known as counterforce matching. Of this tendency Russett and Chernoff (1985: 87) have observed: "Counterforce matching has emerged as the most powerful stimulant of the arms race." The second observation is that once weapons invulnerability is lost by one side, increasing the threat toward the other side does not restore it. Both superpowers are now approaching the capability to threaten first strike destruction of the adversary's land-based missiles. Although this vulnerability does not extend to sea-based forces, nevertheless a vital element of crisis stability appears to be irrevocably lost.

How have arms control negotiations related to these developments? In an assessment of the early works on arms control from the late 1950s, Kruzel (1985) notes that most early thinkers were critically concerned with crisis stability. Some of the themes that emerge from this literature are the need to reduce vulnerability to surprise attack, and the importance of the characteristics of weapons in accomplishing that goal. The early analysts did not place much emphasis on reducing numbers of nuclear weapons, nor did they entertain visions of ending the competition in nuclear arms. The important point was stability, and it was asssumed this problem was largely independent of diplomacy and mainly a function of the force structure on both sides.

Arms control has gotten side-tracked from its original concepts since the early 1970s when SALT I was signed. One symptom of this has been the insistence on counting weapons without apparent concern for what the numbers—either higher or lower—mean in relation to crisis stability. As Nye (1986: 13) has noted: " . . . reducing the risk of nuclear war and reducing reliance on nuclear weapons are not necessarily the same as reducing the number of nuclear weapons." Other departures from the early arms control theory include an almost instinctive pursuit of formal agreements, despite the fact that stability could be promoted through informal understandings, or even without communications altogether. However the real problem is not that arms control has failed to promote stability; worse, it has retarded prospects for crisis stability by the influence it exerts on procurement decisions. In the interests of reciprocity and parity, arms control negotiations encourage a political climate that legitimizes counterforce matching even when the weapons matched are inherently destabilizing. The U.S. MX missile is one such example; it was procured as a bargaining chip to offset Soviet MIRVed ICBMs, even though an increase in U.S. strategic submarines might have been a more stable and less costly response to the Soviet ICBM threat.

Arms control can discourage the procurement of more stable weaponry because of the problems some weapons present for verification. For example, mobile missiles ought to provide security against surprise attack, but they are problematic from the perspective of arms control. Submarine-based cruise missiles pose even greater difficulties for the arms controller; while they might be good retaliatory weapons, there is no way to monitor their presence. As to the difficulties this creates for arms control, Schelling (1985/86: 229) has noted: "The logic is that if you cannot find them (nuclear weapons) you cannot count them; if you cannot count them you cannot have verifiable limits; if limits cannot be verified you cannot have arms control." The conclusion then is that the circumstances that promote arms control may not be those that also promote crisis stability, which in turn is an essential ingredient of crisis management.

The fact that arms control has not dealt sufficiently with the qualitative aspects of strategic weapons becomes even more problematic in connection with the stability of command structures in a nuclear exchange. Recent analyses (e.g., Steinbruner, 1984) suggest that nuclear explosions at a distance of 300 miles above the earth's surface could create an electromagnetic pulse that would produce electrical surges on exposed conductors on the ground. The exact consequences are not known, but the probable results would be major failures of communications, power and electrical equipment. Either superpower could easily effect such explosions (with as little as four or five warheads) over the other party's territory as part of a surprise attack, and the warning time could be less than ten minutes.

The potential vulnerability of command structures to surprise attack is extremely serious for crisis stability, indeed more serious than the vulnerability of nuclear weapons. Nuclear deterrence strategies require effective communications for their execution, both to assure negative control (i.e. to avoid a mistaken launch) and positive control (i.e. to initiate a retaliatory launch). The possibility that strategic communications might be disrupted creates an additional pressure toward preemptive attack. As Steinbruner (1984: 43–44) notes: "Compared with silo vulnerability, command system vulnerability presents a much more powerful incentive to initiate attack before damage has actually been suffered. . . . " In a crisis situation the pressure to preempt could become extremely serious, and if hostilities were to appear likely, one might expect military authorities on both sides to seek approval to initiate a nuclear strike.

Furthermore, the weakness of command structures makes them plausible targets for either a preemptive or a retaliatory strike.

The gravity of the threat to command structures has been recognized in the United States, and has led to pressures to adopt a policy of launching a retaliatory strike on warning that an enemy's nuclear weapons are on the way. Such a policy, even if it were dangerous, could be a deterrent against surprise attack. However, the policy of launch under attack is generally regarded as unworkable, due to the complications of communications and timing, and thus there appears to be no immediate answer to the instability produced by vulnerable communications and command structures.

The vulnerability of command structures is typical of the subjects arms control was originally intended to address, for it is critical to the maintenance of crisis stability. However, recent arms control negotiations which focus on reducing numbers of weapons do not address this problem sufficiently. This threat to crisis stability is not a quantitative problem, for it can be effectively posed by relatively few nuclear warheads operating from intercontinental, intermediate, or submarine-based launchers. It is deeply ironic that even if an arms control agreement were to reduce current numbers of nuclear weapons, the agreement would not necessarily deal with the source of great instability, and therefore great danger, in the current strategic relationship between the superpowers.

Conclusion

The capacity to manage crisis is one of the most important elements of the superpower relationship. Since SALT I, arms control negotiations have not enhanced the superpowers' capacity for crisis management. This is because arms control has focused on the wrong things, especially on reductions of nuclear weapons, and it has not dealt with the important matters, such as how to improve the deterrent stability of nuclear arsenals. Arms control negotiations have not succeeded in establishing a fundamental political and strategic consensus between the superpowers, without which negotiations on any issue of international politics are likely to fail.

Far from promoting a shared consensus between the parties, arms control negotiations have become a source of instability in superpower relations. For example, in negotiations leading up to and including the Reykjavik Summit, both superpowers advanced proposals that ranged from partial to complete elimination of whole categories of weapons. The proposals were accompanied by statements from both sides professing support for the elimination of nuclear weapons together. Compared to the recent history of arms buildups on both sides, these moves seem either cynically designed to manipulate public opinion, or else they reveal that the parties no longer know what they want in arms control. There is an instability to the issues in arms control negotiations that is reminiscent of successive hands in a game of poker; while poker is a captivating form of human competition, it is not a good model for building enduring agreements dealing with fundamental issues of national security.

In negotiating arms control, the parties have both a relationship to contend with and interests to defend. Arms control negotiations now appear to be more relationship-driven than interest-driven, with the result that it is difficult to find stable trade-offs on basic issues around which an overall agreement can be built.[4] The process does not create a political environment conducive to crisis management, since the latter by definition requires the parties to identify and protect high priority national values in the context of a threatening situation. In short, the focus in crisis management is on priorities, whereas recent arms control proposals appear almost indiscriminate.

When negotiations fail it is usually through a lack of political will, but in the case of arms control it may be the method itself that is at fault. Communication between the superpowers is essential, but highly structured formal arms control negotiations may have outlived their usefulness, at least for the near run. One possible substitute might be unilateral action, or "arms control without agreements" (Adelman, 1984/ 85). While this might seem unduly optimistic, the fact is that some aspects of nuclear weapons—such as total megatonnage—have declined since the 1960s without the benefit of explicit agreement. Furthermore, there is no reason why the stability sought in early arms control theory should only be achievable through negotiation, since each side has an interest in developing stable weapons systems regardless of what the other side does. Consistent policy actions toward enhancing weapons stability might elicit cooperative actions from an adversary, although the difficulties of achieving cooperation through unilateral actions—due largely to uncertainty and ambiguity—should not be underestimated (Downs and Rocke, 1987). In any case, unilateral actions are unlikely to make the situation worse than it is at present. Right now the parties pursue negotiation as if it were a requirement for cooperation. Instead, common interests are the basis for cooperation, and arms control negotiations only obfuscate the clear interests both sides have in maintaining crisis stability and political stability in the superpower relationship.

Communications between the superpowers will undoubtedly continue, but it may be better that it concentrate on small, concrete, low profile mechanisms to avert war, such as the establishment of nuclear risk reductions centers in Washington and Moscow. As Ury (1986) notes, negotiations on these matters have made progress in the last decade, at the same time that large-scale arms control negotiations have been foundering. From the perspective of crisis management, it is more useful to have continuous dialogue along a broad range of issues, than to have communication channelled into a fruitless search for major arms control agreements.

Notes

1. The full title of the Interim Agreement is: *Interim Agreement Between the United States and the Union of Soviet Socialist Republics on Certain Measures with Respect to the Limitation of Strategic Offensive Arms.* The Agreement includes a Protocol.

2. Further analysis indicated the reductions were more in the range of 20–30 per cent (Gordon, 1987).

3. The classical goals of arms control are: to reduce risk of war; to reduce costs of war preparation; and to reduce damage should war occur (Kruzel, 1985). Clearly an arms race is inconsistent with the latter two goals, and it is probably inconsistent with the first.

4. Auctions are a common form of relationship-driven negotiation; an extreme example is the dollar-auction game (Shubik, 1971), in which players often unwittingly end up bidding more than a dollar to buy a dollar.

PART THREE

Nuclear Crisis Management

6

Enhancing Crisis Stability: Correcting the Trend Toward Increasing Instability

Charles F. Hermann

Introduction[1]

We live in a dangerous era, when both the United States and the Soviet Union continue to amass nuclear weapons and rely on the threat of their use to deter major war. In such times some encouragement can be found in the repeated expressions by leaders of both countries that they recognize each side would experience catastrophic devastation in a nuclear conflict. The acknowledgement that neither side could escape destruction has been expressed by political leaders ranging from Khrushchev to Gorbachev, from Eisenhower to Reagan. Whatever military leaders and civilian strategists may contemplate as hypothetical contingencies, one observes that politicians of enormously different beliefs, motives, and world views have sensed at a "gut level" that nuclear war as an instrument for achieving political ends makes no sense. Beyond the assurances of their declaratory statements, we have little direct evidence of occasions for decision where Soviet leaders were presented with the option of using nuclear weapons and explicitly rejected the possibility even if it meant accepting possible setbacks, but it certainly is an observable fact that despite various provocations they have not done so even when it meant alienating the Chinese or allowing Egypt to suffer a humiliating defeat. On the American side we know of multiple cases where the idea surfaced and was dismissed (e.g. see Halloran, 1986).

It seems reasonable to conclude that despite occasional flip remarks and endless (and necessary) reexaminations of nuclear deterrence, nuclear war as an acceptable means for achieving policy goals other than political system survival has been repeatedly rejected in actual cases to date and nuclear war has been widely regarded by political leaders at a more general level of declaratory statements as probably suicidal. Because such beliefs seem very widespread, one might conclude, as many have, that in normal times a nuclear war beginning abruptly as a bolt out of the blue in a calculated attempt to achieve potential political advantage appears extremely remote.

Regrettably other causes of nuclear war seem less remote. Among major categories of nuclear war risk are the following:

- demented dominant political leader with dictatorial control over nuclear forces
- accidental or unauthorized use of nuclear weapons
- crises involving threats to core values of a nuclear power[2]

Each of these risks of nuclear war deserves careful attention, but this chapter concerns the third.

From the perspective of policy-makers in a country, an international politico-military crisis exists when they perceive a severe threat to the basic values of their political system from sources that are at least partially outside their polity; when they believe there is relatively short time before the situation (if unaltered) will evolve in ways unfavorable to them; and when they have an increased expectation that in the near future there will be an outbreak of military hostitlies or a sharp escalation of already existing hostilities.[3]

The period of extreme antagonism and severe competition that has marked relations between the Soviet Union and the United States since World War II has been punctuated by such crises. In the most recent years there has been no shortage of provocations by either side—the Soviet invasion of Afghanistan, the American insertion of Marines in Lebanon backed by naval and air strikes against Syrian controlled areas, the Soviet shooting down of a civilian airliner with Americans including a Congressman aboard, the American air strikes against Libya or the shooting of a U.S. Major on duty in East Germany by one of their soldiers. Despite such aggressive acts toward one another, these provocations fail to meet our criteria for a major crisis and lead to the observation that recent years have not entailed the kind of episodes that earlier transpired repeatedly over Berlin, or the Cuban missile crisis, or the potential escalation during the 1973 Arab-Israeli War.

The recent lull in politico-military crises between the Soviet Union and the United States may reflect a growing recognition about the great danger of acute crises in a manner somewhat parallel to that surrounding the use of nuclear weapons in war. Yet to date we have witnessed no wide-spread series of declaratory statements that reflected a sensitivity to the potentially increased danger of crises and, more critically, we have witnessed practices on both sides that make the risks of nuclear war potentially greater in any future crisis.

Both the Soviet Union and the United States have in the past decade engaged in changes in force structure and doctrine that reduce crisis stability. Given our mutual reliance on some form of nuclear deterrence, these developments make crisis as a path to nuclear war a matter of even greater concern than it has been in the past.

Crisis stability can be viewed as a subset of deterrence stability and arises from a country's reliance on deterrence to prevent attacks on itself and on other valued assets. Deterrence stability requires that the threatening capability of strategic forces not be perceived by either party to be neutralized or severely eroded by actions of a potential adversary such as by an initial strike against those forces, or by effective protection of the enemy targets at which they are aimed, or by some development that impedes the will or capacity of the deterrent country's leadership to authorize retaliation. In short, deterrence forces are stable to the degree that they are perceived as capable of inflicting damaging retaliation regardless of the potential adversary's action such as a counterforce first strike. For this reason, such stability is often simplified to the invulnerability of strategic nuclear forces—a perspective that is open to challenge (e.g., Steinbruner, 1978). A strategic nuclear force that has a substantial degree of stability under normal conditions can be adversely affected by a crisis. Thus, crisis instability can be viewed as the extent to which such situations reduce the deterrence stability perceived to exist under normal conditions and create incentives to initiate a strategic nuclear attack.[4]

Crises, as defined, can put stress or special demands on a deterrent force in several different ways:

1. Crises can expose technical features of the force structure or design features of strategic plans that had not previously been understood or had been disregarded. Thus, in the early days of liquid-fuel ICBMs, the process of fueling missiles was protracted and once fueled the missiles had to be launched within a limited period of time or a refueling process introducing long delays had to be initiated. These features could interact adversely within the time pressures of a crisis.

2. Crises may require, or make very desirable, certain actions—such as defensive preparations or demonstrations of resolve—that are highly susceptible to misinterpretation by the adversary. An action intended by the initiator as a prudent defensive response to a

crisis is perceived by the adversary as provocative and offensive. Thus, the Russian desire for a mobilization to show support for Serbia in 1914 was misinterpreted by Germany.

3. Crisis may also change the way policy-makers think. The stress produced by a crisis may cause leaders to believe that they have few options; that their adversary alone has avenues for de-escalating the situation; and that raising questions about the merit of plans proposed by fellow policy-makers is unpatriotic and dangerous.

In summary, crisis stability can be affected by changing the state of weapons systems, by previously unforeseen consequences of forces or plans, or by changes in the perceptions and thinking of policy-makers.

The dynamics that can lead to crisis instability involve some mix of the following:

- Perception by top political authorities that nuclear war is now virtually inevitable. This perception can be compounded by disruption in individual or group reasoning that sometimes results from the stress induced by a crisis. Of particular concern is the perception of some people upon experiencing severe stress in a situation with the adversary that they are helpless and have no further options and that only their opponent has the ability to exercise control and initiate alternatives that can avert disaster.

- Belief that one's own forces are so extremely vulnerable to attack now that little of one's intended retaliatory force would survive the enemy's first strike. This belief may result from "worse-case" type thinking, from actual momentary disadvantage (e.g., a higher than usual number of one's own strategic systems or control arrangements that are down for maintenance or are discovered to be momentarily out of order), from full recognition for the first time by political leaders (although previously known by others) of some of the very real limits on their strategic capabilities and the doctrines governing their use, or some combination of the above.

- Belief that there is a possible decisive advantage in attacking first with nuclear weapons. This belief may be the result of a long-established governmental policy (as for the United States in responding to a conventional attack by Soviet forces in Europe that cannot be stopped by the NATO non-nuclear defense forces) or of the sudden conclusion that nuclear war is inevitable, at which point, as Betts observes (1985a; 59) " . . . the opponent's nuclear force is automatically transformed from a deterrent into a target, which must be attacked to limit the damage that will be suffered from the inevitable exchange."

If war is to be avoided by military deterrence, then it is imperative that in situations where policy-makers perceive great threat, short time, and the likelihood of escalating military action that none of the deterrence arrangements designed to avoid war suddenly act in the reserve way and increase the risk. It is precisely this increased risk in a future crisis—that is, greater crisis instability—that recent actions of both the United States and the Soviet Union have generated.

Recent Sources of Crisis Instability[5]

In considerations of crisis stability it is important to review recent and emerging developments and practices of both the Soviet Union and the United States—many of them quite familiar—that affect the context in which any future crisis involving them would occur. At least four areas require review. They are: changes in the characteristics of strategic weapons, changes in strategic alerts, changes in command and control of nuclear weapons, and changes in strategic plans. Clearly there are connections among these developments, but with respect to crisis stability, each can be viewed as producing some separate effects.

Weapons Systems Characteristics

A discussion of changes in the inventory of strategic weapons of greatest salience to crisis stability might reasonably begin with the American deployment in the early 1970s of MIRVs (Multiple Independently-targeted Reentry Vehicles), which are now deployed by both sides in sufficient numbers and are combined with substantial improvements in warhead accuracy to pose a threat to the survivability of fixed-base ICBMs. The resulting "hard-target kill capability," or ability to destroy with substantial probability hardened missile silos, has put a major portion of each side's strategic force at risk from the other side's possible first strike involving only a portion of its total strategic forces.

MIRVed and highly accurate systems such as the Minuteman IIIs, MXs, Trident D-5s, SS-18s and SS-19s produce a greater pressure on policy-makers than in earlier post-World War II crises for preemptive attack if the likelihood of nuclear war seems pronounced. Because both sides have ICBMs at risk, each will be attempting to calculate whether the other side may be planning to preempt. As a result there will be an increased tendency to interpret any ambiguous military activities as indications of preemption that in turn could trigger decisions to use one's own weapons before they are destroyed.

In recent years the Soviet Union has led the way in the development of antisatellite (ASAT) rockets designed to destroy satellites in space.

Just as the Soviet Union followed the United States in MIRV development, so the United States has followed the USSR's initiative in the pursuit of an ASAT system. ASAT capability on both sides appears unperfected at present. Even if improved, the present generation of such weapons would appear to threaten only low orbit satellites or those in highly elliptical orbits. Although most U.S. strategic satellites are stationed in very high orbit, both countries maintain numerous low orbit military satellites of great importance for intelligence purposes and these systems could be vulnerable in the near future. According to Garwin and his associates (1984: 47): "The ability to destroy low-orbit military satellites, coupled with the fear that the opponent may at any moment attack one's own satellites, could therefore create an irresistible temptation to remove the opponent's satellites. As a consequence the ability to destroy low-orbit satellites promptly could inflame a political crisis or minor conflict that might otherwise have been resolved by diplomacy if there were no antisatellite weapons."

Clearly the destruction of satellites at any time, and particularly during a crisis, would be regarded as a violation of existing treaties and an act of extreme provocation. Even without actual attacks, the knowledge of the presence of antisatellite weapons on both sides will compound tensions in a future crisis. The existence of a substantial antisatellite capability would be perceived as reducing stability in a crisis regardless of whether such weapons were used. Like land-based ICBMs in silos, satellites have become vulnerable, particularly those in low earth orbit.

Optimally the momentous decision about the use of nuclear weapons should be taken under circumstances that promote thoughtful reflection and analysis. The magnitude of the consequences certainly separate this potential decision from all others. Yet both the United States and the Soviet Union push the development and deployment of weapons systems that continuously erode available decision time. Current ICBMs take 25 to 30 minutes to reach most targets in the other country from their present sites. Both sides have available missile systems that reduce warning time to well under ten minutes by the use of submarine-launched ballistic missiles (SLBMs) that traverse much shorter distances from their location in off-shore subs. Pershing IIs and, for European members of NATO, the SS-20s pose equivalent decision-time reducing systems.

The ultimate decision-time reducer will be weapons designed to attack ICBMs or SLBMs in their boost phase. For the present generation of ICBMs, the boost phase begins when the main rocket engines start firing just before lift-off and ends when the final stage rocket engines shut off—an elasped time of three to five minutes. Both sides are currently working on systems designed to attack missiles in their boost phase. To destroy missiles (perhaps up to 1400 in a full scale attack) in the boost phase, the defensive systems must identify rocket launches, track their flight paths, launch interceptor beams or projectiles, and assess what damage was done for possible second efforts—all in under five minutes. Clearly no human decision-making can be introduced in such a highly restricted time frame. In such circumstances computers must determine whether a missile launch is only a test, a manned space mission, or a defective sensor. Its malfunction could not only precipitate a crisis but could also plunge opponents in an existing crisis into vastly greater escalation. Severe consequences could flow from the perception by policy-makers that the other side intended to relinquish to an automated system control over the initiation of strategic defense—possibly involving the detonation of nuclear devices. If the adversary believed the system *would work* and believed in a crisis that war seemed increasingly inevitable, he would know that his first strategic move would have to be massively overwhelming. Both sides would regard the space-based systems designed to attack missiles in their boost phase and the related support equipment as prime targets for ASAT attacks and would encourage preemption. Furthermore, both sides would regard any evidence in a crisis of the defense system's temporary malfunction as a period of acute opportunity or vulnerability. If, on the contrary, an adversary believes that both sides know a strategic defense against ballistic missiles *cannot work* effectively against a large-scale attack and such a system is deployed anyway, then the adversary will assume the defense is part of a first-strike strategy. It would be used against the presumably small number of launched enemy missiles that escaped destruction in the first strike. Such beliefs would reduce crisis stability and encourage preemption by the side not having the system.[6]

In summary, there are some discernible direct effects on crisis stability from these new weapons systems, but the most significant consequences are the second and third order effects. To deal with these weapons, policy-makers take other steps or form new mental images that, in turn, seriously reduce stability in a future crisis. It is important to recognize that every new strategic weapon system does not necessarily erode crisis stability. A mobile, single warhead missile or strategic bomber, for example, would not appear to have such grave effects as those systems described above.

Strategic Alerts in an Era of Essential Equivalence

On three occasions since 1960, the United States has put its global military forces on an increased alert status during a crisis with the

Soviet Union. These include the collapse of the summit conference in May 1960, the Cuban Missile crisis in October-November 1962, and the final days of the Middle East War in October 1973 (See Sagan, 1985). Not much comparable information appears to be publicly available regarding the Soviet Union. To date, however, it does seem that the United States and the USSR have not put their worldwide strategic forces on a very high alert at the same time. The basic military purpose of an increase in strategic alert status is to heighten the preparedness for war by taking steps to reduce the time between a subsequent order to use force and the actual initiation of coordinated military action. At least, the United States has demonstrated its willingness to use a heightened alert status as a means of signaling to the other side quickly and dramatically its revolve to protect threatened vital interests. Clearly that was the intent of the American alert during the Yom Kippur War: to signal rapidly that the U.S. would regard the introduction of Soviet troops into Egypt as contrary to U.S. vital interests. (For a discussion of this strategic alert, see Blechman and Hart, 1982; and Kissinger, 1982.)

Whether the Soviet Union's leadership will elect to follow the American precedent and use an increase in strategic alert status as a means of signaling in a future crisis is unknowable, but the mutual perception of the increased size and relative capabilities of present Soviet strategic forces, as compared to 1973, might invite such action. At a minimum, Soviet leaders may feel they can no longer allow the Americans to engage in such escalation without a comparable response to curb bluffs and communicate that they are equally prepared to defend their vital interests.

If heightened strategic alert status in some superpower crises is to be expected, and is perhaps necessary, that does not alter its implications for crisis stability. This is particularly true if the escalated levels of strategic readiness are mutual. In an acute crisis the American president (and perhaps his Soviet counterpart) could be expected to delegate authority to initiate use of nuclear weapons down the chain of command. This action would be a necessary precaution against a possible enemy attempt to immobilize the strategic system by instantly killing the President, Secretary of Defense, Chairman of the Joint Chiefs and those in the constitutional line of presidential succession with a very small number of nuclear weapons. In contrast to the normal peace time disposition of managers of the strategic system to disbelieve and check repeatedly any information indicating an incoming attack has been launched, in crisis such messages become more credible. Because the authority to initiate use of nuclear weapons would be dispersed, more individuals would be in a position to make separate and independent judgments that this time the message is real. The problem would be most sensitive with submarines placed on a higher alert status. These boats have no physical constraint on launching nuclear weapons outside the boats' crews themselves and experience difficulty with outside communication while making maximum effort to avoid detection. Finally, each side's alert preparations would almost certainly be quickly detected by the other side. (Quick detection by the Soviets is precisely why the United States went to a higher level of strategic alert in 1973 to signal its resolve.) The temptation to respond to the other side's alert with a still higher state of one's own would feed not only the physical changes in the two systems but the psychological state of the respective, enlarged group of policy-makers, each with a finger on the nuclear trigger.[7]

At higher alert levels in a crisis a greater danger arises that action will occur—either unauthorized or actions with unanticipated effects—that will be misconstrued by the other side as moving beyond preparation to a commitment to attack. In the Cuban missile crisis, multiple such actions occurred. With mutual high alerts, the number and reduced tolerance of such events could be extremely troubling.

Finally, simultaneous high levels of alert may complicate the task of orchestrating de-escalations back down to lower alert conditions when such action by one side would appear to give the other very decided advantages.[8]

Command and Control of Nuclear Weapons

The command and control of nuclear weapons or C^3I (command, control, communications and intelligence) have become subjects of increased attention in recent years for both policy-makers and analysts (e.g., Blair, 1985). With respect to crisis stability, two command and control issues seem paramount:

- Elements of command and control remain one of the most vulnerable elements of the strategic system susceptible to a first strike;
- Highly centralized control of nuclear weapons by the highest national authority poses an exceptionally vulnerable target.

Command and Control Vulnerability. The general vulnerability of C^3I results from numerous factors ranging from the "softness" of many elements of the system (e.g., satellite receiver stations, radars, telephone exchanges) to the uncertain effects of nuclear detonations on the performance of electronic equipment and certain radio frequencies (e.g., the ability of the electromagnetic pulse, or EMP, from a high altitude nuclear explosion to create harmful voltage surges over a wide area);

from the increased operational requirements that result from adopting more complicated strategic plans to the increased complexity arising from the tighter integration of more components.

As with so many of the consequences for crisis stability, the main effects appear to flow from the policy-makers' awareness of this vulnerability and their efforts to cope with it. Because each side knows that key elements of the other side's command and control system can readily be disrupted by a modest force and that such an attack might offer a chance of prohibiting a substantial, effective counterattack, there is a temptation to consider a preemptive strike. This is particularly so knowing that one's own side might be made similarly inoperative by an equivalent assault. If war seems likely (which is what a crisis is about), the command and control system may become a factor, not for controlling the situation and promoting a resolution of the crisis, but a pressure for a preemptive nuclear attack.

National Authority Vulnerability. A second dimension of the problem is the vulnerability of the national command authority. Control of nuclear weapons by the highest national authorities has been a widely accepted principle since the beginning of the nuclear age. With the proliferation of strategic systems in geographically diverse locations, the problem of maintaining control has become more complex. In characterizing the evolution of the American system, Bracken (1983) uses the analogy of a rifle trigger and safety catch in which the trigger is inoperative so long as the safety catch is on. "The primary command centers were to serve as triggers, but their ability to fire would be refrained by the viable functioning, and the survival, of the presidential command center. If the safety catch of the system were destroyed, direct operational control would devolve to the primary command centers . . . "(Bracken, 1983: 196–197). Obviously, many steps have been taken to insure the accessibility of the President or his successor to the primary command centers—the constant proximity of the military aide with the authorizing codes, the standby maintenance of the National Emergency Airborne Command Post, and so on.

As with other parts of the command and control system, the centralized control—both the "safety catch" and the primary "triggers"—represent a fairly small number of targets. The Soviet Yankee class submarines off the Atlantic coast of the United States, the American Pershing II missiles in Europe, and nearby American Poseidon and Trident submarines all have missiles with flight times of under 12 minutes capable of destroying the high command centers. The time from the moment of detection of their launch to impact on their targets could in many circumstances be insufficient to remove the designated authorities to safety. In fact, the key subordinate commands also could be subject to similar prompt attacks creating the spector of a society abruptly deprived of its top political and military leadership as the result of a decapitation strike.

Once again the adverse effect on crisis stability partially results from the steps taken to cope with the command and control susceptibility to attack and the resulting perceptions. Bracken (1983) describes the American system designed to meet this problem as one of "cascading authority" whereby through a practice of pre-delegated authority, the ability to authorize an attack is passed to consecutively lower levels of military command before an attack. Assuming higher levels of authority are lost, then by pre-arrangement these officers decide on the use of the weapons under their command. It is the knowledge that the higher authority may disappear suddenly that poses the direct danger of pre-delegated command to crisis stability. Once authority over the use of nuclear weapons has been pre-delegated in a crisis, how does one continuously and confidently assure designated commanders that higher authorities are still safe and retaining authority? After the crisis is over, how is authority firmly recovered? These are the kind of problems posed for crisis stability by eroding decision control.

Strategic Plans

Not only the weapons, the means for their control, and the occasions on which readiness is suddenly accelerated, but also the pre-arranged plans for their use can affect crisis stability. Indeed actual changes or perceived changes in these other factors often motivate changes in strategic war plans. The two current proposals with powerful implications for crisis stability appear to stem from analyses of changing characteristics in weapons and the increasingly recognized problems of command and control vulnerability. The two proposed plans are launch under attack and a preemptive decapitation strategy.

Launch Under Attack. Launch under attack represents a possible response to the perceived growing vulnerability of land-based, fixed-site ICBMs, whose protection through hardening appears to some to be overwhelmed by sufficient numbers of accurate, MIRVed warheads possessed by the other superpower. Such a strategy also offers greater assurance that retaliation can be implemented with an intact command and control system, and, thus, represents a better chance for a coordinated and effective counterstrike. In addition, it recognizes that at the beginning of a nuclear exchange an opponent would act to disperse and otherwise protect moveable strategic systems such as bombers and submarines located at known bases. These are time-urgent targets that one has the best chance of destroying by attacking very quickly before they are moved. (An aggressor might be reluctant to move all these assets prior to his initial attack because it could reveal his intention.)

In a crisis, the possibility of strategic or advanced warning of an impending attack is uncertain and quite likely to be ambiguous. It is only after information processing centers have interpreted signals from intelligence sensors of a ballistic missile attack under way that a tactical warning can be flashed to command centers. If one's own ICBM sites appear to be the probable targets of such an attack, the policy-makers face the much discussed problem of losing a substantial portion of their hard-target, quick response strategic force in less that 30 minutes. Ordering a launch of the targeted systems before they are destroyed by incoming warheads is the proposed plan for launch under attack.

If a launch under attack plan were to have any reasonable hope of success, it would require putting strategic forces on a high state of alert once an international crisis occurs. To minimize delay, launch procedures must be linked very closely to warning sensors. As Bracken (1983: 55) has noted, "tightly coupled systems are notorious for producing over-compensation effects." Information in any part of the system gets repeated and amplified and the costs of any verfications or checks that take more than a moment may insure the defeat of the time-urgent plan. The tendency in any launch under attack plan would be to "switch off" certain normal negative controls under high conditions of alert that might fatally delay its implementation.

Information processing under such conditions would likely appear very different than in the same strategic command and control system under normal conditions or even in a crisis without a commitment to a launch under attack plan. Crisis stability would be sharply degraded as any real or false signals surged through the system. Not only the authorities in the country using such a plan, but also their counterparts on the other side, would be severely affected if they suspected that in a crisis their adversaries were committed to a launch under attack plan.

Preemptive Decapitation. Under the prevailing conditions of mutual deterrence, policy-makers in the Soviet Union and the United States both now and in the future are expected to conclude that no objectives or goals are remotely worth the horrors of nuclear war. But in a crisis would these same calculations prevail under the conditions in which, for example, one side believed the other had adopted a launch under attack policy? Or suppose the policy-makers fully recognized and accepted the implications of the other circumstances described in this chapter. Might they still believe that nuclear war was not worth any of their goals, but conclude that such a war now seemed extremely likely or, perhaps, inevitable? On such an occasion might leaders be tempted to implement a preemptive first strike against the most vulnerable element of the other side's strategic forces—the command and control system—in the belief that it offered a possible chance, however slim, of their own survival? It would be imperative to attack first with a preemptive strike that would be targeted, not primarily against the strategic forces themselves, but the political and military command centers, the strategic communication nodes, and the information processing centers that constitute the brain of the highly integrated force. Such targets appear to be well identified by both sides and their numbers are small. According to Blair (1985: 189): "Half the 400 primary and secondary U.S. strategic C^3I targets could be struck by Soviet missile submarines on routine patrol." Steinbruner (1981–82) suggests that a decapitation strike against the political and military nuclear command and control system offers several advantages. First, it is likely to reduce the damage of any retaliatory response because the response would lack controlled coordination (Should retaliation be undertaken? When? Against what targets?). "Second, it offers some small chance that complete decapitation will occur and no retaliation will follow" (Steinbruner 1981–82: 19).

The consequences for crisis stability of a decapitation strategy are staggering. It imposes powerful incentives on both sides for a preemptive nuclear strike if, in a crisis, war is perceived to be nearly inescapable. It also greatly increases the likelihood of war by loss of control or miscalculated escalation as suggested by Lebow (1987b).

Proposals for Enhancing Crisis Stability

If policy-makers' conscious decisions (sometimes without appreciation of the effects) in both the United States and the Soviet Union have produced the recent developments that increasingly jeopardize stability in a future crisis, then it should follow that they can make decisions to undo these adverse effects. It is most unlikely, however, that any of the described actions were taken deliberately to reduce crisis stability. Rather, greater instability resulted inadvertently from efforts by political and military leaders to realize other objectives. Even if one's sole military purpose is to create the most effective strategic deterrence possible, many criteria must be pursued. Among them are the following:

- The deterrent must be credible to potential adversaries.
- The deterrent must be acquired and maintained at acceptable levels of financial, social, and political burden.
- The deterrent must provide protection to all highly valued assets (e.g., for the United States extended deterrence requires protection of Europe and certain other allies against both conventional and nuclear attack).

- The deterrent, if entailing nuclear weapons, must not make conventional war more likely (i.e., neither side must become so convinced that nuclear war has been prohibited by deterrence that they feel free to initiate conventional war without fearing risk of escalation).
- The deterrent must minimize the possibility of accidental or inadvertent war.

This list by no means exhausts the requirements. Moreover, each of the criteria mentioned can be further elaborated to reveal additional specifications. Such criteria and their elaboration create demands that are contradictory. Some are achieved at the direct expense of others. For example, it is commonly thought that a degree of uncertainty about the conditions that trigger release of a deterrent force contributes to extended deterrence (coverage of all valued assets) and prevents an adversary from believing a conventional war can be waged without the danger of nuclear escalation. Though uncertainty may benefit those requirements, it increases the risk of miscalculation and accidental war. Similarly if strategic deterrence doctrine includes a launch under attack policy, then an adversary may be deterred from considering a preemptive strike, but again the risks of loss of control and accidental war are increased. In brief, the pursuit of these deterrence criteria often entail major tradeoffs. Efforts to fulfill one mean that others may be left unsatisfied. Thus, many steps that could be taken to improve crisis stability will have adverse effects on other deterrent criteria.

Appreciation of this agonizing dilemma has led some thoughtful people to challenge the appropriateness of strategic deterrence as presently conceived as a satisfactory means of war prevention. If all the criteria are necessary to make deterrence work and some are mutually exclusive, then strategic deterrence as a means of war prevention is seriously defective. Although the list of necessary deterrence requirements offered by these individuals might appear different from those indicated above, it is the same essential dilemma that has prompted advocates on both the political left and right to press for alternatives to nuclear deterrence and the present condition it has generated of mutual assured destruction. The results have ranged from advocacy of the strategic defense initiative to the American Catholic and Methodist bishops' respective critiques and calls for disarmament. Thus, one response to the problems of crisis stability is to avoid war by some means other than nuclear deterrence. As important as the search for alternatives is, it is not the focus of this chapter. The remaining task of this essay is to consider means of dealing with crisis stability within the context of a policy of nuclear deterrence.

We will review a variety of proposals for improving crisis stability arranged under three categories. Some approaches entail actions that can be performed unilaterally and presumably could improve conditions even if not reciprocated by the other side. Others are bilateral arrangements that require either the tacit cooperation or explicit agreement of both primary parties. Some arrangements are multilateral and involve an active role for third parties.

Many things that might be useful to try and control a crisis once it occurs need to be planned and initiated long before any crisis happens. These steps, nevertheless, are designed to affect the nature and path of a crisis as it develops. They could be examined under the heading of crisis management—which is beyond our current focus. What will be considered as crisis avoidance are possible steps intended to reduce the likelihood of a politico-military crisis between the superpowers ever happening. How do we protect against another Cuban missile crisis or a 1973 Arab-Israeli War with its rapid escalation? This approach to crisis stability tackles the problem by focusing on the prevention of such potentially risky episodes. We begin by examining actions that one party acting alone can perform.

Unilateral Actions

Reduce Vulnerability of Strategic Forces. This prescription follows from two lines of reasoning. First, vulnerable strategic forces might encourage counterforce preemption. Second, if both sides recognize a particular strategic system as vulnerable, then the party toward which it is directed must assume that it is intended for use either as part of a first strike or for retaliation in a hair-trigger launch under attack mode. Either condition could convert a confrontation into a major crisis.

At the present time the fixed-base ICBMs of the United States and the Soviet Union are becoming more vulnerable. Reducing each side's reliance on such systems by shifting to mobile ICBMs or submarine borne missiles is often recommended as a response (e.g., Allison et. al., 1985: 231). The problem of vulnerability will not be addressed, however, if the vulnerable ICBMs are not withdrawn once the alternative strategic forces become available. In the past, unilateral dismantling of older systems has been difficult to achieve, particularly for the Soviet Union. Furthermore, alternative systems have liabilities. In addition to the obvious cost requirements, the problem of verification of mobile systems has been widely recognized. Nevertheless, building new weapon systems is an approach to deterrence problems to which both sides are accustomed and generally favorably inclined.

Upgrade Strategic Command and Control. The growing recognition that command and control of strategic forces may be the most vulnerable

component of the deterrent force compels advocacy of steps to reduce
its exposure for the same reasons as those for silo-based ICBMs. A great
danger lies in attempted cures that heighten the crisis instability problem.
As we have noted earlier, the pre-crisis delegation of authority to use
nuclear weapons or the tendency to connect even more directly strategic
warning and nuclear response systems can greatly compound efforts at
crisis management.

Steps to build in more redundancy and to harden components of C^3I
represent better responses from a crisis stability perspective. Among
others, Blair (1985) has warned that there are real limits to the degree
that command and control systems can be made less vulnerable. It may
also be the case that command and control upgrades may appear less
attractive to strategic force managers, always faced with budget constraints, than acquiring and maintaining new weapons systems. The
pressure always exists for lower costs, quick fixes in the form of changes
in doctrine and strategy—the very approaches that further erode crisis
stability.

Making Political Leaders Better Informed About Crisis. Lebow (1987b)
makes a strong case that most recent presidents and their top advisers
have devoted minimal efforts to learning about plans for operating in
an extreme politico-military crisis—e.g., learning about evaluation plans,
nuclear options, control procedures, etc. Drills involving the president
have been exceedingly rare. Similarly, there has been little systematic
review of past crises—particularly the points at which major difficulties
in perception, information management, implementation, and communication arose. The neglected consideration of plans or past crises may
breed a false sense of security that someone else has made all the
necessary arrangements and if the contingency arises the president and
his advisors can slip quickly and effectively into the pre-established
crisis management mode.

Some briefings and rehearsal might improve the quality of the decision-
making process and choices made should a crisis arise. (Change in crisis
management planning could be developed in response to the president's
requirements and political judgments that might result from rehearsals.)
But this recommendation is introduced in the crisis avoidance category
because the heightened knowledge by the highest political officials of
the frailty of crisis management might add incentives for leaders to
avoid crises. Few political leaders would admit to a preference for
brinksmanship or management by crisis, but the reluctance of policy-
makers to become acquainted with the details regarding the probable
conditions and decisions that might be required of them can lead to
unwarranted confidence in the ability to handle readily such problems
when they arise. Of course, the biggest obstacle to such rehearsals and

planning is that they demand time of the president and his top associates. Such activities appear to have the quality of being deferrable to a later date. Moreover, because they require leaders to think about the unthinkable, it is likely an unpleasant experience that most would wish to avoid.

Introduction of Unilateral Confidence-building Measures. At least since the time of Osgood's (1962) proposals for GRIT (graduated reduction in tension), suggestions have been introduced for reducing East-West tensions—and for reducing the risk of crisis—by confidence-building measures. Such steps are designed to assure one's adversary of one's intention not to act in provocative or war-like ways. Often this entails making one's actions more predictable and visible (observable) to one's adversary or making the absence of actions predictable and observable. Confidence-building measures can take many different forms ranging from rhetorical gestures (e.g., nuclear no first use declarations, pledges of non-intervention in certain regions) to physical demonstrations (e.g., a moratorium on certain weapons tests, opening installations to inspection by opponent or neutral parties)[9].

Betts (1985: 68) captures one of the basic difficulties of unilateral confidence-building measures, when he observes: "In pre-crisis times the most certain way to prevent tension is to give in to the opponent, but this approach can be counter productive if the other side takes advantage of relaxed inhibitions to expand its influence." This danger— that an opponent will take advantage of a gesture—is one of three. Another is that the opponent will regard the step as meaningless or initiated solely for propaganda purposes. Such actions can also be viewed as designed to create false confidence and invalid assurance that should be responded to with increased vigilance and suspicion. Some of these difficulties can be reduced if the steps are mutual, which is an approach examined in the next section.

Bilateral Actions

Arms control agreements might be viewed as the primary vehicle for bilateral crisis avoidance initiatives. It is important to note, however, that when the primary objective of arms control is to increase deterrence stability, including crisis stability, then the emphasis shifts. Instead of viewing arms control primarily as a means of reducing or eliminating weapons, attention is directed to preventing the conditions that lead to war. As Nye (1984a: 404) observes: " . . . risk-reduction measures are more concerned with the prospects of use of such weapons regardless of numbers." Of course, prohibition of certain weapons or force reductions of certain kinds may be one means to achieving stability, but other means exist as well. Moreover, as has often been noted, reductions to very low levels of some major weapons, without highly confident means of verifying compliance, could actually reduce stability. When the agreed-upon level of a weapon is at or near zero, one side may conclude that the clandestine construction of a very small number that are suddenly revealed in a crisis could provide an enormous advantage. Thus, from the perspective of stability the emphasis in arms agreements must be to constrain the use of weapons under severe circumstances. Numerous stabilizing arms control proposals have been advanced, but a review of several will illustrate major approaches.

Prohibit Strategic Weapons Deployments Near Borders. In the so-called "keep-out zones" or "stand-off zones" approach, the parties agree not to deploy strategic weapons close to the border of their adversary. The purpose of such an agreement is to reduce the vulnerability of national capitals and major command and control centers to sudden knock-out strikes by weapons that offer virtually no time (i.e., less than 10 minutes flight time) for evacuation or other protective measures. Enhancing the survivability of political and military authorities means that a decapitation option would appear less likely to succeed and, therefore, that threat to deterrence would be reduced. Such a strategy also enhances the survivability of the bomber leg of deterrence forces by allowing those on alert time to clear the runway. Lebow (1987b) has suggested a keep-out zone of 2500 kilometers from a nation's capital, although a longer distance might be desirable. Such an agreement, at a minimum, would have to include land and sea-based ballistic missiles, but might also include a ban on the forward deployment of cruise missiles. (See Blair, 1985: 301) Close-in patrolling of nuclear submarines is particularly troubling. It is noteworthy that following the initial deployments of American Pershing II missiles (ballistic missiles with short flight time characteristics) in West Germany, the Soviet Union moved several of its nuclear-armed strategic submarines stationed in the Atlantic closer to the Eastern seaboard of the United States.[10]

As in many arms control agreements, verification of compliance poses a significant obstacle. Fixed-site, land-based missiles such as the Pershing II or the Soviet SS-20 (which threatens European capitals, but not Washington) pose the least problem for verification. Cruise-missiles, which are small and easily moved, are extremely difficult to detect and, thus, to verify. Submarines also pose a problem. Both sides might be reluctant to reveal the circumstances under which a reasonable degree of verification could be achieved with their submarines because such information would reveal valuable data about the status of anti-submarine warfare capabilities. A further problem is that even intercontinental ballistic missiles based over 5,000 miles away afford less than 30 minutes warning and that may not always be enough to insure evacuation of leaders. Nevertheless, in a crisis where some degree of strategic alert and preparation already has been initiated, a keep-out zone agreement might create enough uncertainty about the survival of the adversary's command authority that the temptation to adopt a decapitation strategy would be more easily resisted. This strategy could be further enhanced by the routine dispatch of a top leader from the capital (e.g., the American vice president at the beginning of any crisis). (See Allison et. al., 1985: 231)

Restrict Tests of ASAT Weapons and Submarine Ballistic Missiles in Depressed Trajectories. An alternative to the prohibition on the deployment of certain weapons in a given area is to prevent the maturation of certain technologies judged to threaten stability by agreeing to restrict the testing of such weapons (Drell and Ralston, 1985). Although posing quite different problems for crisis stability, submarine launched ballistic missiles (SLBMs) that do not follow a high-arching trajectory and anti-satellite weapons both illustrate curbs that could be imposed by bans on testing. In each case the technology currently has not been developed to the point where either side has a reliable and threatening system ready for deployment. A prohibition on further testing would likely exclude the emergence of the threat these systems could create.

The elimination of ASAT tests would protect existing satellites, which both sides use extensively for monitoring the other side's compliance with existing treaties and for C^3I. As noted earlier in this essay, the ability to destroy such satellites as a result of ASAT could pose grave problems for crisis stability. Depressed trajectory weapons would create a comparable difficulty to that of deploying weapons close to national command centers—they severely minimize warning time and threaten the ability to command and control a retaliatory strike. The flatter flight path of these weapons reduces the possibility of radar detection.

Agreeing to outlaw a promising technology by banning its testing has always been a problem for major military powers. The problem is particularly acute when one side or the other sees that it might achieve an advantage. In the case of a prohibition on ASAT, it would sharply limit the ability to develop a space-based defense such as the American Strategic Defense Initiative. Thus, there is the added problem of the spillover effects on other weapons programs. The advantage of test bans, however, is that verification can usually be devised with a high degree of confidence, although some related problems such as monitoring the use of high energy lasers or encryption (coding of information from permitted tests) can arise. An ASAT test ban would also leave in place some existing capability in the form of antiballistic missiles (Blair, 1985: 298–300).

Strengthen the ABM Treaty. A third arms control approach for enhancing stability is a total prohibition on certain classes of weapons. The 1972 Anti-Ballistic Missile (ABM) Treaty is a case in point. It uses prohibitions of weapons tests, but goes beyond that to ban operation of radars in certain modes and regulates their location as the major controversy over the Soviet radar at Krasnoyarsk illustrates. (The radar's location appears to be a clear violation of the ABM Treaty.)

Suppose one concludes that the technologies likely to be available well into the 21st century would not allow the United States, or any other country, to deploy a ballistic missile defense having a high probability of destroying almost all missiles in a large-scale attack. Going ahead with such a system would then likely be seen as part of a first-strike strategy. Having only limited defensive capability and itself open to disruption from attack, the ballistic missile defense system could seriously increase the pressure on the adversary to launch a preemptive strike in a crisis. Scenarios like this one reveal the danger for crisis stability.

To prevent such developments, it can be argued that a comprehensive ban on ABMs should be continued and the treaty instrument strengthened. Clearer definitions to prohibit exotic technologies and to sharpen the meaning of what constitutes laboratory testing would be required. Modes of testing radars must be further detailed and what is meant by the periphery of each country also needs tightening.

Such an upgrading of the ABM Treaty encounters opposition on several grounds. If one accepts the assumption that a ballistic missile defense can be designed to be highly effective against a large-scale first strike (or against a strike limited in size by agreements to reduce the size and kind of offensive systems), then its threat to stability may not be so severe. Opponents also argue that Soviet violations have occurred that make further emphasis on this kind of treaty prohibition unwise.

Establish Nuclear Risk Reduction Crisis Center. In 1982 Senators Sam Nunn, John Warner, and the late Henry Jackson amended the Defense Authorization Act to direct the Defense Department to evaluate several ideas for reducing the risk of nuclear crises. One of their proposals was for a joint nuclear risk reduction center. (See Interim Report of the Nunn-Warner Working Group, 1985.) The basic concept entails creation of a bilateral forum for diplomatic and military personnel of the super-powers at which potential or actual confrontation problems and procedures for dealing with them would be discussed. Groups and individuals have explored variations of this proposal (e.g., Betts, 1985b; Blechman, 1983; Landi et al., 1984; Ury and Smoke, 1984; Ury, 1985). Advocates have viewed the proposal both as a means of crisis prevention and as a tool for crisis management, although the avoidance functions will be emphasized here.

The center or centers (there might be one in each superpower capital linked by telecommunications) would involve representatives of both the Soviet Union and the United States. Their purpose would be to work on confidence-building activities in normal times and to clarify positions and avoid unintended provocations in times of increased tension. "In principle its work could involve exchanges of data, discussions of particular issues in force posture and doctrine, and consideration of problematic scenarios and possible joint actions" (Betts, 1985b: 68).

The approach to crisis stability taken in this proposal is bold—to improve crisis stability and avoid superpower crises. Not surprisingly, a proposal that calls for continuous dialogue between the major antagonists about the issues on which their competitive interests may be greatest raises numerous questions. One of the criticisms is that such a center might become a means for planting disinformation and engaging in deception. Another is that each side might be reluctant to commit the kind of high level officials to participation in the center necessary for meaningful exchange. If the center discussion occurred among lower level military officers and diplomats, their flexibility for innovation from official policy would be minimal and the likelihood of their ideas receiving attention within their own governments would be very limited. The center might also be viewed with alarms by allies and Third World countries as evidence of an emerging condominium between the superpowers at the expense of the rest of the world. Although none of these criticisms can be easily dismissed, it should be noted that the center proposal appears to be a logical extension of the Standing Consultative Commission (SCC) created by the 1972 ABM and SALT I Treaties. The SCC, designed to address issues associated with compliance with the treaties, has been generally regarded as a very useful bilateral, professional forum that has worked well. (See Caldwell, 1985; Buchheim and Caldwell, 1986.)

Agree on Code of Conduct for Crisis Prevention. If the concept of a joint crisis center stresses the creation of a structure to assist in the avoidance of crises, then the proposal for a code of conduct or set of rules and norms emphasizes processes for avoiding crises. At the Soviet-American summit meetings in 1972 and 1973, which subsequently appear to have been the high water mark of detente in that era, formal rules for crisis avoidance were adopted. In Moscow in May, 1972, Nixon and Brezhnev signed the Basic Principles Agreement and the following year in Washington they negotiated the Agreement on Prevention of Nuclear War. These bilateral agreements constitute an effort to establish general principles to which both sides pledge to adhere in order to prevent their competition from triggering major crises. These particular documents contain only broad generalities and were accompanied by no mechanisms to encourage compliance or for consideration of how they might be applied in particular situations. George (1983, 1984a), who has led the exploration of this approach in the United States, judges such broad principles of agreement to be extremely unlikely to be effective. Instead he proposes three different kinds of declarations for crisis prevention— norms, rules of engagement, and *ad hoc* ground rules (George, 1983).

Norms are tacit understandings that emerge from experience or lessons drawn from experience. These are practices that both sides may follow without formal agreement. Rules of engagement are explicitly negotiated between the two sides and establish specific actions that would and would not be permitted in a given area or under given conditions. Finally, *ad hoc* rules for escalation control can be devised when the two other arrangements are absent and the superpowers find themselves in a particular situation with clear potential for escalating conflict. These are limitations devised for controlling a specific encounter. All three approaches emphasize agreement on operational features linked closely to well-specified conditions.

The fundamental difficulty is that the mix of common interests and competing interests between the superpowers seems to be perceived on both sides as favoring competition in most circumstances. The desire to gain or maintain a unilateral advantage over an adversary is incredibly powerful. To reach and abide by an agreement that constrains those opportunities in exchange for the possibility of avoiding a crisis that has not yet occurred (and may not happen soon) requires actions that meet strong political and military resistance. Nye (1984a) notes that specific qualities of the superpowers—the secretive nature of the Soviet society and the relatively frequent shifts and inconsistencies in American policy—compound the problem of perceiving and sustaining reciprocity of compliance with crisis avoidance procedures. Thus, each sides tends to believe that what it must forego in way of unilateral advantage is not equal to what the other may yield if it complies at all.

Multilateral Actions

We will not emphasize multilateral arrangements for crisis avoidance, but wish to acknowledge the desirability of further exploration of this approach. It is noteworthy that U.S.-Soviet crises frequently have involved third parties including their allies and Third World countries who often become the subject of the crises. In fact, without their competition in these areas, the Soviet-American rivalry would have created many fewer occasions for crisis. Clearly the need to coordinate with allies or take into account the parties in any region in which a superpower crisis arises, recommends consideration of multilateral approaches. Furthermore, the conflict management literature traditionally has assigned a major role to third parties as brokers, mediators, and arbitrators. Some variations of the Nunn-Warner proposal for a crisis avoidance center envisioned it as having multilateral participation. (See Ury, 1985.) Landi and associates (1984) have proposed that the Soviet Union and the United States establish a series of bilateral direct communication links that could be combined into various multilateral networks as a particular potential crisis situation warranted.

One intriguing multilateral idea proposes the establishment of an international monitoring agency to provide surveillance of the strategic weapons of the Soviet Union and the United States. Proposed by Lebow (1985a), the multilateral monitoring agency would provide independent verification of the status of each side's strategic forces using state of the art satellites and other technology. The purpose would be to provide a check on each side's own early warning system to reduce the likelihood that system failures could lead to launching an attack by mistake. It might also make either side's efforts to prepare for a preemptive attack more difficult to conduct without detection and worldwide reporting. Knowledge of such additional monitoring and verification would serve as a further deterrent. The computers, satellites, and associated technology necessary to perform the job with sufficient reliability to be credible would be expensive and would likely require the active assistance of the antagonists themselves. The superpowers could be expected to be reluctant to openly share state of the art technology for surveillance. Yet they might feel pressured to participate by other nations or other advanced technological societies might be able to supply the necessary capability.

Conclusions

For approximately the last one and a half decades both the United States and the Soviet Union have initiated a variety of actions with respect to their strategic nuclear forces that have reduced crisis stability. As noted, these changes have incuded:

- Deployment of certain weapons systems with destabilizing characteristics;
- Command and control configurations whose vulnerability produces instability;

- Established practices of force generation in response to strategic alerts (admittedly dormant during recent times), that if used in the future could be destabilizing;
- Changes in doctrine and strategy—both proposed and adopted— that could be destabilizing in a crisis.

Not all changes have decreased crisis stability. Although there have been some actions that have contributed to improved crisis stability, the judgment must be that on balance the net effect of all changes in the configuration of strategic forces has been to reduce crisis stability. This conclusion does not mean that any major crisis in the future between the United States and the Soviet Union must inevitably result in a breakdown of deterrence and the initiation of war. The point is that both sides have made it more difficult to end an acute crisis without war. In sum, the nuclear war risk is greater.

The changes that have increased the risk of war in crisis do not appear to result from callousness or indifference to crisis stability. Rather the effects seem to be the inadvertent consequences of pursuing other objectives to strengthen deterrence and conserve resources.

Dangers to crisis stability have sparked numerous prescriptions for corrective action. Table 6.1 summarizes the options reviewed in this essay. An examination of this sample of proposals for enhancing crisis stability leads to several observations.

1. The approaches are diverse. Some assume a direct approach and seek to alter the immediate source of the problem. Thus, for example, the proposed ban on ASAT tests or the initiative to improve C^3I deal with the specific developments that have generated stability problems. Other proposals tackle the problem indirectly by advancing offsetting measures to deal with possible effects. The proposal for submarine stand-off zones illustrates an indirect approach to dealing with strategic plans of decapitation or preemption in general. Still other proposals seek to eliminate the problem by minimizing the occurrence of situations that could alter normal stability. In other words, if we could avoid acute superpower crises entirely, we would not have to worry about their effects on deterrence stability.

2. The emphasis seems to be on crisis avoidance. Whether the proposals take a direct or indirect approach, there appear to be a greater range of recommendations for initiatives in the category of crisis avoidance than for crisis management. No systematic review of the literature has been undertaken to confirm this conclusion, but certainly the range of approaches would appear to be greater in principal for averting such situations as opposed to getting out once they have occurred. It would be a mistake, however, to infer that exploration of the topic of crisis

TABLE 6.1   SUMMARY OF PROPOSALS FOR ENHANCING CRISIS STABILITY

Proposal	Purpose	Possible Liabilities
MULTILATERAL ACTIONS		
1. Create an International Strategic Missile Monitoring Agency	a. Guard against breakdown of either side's independent strategic warning system that might lead to accidental war and to further discourage any attempts by either side to engage in covert war preparations.	Technology might require participation of U.S. and USSR who could be expected to resist sharing such technology; costs of reliable system would be high.
BILATERAL ACTIONS		
1. Prohibit Strategic Weapon Deployments Near Borders	a. Prevent decapitation strike against political and military leaders	Verification difficulties with some weapons (e.g., cruise missile).
	b. Enhance survivability of second-strike forces (e.g., enable bombers to be flushed)	Could expose state of ASW capabilities. Limits to how much time for evaluation can be achieved even with keep-out zones.
2. Restrict Tests of Submarine Ballistic Missiles in Depressed Trajectories and ASAT Tests	a. Prevent decapitation strike	Constrains other programs such as SDI.
	b. Maintain survivability of C^3I and related satellites	Banning technology at test stage has been difficult.
3. Strengthen the ABM Treaty	a. Discourage preemption by prevention of the development of a ballistic missile defense which would be perceived as being used in conjunction with a first strike	SDI not provocative if it can be made to work against large scale attack. Soviet violations of ABM Treaty challenges utility of that approach.
4. Establish Nuclear Risk Reduction Crisis Center	a. Avoid crises by continuous discussion and information exchange between Soviet and American diplomats and military officers	Could foster deception; staffing by officials with sufficient seniority to be flexible would be difficult; might generate alarm among allies and Third World.

(TABLE 6.1)

Proposal	Purpose	Possible Liabilities
BILATERAL ACTIONS (cont.)		
5. Agree on Code of Conduct for Crisis Prevention	a. Avoid crises by negotiating agreement to adhere to certain codes of conduct to limit superpower competition	Requires each to forego unilateral advantage which may not appear to be reciprocated equally; secret nature of Soviet society and inconsistency of U.S. policy heighten in each other's suspicion.
UNILATERAL ACTIONS		
1. Reduce Vulnerability of Strategic Forces	a. Reduce perception of weapons' mission as being for first strike	Older systems are not always destroyed, so purpose is defeated. New weapons accelerate arms race and overall costs; mobile ICBMs are difficult to verify.
2. Upgrade Strategic Command and Control	a. Curb adversary's incentive for a decapitation strike in particular and preemption in general b. Reduce the necessity for immediate use of retaliatory strategic forces (increase decision time)	Given the nature of C^3I, there are significant limits to which some components can be protected at reasonable costs. Military may resist heavy expenditures that come at the expense of maintaining existing weapons or aquiring new ones.
3. Have Political Leaders Better Informed About Crises	a. Increase incentive to avoid crisis by more realistic understanding of difficulties in maintaining control b. Improve crisis management	Training time of president and top advisors difficult to schedule; subject is unattractive and appears less pressing than other business.
4. Introduce Unilateral Confidence-Building Measures	a. Provide adversary with assurances that one does not intend to act in provocative way — particularly to minimize unintended provocations or uncertainties	Opponent may take advantage of assurances, or may regard them as meaningless or deliberately designed to be misleading.

management to enhance crisis stability should not be vigorously explored. Certainly, the crisis management proposals make clear that preparations for their use, e.g., upgrading the hot line, must be in place before the crisis.

3. All the proposals involve tradeoffs. No effort has been made to enumerate every objection that could be raised to each proposal for enhancing crisis stability. It has been possible, however, to illustrate that each approach poses difficulties. Some directly affect other deterrence criteria, such as uncertainty. Others have substantial financial and/or political costs.

Where does this leave us? Three major questions appear to be central for the future examination of crisis stability.

1. What priority should be given to improving crisis stability relative to other requirements for effective deterrence? This question requires us to weigh the evidence as to how serious we regard the threat to stability as well as to articulate the other requirements for avoiding nuclear war.

2. What are the criteria by which proposals for enhancing crisis stability should be appraised? We need to engage in a serious assessment exercise in which major proposals are evaluated in a comparative perspective rather than in isolation.

3. Have the risks associated with major superpower crises become so great that, like major war itself, they are no longer acceptable instruments for the pursuit of national policy? It is unlikely that leaders would admit to pursuing a national policy through crisis confrontations. Nevertheless, they have not adopted the same kind of shared norms concerning the unacceptability of acute crises that now appear to apply to the use of nuclear forces. If acute crises are now too risky to contemplate, how can that conclusion be reached in a timely fashion by the leadership in both the United States and the Soviet Union?

Notes

1. An earlier version of this paper was presented at the XIIIth World Congress of the International Political Science Association under the title: "The Ultimate Crisis in the Nuclear Era."

2. Other classifications have been proposed. For example, Allison, Carnesale, and Nye (1985: 10) suggest the following general paths to war: accidental or unauthorized use, surprise attack, preemption in crisis, escalation of conventional war, and catalytic war. Although important insights can be gained by considering such distinctions, the last three categories can be regarded as further differentiation of what has been referred to here as war resulting from crises.

3. For evidence in the movement toward consensus on a definition of crisis, at least from a decision-making perspective, compare Hermann (1972), Young (1977), and Brecher (1978). The definition of crisis used here is a variation on Brecher's modification of my own earlier efforts. I accept his introduction of the expectation of military hostilities as particularly appropriate for delimiting the class of problems to be examined in this essay.

4. For further discussion of crisis stability, see Mearsheimer (1986: 7), Snyder (1961: 104–110), and Schelling (1966: 221–259).

5. This section is a condensed version of a chapter entitled, "Trends Toward Crisis Instability: Increasing Danger of Nuclear War," prepared by the author for a forthcoming book edited by Stephen Cimbala, *Challenges to Deterrence in the 1990s* to be published by Praeger.

6. This analysis applies to space-based or space-supported ballistic missile defenses designed to attack the boost phase of enemy missile launchers. Ground-based, point-defense might enhance crisis stability with respect to increasingly vulnerable silo-based ICBMs. Without such defense ICBMs may be recognized by both sides as increasingly valuable only if they are launched before they are attacked. If they can be restored as second-strike, retaliatory weapons by ballistic missile defense, it would reduce the possible "use them or lose them" pressure on policy-makers in a crisis.

7. In his book, Lebow (1987) envisions three broad ways in which a superpower crisis could result in war—preemption, miscalculated escalation, and loss of control. In his view increased strategic alerts above normal levels represent a primary means by which the sides could lose control.

8. Several readers of an earlier version of this paper correctly noted that there has been no trend toward increased use of strategic alerts, but on the contrary they have occurred less frequently—none since 1973 despite incidents such as the invasion of Afghanistan or the Soviet shooting down of the Korean airliner. Perhaps there is increased sensitivity in the policy community to the implications of strategic alerts. The assumption of this essay remains, however, that a higher level of strategic alert in the late 1980s would be far more serious than in 1973 because of the changing nature of the force systems of the two sides and the greater likelihood that the expanded Soviet capability would mean that they would respond with a higher alert level of their own.

9. A considerable literature exists on confidence building measures (CBMs). (For an introduction see Holst, 1983). Most of the analysis to date, however, has focused on theater operations (particularly between NATO and WTO) rather than on strategic forces. An exception is Vick and Thomson (1985) who discuss the use of CBMs in each of the three legs of the triad (ICBMs, bombers, submarines) to reduce the crisis of strategic nuclear war. Many CBMs assume mutual adoption by both sides rather than unilateral steps. In his initial work, Osgood (1962) assumed that each step would be unilateral but there would be expectations of a responsive step by the other side—sooner or later. The unilateral first step would remain in place until there was a response. When a responsive step occurred, then the initiator would take an additional step. Thus, he envisioned sequential unilateral measures.

10. Both the Soviet Union and the United States keep submarines carrying ballistic missiles on patrol off the coasts of the other country. Apparently the Soviet Union has not kept its three ballistic missile submarines that normally patrol in the mid-Atlantic at the closer range demonstrated in January and February 1984 (after the beginning of American deployment of Pershing II missiles in Europe). Instead they have moved back to the "box area" roughly 1,000 to 2,000 miles off the U.S. eastern coast. This may be to reduce detection of their exact location by the U.S. Navy. (See the *New York Times*, October 6, 1986: 6.)

7

Approaches to Nuclear Risk Reduction

Joseph S. Nye, Jr., and William L. Ury

So long as nuclear weapons exist, there will always be some chance of their use. It is impossible to think clearly about avoiding nuclear war without thinking in terms of probability and risk. Even efforts to abolish nuclear weapons could raise the risks of nuclear use under some political conditions. Most people do not believe that any objective would justify the loss of half a billion lives or the end of life itself. But many would be willing to raise the likelihood of major nuclear war from one chance in ten thousand to one chance in a thousand if that were necessary to preserve their way of life, or to avoid a conventional World War III. Some risks are unavoidable if we want to lead certain types of lives. At the personal level, we accept that fact whenever we enter an automobile. But we should try to reduce unnecessary risks as much as possible.

The Likelihood of Nuclear War

How likely is a major nuclear war between the United States and the Soviet Union before the end of the century?

_____ Almost certain
_____ Approximately even
_____ 1 in 10
_____ 1 in 100
_____ 1 in 1,000
_____ 1 in 10,000
_____ Almost no chance

Over the past two years, we have put this question to dozens of groups. In most groups of fifty or more, at least one respondent selected each answer—from "almost certain" to "almost no chance."

Specialists in national security are much more optimistic in their responses than the general public. A majority of the general public says it believes nuclear war is likely before the end of the century. Specialists' answers cluster between 1 in 100 and 1 in 10,000.

Not much is proven by this finding. The beginning of wisdom is the recognition that in this realm there are specialists but not experts. Fortunately, since Hiroshima and Nagasaki, we have had no experience with nuclear wars.

This does not mean, however, that one person's estimate is as good as another's. Some are based on more careful and sustained appraisal than others. Choices must be made among actions to reduce risks of war, and such choices necessarily reflect estimates of risks. Two decades ago, the British scientist and novelist C.P. Snow predicted nuclear war within a decade as a "mathematical certainty." Some of his defenders say that if he is right within a century, his prediction will have been justified (Powers, 1982b: 17). But the difference between a century and a decade may make all the difference in the world when it comes to shaping policies to avoid nuclear war.

Is the current situation more or less risky than the previous period of heightened public concern, 1958–62, when Snow made his prediction? Are things worse or are we just more worried? Some observers argue that the chance of nuclear war is lower today than in 1962. They point to technical improvements such as permissive action links, improved command, control, and communication, national technical means of verification, and political factors such as U.S. and Soviet experience in managing crises. They also note that current Soviet leaders seem more cautious than Khrushchev was, though that could change on either side in the future. Others believe that risks are higher now, pointing to the loss of American nuclear superiority; the greater Soviet capability to support forces in Third World areas; the deployment of vulnerable weapons and support systems that place a premium on preemption; doctrinal stress on protracted war-fighting; and the deterioration of U.S.-Soviet political relations.

A recent analysis by the Avoiding Nuclear War Project of Harvard's Kennedy School provides support for both positions. One is struck, however, by how difficult the authors found it to paint plausible scenarios for reaching a major nuclear war along various paths. If these authors are correct, it is not easy to start a major nuclear war. Paul Bracken concludes that the risks of purely accidental nuclear war are much lower today than two decades ago. But he also warns that the continuing development of complex and tightly coupled strategic systems in the United States and the Soviet Union reduces the time in which diplomacy can work and increases the potential effects of accidents and misperceptions when both systems are on alert during a crisis (Bracken, 1985: 25–53). Stephen Meyer points out that, despite our concern, the probability of surprise of preemptive attack was actually close to zero in the 1950s and 1960s because the Soviets did not have the capability Americans attributed to them (Meyer, 1985: 167–205). Today they have that capability, and the dangers of preemptive attack will depend on the conditions that Betts describes in his study of surprise and pre-emptive attack (Betts, 1985a: 54–79). Harry Rowen argues that concern about catalytic nuclear war is justifiably lower today than twenty years ago, but those risks may rise in the future if we follow imprudent proliferation policies (Rowen, 1985: 148–163).

In sum, risks of nuclear war along the different paths change over time. When we allow for combinations of the paths, we see that risks are higher than for any one path alone. In our own assessment of overall risk, we are closer to the specialists than to the general public. But whether the odds are 1 in 100 or 1 in 1,000, they are still too high. Given the consequences of a major nuclear war, a chance of 1 in 1,000 must motivate urgent action.

Three Ideal Types: Hawks, Doves, and Owls

Thinking about the risks of nuclear war quickly leads to the question: What is to be done? The current policy debate clusters answers to this question under two dominant caricatures: the Hawk and Dove.[1] While neither exactly captures the thought of any individual, these simplifications do highlight central predispositions. They provide starting points for answers to questions about causes of war in general, the likely cause of nuclear war in particular, and the preferred posture for preventing a major nuclear war.

Hawks see the proximate cause of war as one-sided weakness— weakness that tempts an aggressive adversary to exploit advantage. The classic example is Munich. This symbol of unsuccessful appeasement conveys two lessons: (1) Britain and France's unwillingness to resist encouraged Hitler's demands; and (2) early resistance to a more ambiguous threat, during the remilitarization of the Rhineland or even over Czechoslovakia, might well have led to Hitler's ouster at the hands of his generals and might thus have prevented a world war. To avoid war, and nuclear war in particular, hawks believe we must make our commitments and interests absolutely clear, and establish a posture of superior military strength (or the closest approximation domestic politics will support). By making it clear that we cannot be beaten at any level of violence (an escalation ladder), we insure that they will never calculate that war could serve any rational goal. When crises arise, Hawks counsel resolve and steps to make our deterrent threat credible. The motto is "peace through strength."

The Dove shares the Hawk's belief in rational calculus, but worries about a different danger. For Doves, the primary cause of war lies in the "mad momentum of the arms race" that becomes provocative and thus undermines deterrence. Doves worry about arms in themselves and the irrestible momentum of military preparations both because the psychology of arms races prevents conciliation and because threats that are intended to deter may instead provoke. To avoid war, Doves prescribe a policy of communication, conciliation, and accommodations. In crisis, Doves counsel caution and compromise.

Doves worry that increasing military strength and threat may not strengthen deterrence, but cause it to break down under some circumstances. At some point, greater military strength is transformed from a deterrent threat into a provocative threat. The leaders of the threatened country may feel themselves backed into a corner, their very existence threatened. Rational leaders may then decide to go to war despite horrible consequences if that seems the least bad alternative. They may decide to gamble on a preventive war and surprise attack now rather than suffer sure defeat later. The appropriate policy in such circumstances is conciliation and reassurance of the adversary, rather than increasing military strength.

Hawk and Dove share a common set of assumptions about the logic of the process by which war might come. Both see war as starting deliberately. Both assume that national leaders with accurate information carefully calculate risks, costs, and benefits, and control the actions of their governments. In essence, the Hawk and the Dove disagree about the right point for an effective deterrent policy along the spectrum that stretches between threat and conciliation. They roost on the same rational branch, and argue about the best place to sit on it.

Some people—we call them Owls—are preoccupied by a very different set of concerns. Owls worry primarily about loss of control. They place more weight on nonrational factors in history. In the Owl's view, a major war would not arise from careful calculations but from organizational routines, malfunctions of machines or of minds, misperceptions, misunderstandings, and mistakes. While Hawks and Doves focus on deterrence of deliberate choices and often cite World War II, Owls are more impressed by World War I, the assassination at Sarajevo, the leader's misperception of the military situation and the inadvertent escalation caused by interlocking mobilization plans.

Owls believe that crises or conventional war could create the circumstances in which an unintended nuclear war might occur. Under those conditions, one danger is misperception of the real situation, such as a false belief that war is inevitable or a false warning that the other side is about to strike. A second danger is mental deterioration of leaders under stress. The extreme case would be a leader (or key subordinate) driven to madness. A more likely situation would be constrained rationality under stress as tired or anxious leaders feel they have no options, become rash or fatalistic, and are bolstered in their views by other members of their inner group. A third danger originates in the difficulty of controlling large complex organizations in time of crisis. During the Cuban missile crisis President Kennedy found he was unaware of the timing of surveillance flights near the Soviet Union; and in the enforcement of the blockade, the Navy followed its standard operating procedures in a manner that was impossible for him to control in detail. A fourth danger emerges when multiple events arise simultaneously. Systems that have been designed with enough slack for one crisis will find themselves stretched taut when crises overlap. Leaders' attention is torn in different directions and stress multiplies. Finally, there is the danger of accident. While Hawks argue that pure accidents are unlikely to lead directly to nuclear war, Owls point out that accidents that happen in the midst of a crisis (or a conventional war) occur when the safety catches have deliberately been released. As Bracken shows, it is when accidents coincide with other factors that they might lead to nuclear war.

The Owl is not an intermediate species between the Hawk and the Dove. Their emphasis on nonrational factors means Owls rely on a different logic of how war begins—they roost on a separate branch.

In summary, Hawks worry that deterrence may fail if a potential aggressor calculates an opponent's weakness and has an opportunity to take advantage of it. Their policy remedy is to enhance the threat of retaliation by building military strength. Doves worry that deterrence may fail by slipping into provocation. Since additional threats may create a sense of inevitable war, the best remedy is conciliation and reassurance. Owls worry about deterrence because of the nonrational factors that degrade rationality as stress mounts and time is compressed during a crisis. They think the appropriate policy is to avoid crises and increase controls. Table 7.1 summarizes the three perspectives.

Three Potential Errors

Which of these approaches is right? All three are! Each captures an important insight about the potential initiation of nuclear war, and each rests on evidence from the world wars of our century. Yet all three also contain serious potential flaws. Hawks generally accuse Doves of spurious appeasement; Doves are quick to point out the Hawk's flaw of provocation

Table 7.1   THREE CARICATURES: HAWKS, DOVES, AND OWLS[2]

Caricature	Primary Cause of War	Dominant Metaphor	Recommended Policy	Potential Error
Hawk	Weakness	Munich	Strength/ Superiority	Provocation
Dove	Provocation	Pearl Harbor	Conciliation	Ineffectual appeasement
Owl	Loss of control	World War I	Strengthen controls	Paralysis

Source: Hawks, Doves, and Owls: An Agenda for Avoiding Nuclear War, edited by Graham Allison, Albert Carnesale, and Joseph S. Nye, Jr. (New York: Norton, 1985).

and inadequate reassurance. In recent policy debates, these arguments have been buttressed by references to the two world wars, that "richest source of parables to help us see where we are going" (Dyson, 1984: 15). But valuable as parables are, history has often been distorted in recent policy debates.

Doves often cite the arms race that preceded World War I as a causal factor, but the evidence is ambiguous (Kennedy, 1983: 163–177). The Anglo-German arms race was largely over by 1912. While it had sowed suspicion in both countries earlier in the century, relations between Britain and Germany were actually improving before 1914. A more serious issue was German concern over Russian military and railway improvements, which led some Germans to favor a preventive war in 1914 to avoid a less favorable situation in 1916. But this could have been countered by a switch from an offensive to a defensive strategy (Van Evera, 1984).

A stronger example for the Doves' position comes from Japan's experience in World War II. It is also useful in correcting the Hawk's Europe-centered views of World War II that have characterized recent policy debates. Contrary to popular American mythology, Japan did not attack Pearl Harbor because the United States looked weak or because Japan expected to defeat the United States in the war. On the contrary, Japanese leaders were pessimistic about their ability to defeat the United States. But they were even more pessimistic about their ability to survive if they did not go to war. The United States attempted to deter Japan from further expansion in Asia through policy statements and an oil embargo, but these measures instead convinced the Japanese leaders that their economy and war-making capacity would be strangled within a year in any case. A war now with a high risk of loss was better than certain defeat later. In the minds of Japan's military and expansionist

leaders, the American threat had turned from a deterrent into a provocation, and that led to preventive war and surprise attack.[3]

Doves fear a situation in which the Soviet Union is backed into such
a corner, and the Marxist historical optimism of the Soviet leaders turns
to a pessimistic view of historical decline: "A bear cornered is even
more dangerous than a bear on the prowl." If the Soviet empire in
Eastern Europe begins to crumble, and difficulties mount at home, a
dramatic new turn in the arms race could tip the American threat from
deterrence to provocation in Soviet eyes. Suppose, for example, that the
United States seemed on the verge of a breakthrough in strategic defense
technology that would disarm the Soviets and allow the Americans to
coerce them. The Soviets might then take great risks of starting a nuclear
war in a crisis, believing that the situation would become intolerable
in a few years in any case. The appropriate policy in such circumstances
would be conciliation and a bilateral or unilateral dampening of the
arms race in strategic defenses.

If provocation is the potential fatal flaw in the Hawk's mentality,
spurious appeasement is the equivalent flaw in the Dovish prescriptions.
A clever adversary can deceive the Dove, as Hitler did Neville Chamberlain in 1938. And if defenses have not been adequately strengthened,
as British and French defenses were not in the 1930s, last-minute efforts
to switch to deterrence, as the British and French tried over Poland in
1939, will lack credibility.

Owls are not always wise; they too make mistakes. Their dominant
concern is with the unintended triggering of war in a crisis, and their
preferred solution is better safety catches to prevent the hair trigger
from ever going off. Their potential policy failure is paralysis and the
sticky or frozen safety catch. If controls are so cumbersome that an
opponent concludes that nuclear weapons could never be used, the
weapons lose their deterrent effect. An aggressor might be tempted to
undertake a rash action such as nuclear decapitation of the enemy's
leadership on the belief that the remaining weapons cannot be unlocked.
If the Owl's safety catches appear to be very sticky or frozen, we are
thrown back into the Hawk's world.

Balanced Deterrence

Actual situations are unlikely to conform exactly to the paradigm of
the Hawk, the Dove, or the Owl. Pure types rarely exist in the real
world. Whatever their value as a source of parables, neither of the two
world wars of this century was a pure case. World War I was not purely
accidental. Confronted by Slavic nationalism, Austria deliberately chose
war rather than face its probable disintegration as an empire. But it

wanted a small war, not a world war. And when the Kaiser backed Austria, he expected the Russians to back down as they had in a similar crisis over Bosnia five years earlier. What was supposed to be a diplomatic crisis or small war became a world war through a combination of miscalculation and inadvertence. Actions to strengthen deterrence, such as threats of mobilization during the crisis, merely made matters worse. Similarly, while Hawks see World War II as an instance of planned aggression, the scale of the war went far beyond Hitler's plans. But the efforts to appease Hitler in the 1930s and the failure to establish a credible deterrent certainly played a significant role in the onset of the war. And as we have seen, American efforts to deter Japan instead provoked preventive war and surprise attack.

In an actual crisis situation, the interaction of rational and irrational factors will make all three approaches relevant. What starts out as rational is likely to become less so over time. And accidents that would not matter much in normal times or early in a crisis may create "crazy" situations in which choice is so constrained that "rational" decisions about the least bad alternatives lead to outcomes that would appear insane under normal circumstances. As Thomas Schelling has written, "It is not accidents themselves . . . that could cause a war, but their effect on decisions. . . . If we think of the decisions as well as the actions we can see that accidental war, like premeditated war, is subject to deterrence" (1966: 227–229). A major nuclear war is less likely to start purely by accident or purely by calculation than by an unfolding combination of the two in a crisis.

In terms of policy for avoiding nuclear war, Hawks, Doves and Owls each have part of the truth, but not the whole. Each camp's prescriptions, taken to an extreme, could lead to fatal errors. What we seek is *balanced deterrence*, not simply deterrence by increased threats or by greater conciliation, or by shifting the burden of uncertainty about loss of control. As Figure 7.1 suggests schematically, the crucial policy task is one of balance and synthesis—avoiding the three polar errors.

An Illustration of the Owls' Approach:
Crisis Control

While each perspective has merit in certain circumstances, too little attention has been devoted to the Owls' approach in recent debates over security in the nuclear age. Much more could be done about preventing and managing crises in a manner that would reduce nuclear risks. In the balance of this chapter, we seek to illustrate the Owls' agenda by discussing the approach of crisis control.

Figure 7.1   Balanced Deterrence Avoids Polar Errors

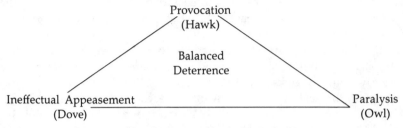

Source: *Hawks, Doves, and Owls: An Agenda for Avoiding Nuclear War,* edited by
Graham Allison, Albert Carnesale, and Joseph S. Nye, Jr. (New York: Norton,
1985).

Various kinds of policies can affect the risks of nuclear crises. First,
force structure and force deployments can contribute to make crises
either more or less risky. Configuring both sides' arms to maximize
"crisis stability" is one of the classical objectives of arms control. Second,
military doctrine and grand strategy can affect crisis risk for similar
reasons. An obvious example is doctrine for the initial use of nuclear
weapons. Third, aspects of overall foreign policy also contribute to
making crises more or less likely and more or less dangerous. Obviously,
greater aggressiveness will make crises more probable and more dangerous. But the superpowers' general perceptions of each other are also
important—for example, whether each perceives the other as interested
in forestalling and/or quickly resolving severe confrontations, or as more
likely to try to exploit them. Finally, a nuclear crisis can become more
or less probable and dangerous as a result of the design of decision-
making processes. The adequacy of communications, negotiations, internal decision-making processes, and prior consultations with the other
side may make a considerable difference should a crisis occur.

It is on this last area of "crisis management" or "crisis control" that
we would like to focus. The challenge of nuclear crisis control is to
shape U.S.-Soviet decision-making during and immediately preceding
crises so as to reduce the risk of nuclear war while at the same time
preserving other vital national interests.

Steps Taken Toward Crisis Control

Recognition of the dangers of runaway escalation and of the difficulties
of decision-making in crises have already led Washington and Moscow
to undertake some measures to help control crises. The most well-known
is the Hotline, formally termed the Direct Communications Link, which
was created in 1963 in the wake of the Cuban missile crisis. During
that crisis, the two sides were compelled to improvise awkward and

roundabout ways for President Kennedy and Premier Khrushchev to communicate, such as passing notes through a news reporter. The Hotline was created to allow direct, prompt and confidential communication at the head of state level.

Since then, additional steps have been taken; a chronology follows:

- 1971. The Hotline was made more reliable. Two satellite links were added; the sea and land link was kept as a back-up.
- 1971. The United States and the USSR signed the so-called Accidents Agreement. The terms of the Agreement commit each side to notifying the other at once in the event of an accidental unauthorized occurrence that could lead to a threatening detonation; to give notice of any missile test firings in the direction of the other's homeland; "to act in such a way as to reduce the possibility" of actions being misinterpreted should a nuclear incident occur; and to maintain and improve internal arrangements intended to prevent unauthorized or accidental nuclear war.
- 1972. The Incidents at Sea Agreement created navigation rules for naval vessels and procedures for coping with accidental collisions and near-misses.
- 1972. The Basic Principles Agreement attempted to create a mutual understanding about the ground rules for Soviet-American involvement in the Third World.
- 1973. The Prevention of Nuclear War Agreement was signed. This agreement required consultation between Washington and Moscow in any situation carrying a higher than normal risk of nuclear war.
- 1975. The Helsinki Final Act was signed as part of the CSCE process. "Basket One" of the Act includes two confidence building measures: a requirement of prior notification of major military maneuvers in Europe and provisions for the exchange of observers at these maneuvers.
- 1984. The Hotline was improved again, gaining the capability to transmit whole pages of text, photographs, and graphics.
- 1985. A Common Understanding was reached at the Standing Consultative Commission in Geneva to consult via the Hotline in cases of a nuclear incident instigated by a third party, or an unknown or unauthorized group of individuals who have obtained a nuclear weapon (Arms Control and Disarmament Agency, 1980: 112).

Growth in American Interest

The first half of the 1980s witnessed a considerable growth in interest in ways to go beyond these existing agreements. In part this interest was inspired by a realization among some U.S. senators and experts of the potentially increasing dangers of a nuclear crisis. In part it may have been a response to the intense and widespread popular concern at the time with preventing nuclear war, and to the dissatisfaction felt by many with traditional arms control.

In 1981 Senator Sam Nunn asked the Strategic Air Command (SAC) to study how the U.S. could identify accurately a nuclear attack from a third party that was disguised as Soviet in origin, and some related questions. SAC reported that dramatic improvements in nuclear crisis control were needed on the part of both the United States and Soviet Union (Congressional Record, 1982: S3963).

In 1982 Senators Nunn and Jackson, later joined by Senator Warner, proposed that the U.S. and USSR jointly create a "military crisis control center" (Congressional Record, 1982: S3963). Such a center, perhaps located in a neutral country, would be staffed by personnel from both nations and would monitor the nuclear weapons of third parties and terrorist groups.

In September of that year, the Senate, at the initiative of Senators Jackson and Nunn, added an amendment to the FY83 DOD Authorization Act, directing the Defense Department (DOD) to conduct a study of initiatives for improving controls on the use of nuclear weapons, especially during crises.

Secretary of Defense Weinberger responded with a DOD Report on 11 April, 1983. The report made several positive proposals: to the Hotline should be added a high-speed facsimile capability but not voice or video. (This was the proposal subsequently accepted by the Soviets and implemented). A high-speed data link should be added from each national capital to the embassy in the opposite capital. And a Joint Military Communications Link would connect the two national military command centers with a high-speed facsimile transmission capability. This link, said the report, could be used for crisis communications not requiring the attention of the head of state, for transmitting urgent technical and military information in a crisis, for communicating in a terrorist incident, and for some non-crisis functions. In the spring of 1984, Senators Nunn, Warner and Bradley introduced a Senate Resolution commending the Administration for the steps it had taken, and urging that negotiations be opened toward making "risk reduction centers" the next step. On June 15, Sen. Res. 329 passed 82-0.

Three months later, in a speech at the United Nations, President Reagan proposed institutionalizing regular cabinet-level meetings as well as "periodic consultations at policy level about regional problems . . . to help avoid miscalculation [and] reduce the potential risk of U.S.-Soviet confrontation" (*New York Times*, Sept. 25, 1984: A10).

On May 8, 1985, in a speech to the European Parliament in Strasbourg, President Reagan proposed instituting "regular, high-level contacts between Soviet and American military leaders to develop better understanding and to prevent potential tragedies from occurring." He went on to re-propose a "permanent military-to-military communications link . . . to reduce the chances of misunderstanding and misinterpretation." "Over time," he continued, "it might evolve into a 'risk-reduction' mechanism for rapid communication and exchange of data in time of crisis" (*New York Times*, May 9, 1985: A22). At their summit meeting in Geneva in November 1985, President Reagan and General Secretary Gorbachev agreed to have experts from both countries study the proposal for risk reduction centers. As of this writing—September, 1986—this joint study is proceeding with a view towards reaching agreement.

Soviet Views

At various times, the Soviets have expressed suspicion about American motives in advancing crisis control as a subject for negotiations. In Soviet eyes, Washington may have wanted to create a distraction from the issue of limiting nuclear weapons, which divides the USSR and the United States so deeply. Moscow has suspected Washington of wanting a visible success on the crisis control front, as a way of diverting world public opinion from an American weapons build-up, which the Soviets believe world public opinion opposes. A *Pravda* article commenting on President Reagan's Berlin speech of November, 1982, on reducing the risk of miscalculations, asked rhetorically: "If a hundred MX missiles are complemented by ten telephones—red or blue—directly linking Moscow and Washington, will that make those missiles any less dangerous?"

The Soviets have also expressed some skepticism about the substance of crisis control. Some officials and academics have questioned whether a center, for instance, could be misused to make it easier for one side to escalate a low-level crisis. They have suggested that the superpowers already have some crisis control procedures in the form of the Hotline and the 1971 and 1973 agreements; they have not been convinced that more are needed. And they have pointed out that mere technical improvements cannot make up for a hostile and dangerous overall relationship between the two superpowers.

At the same time Soviet officials and scholars acknowledge that the superpowers share a true common interest in controlling crises. The Soviets have long been concerned about accidental war, including the possibility that another nation might deliberately draw the superpowers into a mutually annihilating nuclear war. Growing Soviet apprehension about the dangers of inadvertent escalation and increasing interest in crisis control were reflected in the Soviet decision to explore the creation of risk reduction centers.

Risks of Crisis Control

Crisis control contains a basic paradox. The very information and procedures that leaders should have during a crisis in order to control and end it are often the same things that, if available before the crisis, might lead to overconfidence. Having crisis control machinery could conceivably cause leaders to relax in times of crisis or even to take risks they would not take without the machinery.

A more concrete danger of many possible measures lies in their vulnerability to misuse. Unless adequate safeguards are adopted, joint centers, for instance, could be used for gathering intelligence or for sending false information at a critical time. Moreover, unless allies and friends are carefully consulted, U.S.-Soviet crisis control measures could be misinterpreted as collusion by the superpowers to control the world.

Going Beyond the Hotline

Below are five concrete measures that might extend our current system for crisis control:

Risk Reduction Centers in Washington and Moscow

If a nuclear bomb suddenly were to detonate in San Francisco, American suspicions would naturally fasten on the Soviet Union. But the bomb might have been exploded by a third nation, a terrorist group, or through a Soviet accident. In such a case, American leaders would want proof and the Soviets would surely want to cooperate. No one would want to go to war over a mistaken assumption.

The Hotline—even the "enhanced" one—might be inadequate for the delicate tasks of interpreting and authenticating information. It might be valuable to the leaders of both countries in such a situation to have on call a group of highly trained military and diplomatic experts from both sides who already knew each other and had prepared together for just such a crisis. Hence the usefulness of U.S.-Soviet risk reduction centers in Washington and Moscow, connected by instant video communication and staffed with American and Soviet specialists. A modest version of this concept was agreed upon by the United States and the Soviet Union on September 15, 1987.

In advance of a crisis, this joint professional working group could anticipate potential crisis triggers and develop technical procedures for handling them. The centers' officers, moreover, might serve as a support staff to ongoing Cabinet-level talks with the USSR on crisis prevention and control, thus helping to ensure the centers' relevance to policy-makers' concerns and increasing the likelihood of the staff's expertise being tapped in time of crisis.

Unless handled with considerable care, risk reduction centers could potentially involve certain problems, including disinformation at critical moments, intelligence leaks, added bureaucracy, and foreign perceptions of U.S.-Soviet condominium. The centers therefore might best be implemented in increments. The centers at first might have a narrow mandate, derived from the Accidents Agreement (1971) to develop measures to prevent and control crises arising inadvertently, such as from accidents, a nuclear war in the Third World, or nuclear terrorism.[4]

Crisis Procedures

Agreed-upon crisis procedures such as the Hotline and the Incidents at Sea Agreements make it technically possible both to head off potential crises and to cope more effectively with any that do occur. Such essentially non-political procedures are in both sides' interest and could and should function even in times of tension.

Successful crisis procedures created to date provide a basis for developing additional ones. To prevent crisis, the U.S. might consider proposing further "incidents agreements" for accidental ground and air intrusions (like that of Korean Airlines Flight 007) and limited but regular consultations on the possibility of nuclear terrorism. The meetings between the American and Soviet generals held in the wake of the shooting of Major Arthur D. Nicholson in March 1985 might be regularized and expanded to pro-active (rather than reactive) study of potential incidents in Germany.

To contain crises, the superpowers could adopt such measures as procedures for coping with nuclear detonations whose source and motive are unclear; procedures to signal peaceful intent in time of heightened expectation of war; prearranged procedures to facilitate face-to-face negotiations in times of crisis; and enlargement of the existing crisis codes for instant and accurate Hotline communication. For halting inadvertently triggered hostilities, the U.S. might consider a discussion of contingency procedures for a cease-fire and return to *status quo ante*, as well as an East-West communications channel for the supreme commanders in Europe.

In particular, Washington and Moscow (or any two potential adversaries) might agree in advance on a crisis consultation period in the event certain specified contingencies occur. In the case of the superpowers, an unlikely but exceedingly dangerous possibility is the single nuclear detonation on either's territory, the purpose, and perhaps even the origin, of which is not immediately clear. Agreements currently in force require the superpowers to "notify" each other if such an event is imminent, and to "consult" over any imminent risk of war. A feasible next step is to define a period during which no hostile action will be taken, assuming only one or a small number of detonations occur. Although such a period would be unenforceable, top leaders on both sides would have strong incentives to observe it, and even to seize upon it as a means of preventing otherwise uncontrollable escalation.

The essential value of these agreed-upon crisis procedures lies in making sure that when the leaders of each side want to avoid or defuse a crisis, they will not fail for simple lack of the machinery to do so.

Regular Cabinet-Level Talks on Preventing Nuclear War

Agreement on crisis control measures is likely to be in incremental steps. Moreover, as new potential dangers arise, new measures will be required. All this suggests the need not for one-shot negotiations, but for ongoing regular talks. As noted above, President Reagan proposed Cabinet-level discussions in his speech to the United Nations in September, 1984.

Some agreements, because of their delicacy and susceptibility to misinterpretation by others, would remain necessarily informal. Indeed, useful discussion would likely revolve not just around possible agreements, but around basic assumptions and the intentions of each side, so as to reduce the chance of miscalculation and misunderstanding. Because of the informal nature of these exchanges, they might best take place between those who would later be centrally involved in the crisis decision-making process, such as the American secretaries of state and defense and their Soviet counterparts. Should a crisis occur, officials already would have a working relationship with their opposite numbers, a wish frequently expressed by American participants in past crises.

Such talks carry, of course, a certain risk of misunderstandings and false confidence. While this calls for considerable caution in the talks, it probably does not outweigh their potential benefits.

Briefing for the President

While the president receives some preparation for fighting a war and using nuclear weapons, apparently little preparation is provided for defusing a nuclear crisis safely and successfully. Yet decisions in a nuclear crisis would likely be the most important decisions a president would ever make. Controlling such a crisis, moreover, is like launching a mission to the moon: an extremely complex system must work perfectly the first time.

A given president will likely make real "hands-on" crisis decisions only once, if ever; no practice is possible. But it is possible to transfer to a new president and a new staff the accumulated wisdom and experience of past nuclear crises in the form of an intensive briefing over several days. Participants in those past crises, most of whom are still alive, could discuss the lessons they learned, assisted by experts in military affairs, history, and international relations. The president and staff members might also observe or participate in one or more simulations of an emerging crisis to explore the difficulties of keeping a crisis under control. Such a briefing might usefully take place in the pre-inaugural period.

Enhanced Roles for Third Parties in Defusing Regional Conflicts

Perhaps the most likely source of superpower confrontation is a regional crisis in the Third World which draws in the superpowers. Regional mediation before the U.S. and USSR become directly involved may be the most effective means of forestalling escalation. While there is a long history of third-party efforts, their effectiveness could be enhanced.

Potential third parties include regional organizations like the OAU or OAS, neutral countries, or the U.N. One of the most successful efforts in recent years was the British mediation of the Zimbabwe-Rhodesia conflict, which threatened to escalate into an East-West crisis (Napper, 1983: 169).

An international mediation service could be created with senior, globally respected figures who could help mediate conflicts before they become crises. There might also be constituted a "Rapid Deployment Peacekeeping Force" made up of soldiers from many countries and able to arrive quickly in a trouble spot to separate antagonists before fighting begins or is renewed. Greater use should also be made of regional congresses, which can bring together adversarial and mediating nations and groups in search of a resolution, or at least a containment, of a local crisis.

A Stabilization Strategy

The centers, crisis procedures, cabinet-level talks, presidential briefing, and enhanced third party roles, together with the Hotline and other existing crisis control measures, would add up to a "crisis control system." Such a system would be intended to help head off, or escape from, crisis situations that had arisen at least partly inadvertently. But what if the other side had deliberately initiated the crisis to make a unilateral gain? How can one defuse a dangerous crisis while protecting vital national interests?

One possible approach, which may be labelled a "stabilization strategy," involves two elements: blocking or freezing offensive military action so as to deny the other side any gains by arms, and simultaneously initiating immediate negotiations to protect both sides' essential interests in security and national stability. Blocking military action helps gain time for decision-making and reduce the perceived stakes; negotiation helps reduce dangerous uncertainty and expand the options available for a peaceful resolution. These steps usually require preparatory measures, which ideally would head off crises even before they start.

Khrushchev's sending missiles to Cuba in October 1962 offers a good example of a crisis challenge for unilateral gain. Kennedy's response offers a fair illustration of a stabilization strategy. His skillful combination of military blocking action—the naval quarantine around Cuba—and high-level personal communication and negotiation succeeded in defusing the crisis while protecting vital national interests.

In some instances it may be possible to block the other side without counter-escalating in a way that threatens its security. Land mines and tank barriers along borders, the inter-position of third forces, and other defensive techniques might reduce the risk to one's own vital national interests without increasing the risk to those on the other side. Developing additional techniques of this kind is a promising area for military R&D.

In Sum

Such crisis control measures are not the only items on the Owl's agenda, but they serve to illustrate it. Nor is the Owl's agenda the only one way to reduce the risks of nuclear war, but in our view, insufficient attention has been paid to the inadvertent and non-rational causes of nuclear war. While this approach will not solve all the problems of nuclear risk reduction, more political imagination and policy effort should be invested in the Owl's approach and, in particular, in crisis control.

Acknowledgments

This paper was originally presented at the XIIIth World Congress of the International Political Science Association. The first half of the paper is drawn from Chapter 8 of Graham Allison, Albert Carnesale and Joseph S. Nye, Jr. (eds.), *Hawks, Doves and Owls: An Agenda for Avoiding Nuclear War* (Norton, 1985). The second part summarizes key recommendations of a report done for the U.S. Arms Control and Disarmament Agency in March 1984 entitled *Beyond the Hotline: Controlling a Nuclear Crisis*, by William L. Ury and Richard Smoke. The report's findings are discussed in *Beyond the Hotline: How Crisis Control Can Prevent Nuclear War* by William L. Ury (Houghton Mifflin 1985; Penguin 1986).

Notes

1. Robert Jervis refers to believers in "deterrence and spiral models" in *Perception and Misperception in International Politics* (Princeton: Princeton University Press, 1976). Glenn H. Snyder and Paul Deising refer to "hard and soft liners" in *Conflict Among Nations* (Princeton: Princeton University Press, 1977). Like the terms in the current public debate, these dichotomies are inadequate because they compress two different causal views (Dove and Owl in our parlance) under one label (whether it be "Dove," "Spiral," or "soft").

2. These perspectives are defined by views of precipitating causes (calculated versus nonrational) and intermediate causes (too little threat versus too much threat) of failed deterrence. Logically there are four possible positions: calculated onset/too much threat—Dove; calculated onset/too little threat—Hawk; non-rational onset/too much threat—Owl; nonrational onset/too little threat—pure accidental war. Since there seem to be no historical instances of purely accidental war, we have described only three perspectives. Moreover, Owls are likely to include the policy implications of accidental war in their own worries.

3. This issue is discussed in detail in Scott Sagan, *The Failure of Deterrence: Pearl Harbor and Nuclear Strategy*, unpublished manuscript, Avoiding Nuclear War Project, Harvard University, 1983.

4. For further discussion of the joint center concept, see: Richard K. Betts, "A Joint Nuclear Risk Control Center" (Washington, DC: Brookings Institution, 1983); Barry Blechman, "U.S.-Soviet Nuclear Risk Management Centers," in *Avoiding Inadvertent War: Crisis Management*, ed. Hilliard Roderick (Austin, Texas: Lyndon B. Johnson School of Public Affairs, 1983), pp. 78–88; and William L. Ury and Richard Smoke, *Beyond the Hotline: Controlling a Nuclear Crisis* (A Report to the United States Arms Control and Disarmament Agency) (Cambridge: Harvard Law School Nuclear Negotiation Project, 1984).

PART FOUR

Crisis Management in Regional Context

8

The Managed and the Managers: Crisis Prevention in the Middle East

Janice Gross Stein

Introduction

The prevention of crises between the superpowers may be as important as their management but it is far more difficult to accomplish. Although the management of crises that grow out of regional wars among allies has been extensively considered, we know considerably less about the attempt of the superpowers to prevent crises by preventing war among their allies. We examine this dimension of crisis prevention, the attempt by and the capacity of the superpowers to restrain their allies from initiating war.

Crisis prevention is inherently more difficult than crisis management for two sets of reasons. First, superpowers frequently have a low incentive to engage actively in crisis prevention before a crisis is upon them. They support regional allies to reap political advantage and may be unwilling to face the unpleasant consequences of restraining their allies. The superpowers also may not be equally committed to crisis prevention under all kinds of circumstances; the balance of interests will vary through time and place as will their estimates of the probability of war (George, 1984a: 131–132, 1985a). Indeed, Alexander George, the foremost analyst of crisis prevention, argues that in the nuclear age crises at times are a substitute for war; they offer the two superpowers the opportunity to change the status quo and achieve their objectives, even though at a high risk (1983; 1984a: 131–132; 1985a). When superpowers are not highly motivated to prevent crises, the task becomes inherently more difficult.

Second, the emphasis on the avoidance of war is not universally shared by all members of the international community. Although the two great nuclear powers seek to avoid war, at times their smaller allies may consider the use of force an optimal instrument to achieve their goals. Equally dangerous, if smaller allies want crucial military, political, or economic resources from the superpowers to help them manage their own conflict, they may deliberately seek to create and exploit crisis between the superpowers to focus attention on the regional conflict. Under these circumstances, superpowers may misjudge their allies, underestimate the differences in interests and priorities, and overestimate their capacity to "manage" their friends.

In part because smaller allies at times seek not to avoid war but to provoke crisis, crisis prevention may be difficult even when the superpowers are highly motivated. Effective communication and control between superpower and ally is necessary but not sufficient. Leaders in Washington and Moscow must control not only their own military forces and bureaucracies as they communicate with each other, but they must simultaneously persuade their allies to refrain from a use of force and to compromise their fundamental objectives. They must attempt to manage an adversary who shares their aversion to war and, equally important, to restrain their ally who may well consider the use of force an acceptable, if not preferred, instrument of conflict management.

More important than improved communication and control, however, is attention to the needs and grievances of allies. Frequently, it is these needs and grievances which make a resort to force attractive to them. If superpowers are to prevent crises that grow out of intense conflict between regional allies, they must confront the basic differences in their own and their allies' agendas. In crisis prevention, the issues go beyond "management" to "politics" and "interests."

Despite these difficulties inherent in crisis prevention, when the superpowers have seen a war between their allies in the Middle East as a likely and serious source of confrontation, they have tried, at times strenuously, to prevent the use of force. They did so in part because the Middle East traditionally has been a dangerous flash point, a region where the balance of interests between the two superpowers is ambiguous. Unlike Europe, there are no clearly demarcated spheres of influence. On the contrary, relative advantage varies as the influence of one or the other superpower waxes or wanes. Yet, the Middle East is important strategically to both the United States and the Soviet Union. In trying to "manage" their allies to prevent crisis, the superpowers face the critical trade-off between losing the confidence of their allies but controlling the risk of war and confrontation, or meeting their allies' demands but increasing the likelihood of regional war and superpower crisis.

Research Design

Our analysis of crisis prevention includes only those cases where one of the superpowers worried that a resort to force by its regional ally might provoke a crisis with the other superpower. We use crisis in its broadest sense: leaders perceive a threat to basic values and anticipate only a limited time to respond (Brecher, 1977: 1980). Crisis may be more or less acute as leaders perceive varying intensities of threat. An acute crisis occurs between the two superpowers when one perceives a high probability of confrontation with the other. Because both Moscow and Washington fear the "autonomous risk" of war, because they see a war between Israel and the Arab states as a likely and serious source of confrontation, the prospect of a major war in the region is generally sufficient to trigger an attempt by one or the other superpower to restrain its ally from the use of force.

This study looks at the "vertical" linkages between superpower and regional ally rather than at the two sets of "horizontal" linkages between the two superpowers and among regional powers. Drawing from the literature which treats the management of an adversary in an attempt to avoid war, we examine three critical dimensions of the relationship between superpower and ally across four cases: their pattern of communication; organizational coherence and political control in the two governments; and relative asymmetries of interest and differences in their political agendas. We pay special attention to the impact of these three factors on the capacity of the superpowers to restrain their allies in the critical stage of the initiation of war.

We look at four attempts at crisis prevention in the Middle East to assess the difficulties of simultaneous management of an ally as well as an adversary. In all four cases, one or the other superpower tried and failed to prevent an ally from using force. In all four cases, the initiation of war by a regional ally did, consistent with superpower expectations, generate or compound a crisis between the two superpowers.

The most intense crisis occurred in the context of a short but fierce war between Egypt, Israel, and Syria in October 1973. On 24 October, the United States alerted its forces to deter the Soviet Union from using limited military force to assist beleaguered Egyptian armies. Although much is now known about the management of this crisis, analysts have paid less attention to Soviet difficulties in restraining Egypt than they have to the pattern of communication between the two superpowers once war broke out. In an earlier, somewhat less acute crisis in June, 1967, American and Soviet leaders resorted to the hot line for the first time, as they struggled to terminate a war between Egypt, Syria, and

Israel. Here we look at the intensive American attempts to restrain Israel from initiating the war.

The other two crises, less acute, were embedded in cases of protracted conflict in the Middle East. During the war of attrition between Egypt and Israel in 1969–1970, the Soviet Union threatened to intervene to protect the Egyptian heartland from strategic bombing by Israel's air force, the United States tried unsuccessfully to deter the introduction of Soviet forces, and as the United States attempted to end the fighting between Egypt and Israel, Israeli and Soviet forces engaged in aerial combat over the Suez Canal. We look at the Soviet attempt to prevent Egypt from initiating a war of attrition. The civil war in Lebanon, which began in 1975, threatened several times to explode into a full-scale war between Israel and Syria. It did so on June 6, 1982, when Israel's army invaded Lebanon and, three days later, began military operations against Syrian forces in the eastern sector of the front. American officials immediately became concerned about the widening of the war, the possibility of Soviet intervention on behalf of Syria, and the probability of a crisis with the Soviet Union. We consider the American attempt to "manage" Israel in the six years preceding Israel's decision to use large-scale force in Lebanon against Syria and the PLO, both allies of the Soviet Union.

A word of caution is appropriate. The conclusions from this investigation must be treated with reservation, largely because of the bias in selection of cases for analysis. We deal only with cases where one of the superpowers failed to restrain its ally from going to war. We do so because it is extraordinarily difficult to identify instances where superpowers do persuade their allies to refrain from a use of force; regional leaders usually do not speak or write of such decisions. Moreover, it is generally difficult to analyze counterfactual evidence, to explain what did not happen.

Within these limits, the research design does permit some carefully controlled comparisons (George, 1982). The outcome of the four cases was similar: in all four, an ally went to war against the explicit advice of a superpower. Yet, the four cases do differ in important respects. In two, Egypt, an ally of the Soviet Union, initiated war and in the other two, Israel, a protege of the United States, resorted to force. Two of the crises were acute and occurred in the context of short but intense wars while the other two were less acute and occurred during protracted conflict. Using the "logic of agreement," we can discount the importance of many of the differences in these cases and concentrate on the similarities in an explanation of the failure of the superpowers to prevent their allies from resorting to force.

Initiating the Use of Force: Managing the Managers

Soviet Attempts to Restrain Egypt

In 1969, when President Nasser of Egypt decided to launch a war of attrition against Israel's forces stationed along the Canal, he did so against Soviet advice (Bar-Siman-Tov, 1980: 46, 47). The Soviet leadership repeatedly turned down Egypt's requests for offensive weapons in an effort to "persuade" Egypt not to initiate military action.[1] They insisted that all diplomatic options be explored and, to advance the prospects of negotiation, agreed to participate directly in two-power meetings with the United States and in four-power discussions with Great Britain and France as well (Heikal, 1975: 56–57).

In December, 1968, Foreign Minister Gromyko went to Cairo to persuade President Nasser not to resort to war and to propose a plan for a comprehensive settlement of the Arab-Israel conflict. Although the president of Egypt rejected the terms, he did agree to refrain from launching a major attack along the canal for three months. The Soviet Union had bought a limited amount of time, but in a revealing aside to the Soviet foreign minister, Nasser reportedly warned: "If I do not do something soon, the people will hang me" (1968).

The communique at the end of the visit masked the fundamental divergence between Egypt and the Soviet Union and the growing tension in their relationship. Soviet statements continued to emphasize the importance of a negotiated settlement of the crisis while Egyptian officials and commentators spoke pessimistically about the prospects of diplomatic efforts and the inevitability of war. The president, speaking to the National Assembly, insisted that " . . . no progress can be made by military or political action unless the military front is the starting point . . . "(1969). Despite the intense differences between Egypt and the Soviet Union, however, in February a large number of Soviet freighters arrived in Egyptian ports bearing arms. Shortly thereafter, in March, 1969, Egypt launched a war of attrition along the canal front.

President Nasser chose to use force in large part because he could see no acceptable alternative to a situation he considered intolerable. He had long refused to negotiate with Israel, and became even more adamant after 1967 as Egypt's military inferiority became apparent and Israel's forces remained in the Sinai peninsula. Yet, the president considered that the Egyptian public would not long sustain a policy of inaction; the general demoralization that followed the humiliating military defeat of 1967 would explode into political violence.[2]

A paradox is immediately apparent. The Soviet Union, for all intents and purposes the exclusive military supplier of the Egyptian armed forces, was unable to prevent President Nasser from resorting to military force. On the contrary, the president felt able to use force in part because he considered that the Soviet Union provided a safety net. Crucial to his strategy was his estimate that the presence of Soviet military advisers would constrain Israel from escalating the war. It was Soviet military and political support which allowed the Egyptian president to defy the wishes of the Soviet Union and to initiate the military conflict which would provoke a crisis between the two superpowers.

The Soviet failure to restrain Egypt cannot be attributed to inadequate or faulty communication. During the crucial three months before the outbreak of war, the Soviet foreign minister visited Cairo for extended talks with the Egyptian president and there were frequent exchanges at lower levels. Nor is there any evidence of misunderstanding between patron and ally. Both publicly and privately, Egypt was unequivocal and vociferous in its rejection of a negotiating strategy endorsed by the Soviet Union. Its bargaining strength with the Soviet Union grew out of its desperate weakness, its military vulnerability to Israel and the political vulnerability of the regime at home.

The inability of the Soviet Union to "manage" its ally is even more striking in October, 1973. Repeatedly in 1971 and 1972, the Soviet Union refused to supply the offensive military equipment, particularly long-range bombers, necessary for a full-scale Egyptian military offensive against Israel. In July 1972, Soviet opposition to a use of force by Egypt provoked President Anwar el-Sadat to expel Soviet military personnel in order to free the Egyptian army to prepare for military action. The Soviet Union suffered considerable damage to its reputation as ally and patron in the Middle East and its response was predictable: although it still refused to supply advanced bombers, it dramatically increased its shipments of military equipment to the Egyptian army (Golan, 1977 and Kolkowicz, 1981). As the Egyptian Under-Secretary of State for Foreign Affairs noted: "Clearly, the Soviets had got the message that they could not take Egypt for granted and had to take positive measures to maintain good relations" (Fahmy, 1983: 9). That spring, the president of Egypt voiced his satisfaction with the pace of arms shipments from the Soviet Union and warned of the coming battle.[3] In the summer of 1973, the Soviet Union delivered the long-promised SCUD missile which, though inaccurate and crude, could strike at Israel's population centers.

Two months later, despite Soviet disapproval and with only a few days notice to the Soviet leadership, Egypt and Syria launched a coordinated attack across the ceasefire lines. The record suggests that Egypt was far more adept at "managing" the Soviet Union than was the Soviet leadership at restraining Egypt. The Soviet leadership faced the classic trade-off characteristic of crisis prevention: they tried simultaneously to avoid the loss of their most important ally in a strategically important region and to prevent the outbreak of a conventional war which could escalate to a confrontation between the two superpowers. Indeed, at his summit meeting in June, 1973 in the United States with President Nixon, Secretary-General Brezhnev warned indirectly of the growing probability of war in the Middle East (George, 1984a: 144). When they were forced to choose between the two competing purposes, however, they chose to avoid the loss of their ally. From the spring of 1973 on, their commitment to crisis prevention was inherently less vigorous as they increased arms shipments to Egypt.

The Soviet Union faced the dilemma it did in large part because Egyptian objectives were not only different from but diametrically opposed to those of the Soviet Union. The president of Egypt intended, through the use of conventional force against Israel, to provoke a crisis between the superpowers and thereby to inflate the costs to them of perpetuating a status quo that was intolerable to him. His strategy was a limited use of military force to change the political context of negotiation, to demonstrate to the two superpowers that continued immobility could be dangerous to them as well as costly to Egypt, and to interest the rival of the Soviet Union in committing itself to a diplomatic resolution of the crisis in the Middle East.

Paradoxically, the nascent process of detente between the two superpowers, their attempt to improve the management of regional crises to reduce the danger of a confrontation between the two nuclear powers, intensified the Egyptian desire to resort to force to provoke precisely such a crisis. Sadat insisted that Egypt's interests were most directly threatened by the process of detente between the two superpowers, by their joint interest in avoiding a major crisis in the Middle East. The Egyptian Under-Secretary of State for Foreign Affairs, Ismail Fahmy, was most explicit:

> I suggested that the superpowers were contributing to the maintenance of "no peace, no war," because a permanent settlement in the Middle East had low priority for them. Detente was likely to make this priority even lower, as the two superpowers would now be preoccupied with safeguarding their rapprochement. As a consequence, the Soviets would become even more reluctant to provide Egypt with the arms it needed for a new confrontation with Israel (Fahmy, 1983: 6).

Fahmy also put Soviet attempts to persuade Egypt to refrain from the use of force in its regional context:

> . . . it was clear that the Soviet advice to the Egyptian side not to start military operations was due to Moscow's fear that once a war started

events might lead to a greater confrontation between the two superpowers in the Middle East (1983: 7).

In 1973, the paradoxes are even more striking than they were in 1969: the Soviet Union was effectively unable to "manage" Egypt. Moscow first suffered a diplomatic humiliation, then conceded substantially on the issue of arms supplies, and, ultimately, failed to dissuade Egypt from initiating a conventional war. The reasons for the failure are instructive. The Soviet Union did not fail to prevent the initiation of war because of inadequate control of its own institutions or because of weaknesses in its policy process. Nor did Moscow fail because it had inadequate lines of communication with Egypt. The roots of the failure go far deeper. The urgent need of the Egyptian leadership to break a stalemate it could not tolerate, the disruption of its domestic economy and social fabric, the growing political discontent, the extraordinarily high costs of inaction which outweighed the risks of the use of military force, drove the Egyptian leadership to a strategy of crisis creation (Stein, 1985: 34–59).

Not only was the Egyptian leadership driven, but in the nine months that preceded the outbreak of war, the Soviet Union implicitly moderated its opposition to a use of force. It did so tacitly by increasing the scope and pace of arms deliveries to Egypt. The Soviet Union was caught badly between two unpleasant options: sacrificing its most important ally in the Middle East or increasing the risk of confrontation and crisis with the United States. Confronted with the certainty of the former, it chose to risk the latter. In large part because President Sadat succeeded in structuring the Soviet dilemma in precisely this way, the Egyptian record as a "manager" is far more impressive than that of the Soviet Union.

American Attempts to Restrain Israel

The United States succeeded no better in restraining Israel in the two crises of 1967 and 1982. In 1967, the United States moved swiftly to try to manage the growing crisis between Egypt and Israel and prevent its escalation. After President Nasser asked United Nations peacekeeping forces to withdraw on 19 May, 1967, at Israel's request President Johnson wrote immediately to Premier Kosygin, affirming American support for Israel and suggesting a "joint initiative of the two powers to prevent the dispute between Israel and the U.A.R. and Syria from drifting into war" (cited by Quandt, 1977: 40–41).

The president also wrote on 22 May to Israel, Egypt, and Syria, urging the deescalation of troop movements, respect for free navigation, and reliance on the United Nations to resolve the growing crisis (Quandt, 1977: 42 and Eban, 1977: 334). That same day, President Nasser escalated the crisis by announcing a blockage of the Straits of Tiran. Israel had declared ten years earlier that it would retaliate with force were the Straits to be blockaded and the United States had acknowledged its right to do so (Stein and Tanter, 1980: 163–164).[4] Acting on behalf of the President, Undersecretary of State Eugene Rostow immediately urged Israel to make no decision for forty-eight hours and to consult with the United States in the interim. President Johnson reiterated his earlier warning that he would not be responsible for any action on which he was not consulted (Eban, 1977: 334).

After an exhaustive debate, Israel's cabinet voted to delay military action for forty-eight hours so that Foreign Minister Abba Eban could explore the position of the United States. The evidence suggests that, in the initial phase of the crisis in the Middle East, the United States was able to restrain its ally: Israel's leaders were unwilling to use military force without attempting to secure American support. A crucial component of the American success was not only the negative sanctions but also the positive inducements: the United States warned repeatedly against unilateral action but also hinted at multilateral action to open the Straits.

By the time Eban arrived in Washington, Israel's military intelligence had increased its estimate of the likelihood of an Egyptian attack. Eban was instructed to explore American willingness to reinforce deterrence by promising to come to Israel's defense. By requesting a statement that an attack on Israel was tantamount to an attack on the United States, Israel's leaders were acknowledging implicitly their inability to deter after they had failed to respond with force to the blockage of the Straits, a declared *casus belli*. Paradoxically, Israel's leaders hesitated to use force not because they considered their military capabilities inadequate— Israel's senior military officers had no doubt about their capacity to prevail in a military confrontation—but rather because they anticipated the need for American support both to deter the Soviet Union should it intervene on behalf of Egypt and in the postwar bargaining. A request to the United States to deter Egypt and Syria from attack, however, gave the United States the opportunity to restrain its ally, to insist that Israel itself refrain from military action (Stein and Tanter, 1980: 182).

In an intensive series of meetings in Washington among Israel's foreign minister, the secretary of state and his senior advisers, and, finally, with President Johnson, the United States pointedly refused to make an open-ended commitment to Israel's defense. However, the United States asked the Soviet Union to use its influence with Egypt to prevent an attack and summoned the Egyptian ambassador to the State Department to make a similar request (Quandt, 1977: 49).[5] At the same time, the president warned vigorously against unilateral action by Israel and insisted that Israel would bear the consequences if it resorted to force. The president warned, moreover, that he " . . . was not prepared to act in a manner . . . [that would] bring about the intervention of the Soviet Union" (Eban, 1977: 358 and Foreign Ministry sources, cited by Brecher, 1975: 390–391). Johnson did promise to try to organize an international maritime flotilla to open the Straits, but warned of the imperative of full Congressional support and the need to consult with the United Nations.

As Israel's leaders were considering the American request, Premier Kosygin appealed to Israel to refrain from a use of force.[6] The Soviet note was moderate and did not weigh heavily in the deliberations of Israel's leaders. More relevant were two messages from the United States. The president wrote that he had received a note from the Soviet Union indicating that it had information that Israel was preparing to attack: "The Soviets state that if Israel starts military action, the Soviet Union will extend help to those attacked" (Foreign Ministry sources, cited by Brecher, 1975: 398). Johnson concluded by telling Prime Minister Eshkol that, "Israel just must not take preemptive military action and thereby make itself responsible for the initiation of hostilities" (cited by Eban, 1977: 370). The secretary of state attached an optimistic report on the organization of a naval escort.

The prime minister, convinced of the importance of American support, persuaded his colleagues that Israel could not resort to force as long as the United States was actively involved in organizing international maritime action. Like the Soviet Union in December, 1968, the United States had bought time but, again, in a dilemma analogous to that of Soviet leaders, if the time were to be used effectively to prevent a use of force, American officials had to address the issues that had generated the crisis in the Middle East.

This they did not do. Events moved more rapidly than did American officials. A joint defense pact between Egypt and Jordan raised the possibility of a two-front war. Not only did Israel's estimate of the military threat increase, but its estimate of the probability of international maritime action declined. Even though State Department officials remained optimistic, the United States encountered considerable difficulty in organizing an international naval flotilla.

Not only the United States but also the Soviet Union tried to deter Israel from using force. A note delivered to Israel's ambassador in Moscow warned of the dangers of initiating military action: "Should the government of Israel take upon itself the responsibility for an outbreak of war, it will have to pay the full price for the results" (cited by Dayan,

1976: 274). Crucial to Israel's decision-makers was the probability that the United States would deter the Soviet Union. On this critical issue there was some uncertainty: Ambassador Harman, who met with Rusk and Eugene Rostow at the State Department, reported that they were equivocal both in their estimate of Soviet intentions and of the likely American response, but Israel's foreign minister was far more optimistic.[7]

Persuaded that the United States would not succeed in organizing an international naval escort, alarmed by the growing concentration of Egyptian troops in the Sinai peninsula as well as by the prospect of coordination among Arab armies, and confident of American support precisely because they had delayed the use of force at the request of the United States, Israel's leaders chose to launch a preemptive air and ground attack against Egypt. Analysis of Israel's decision-making suggests that this factor was critical (Stein and Tanter, 1980: 241–252). The onset of war and the imminent defeat of Arab armies quickly provoked a major crisis between the United States and the Soviet Union.

Why did the United States fail to restrain Israel? There was more than adequate time for clarification of intentions, intensive face-to-face communication, and coordination of strategy. Both the United States and Israel had access to good if not excellent intelligence about each other's political processes and decision-making procedures. Indeed, the multiple channels of communication and the extensive high-level meetings in the last two weeks of May were unprecedented.

Nor did the United States encounter opposition from the rival super-power. The Soviet Union did commit a major blunder in transmitting to Egypt false intelligence information of a concentration of Israel's forces on the Syrian border. It did so in an effort to encourage Egypt to engage in a limited show of force to deter Israel from a retaliatory raid against Syria and, indeed, it provoked the initial movement of Egyptian forces across the Canal into the Sinai peninsula. It opposed further moves by Egypt, however, and attempted to forestall a blockade of the Straits. Very quickly, however, the Soviet Union and, indeed, Egypt lost control as Nasser's Arab constituency escalated its demands and Egyptian public opinion responded. It is not surprising that the Soviet Union could not restrain Egypt from escalating a crisis that it had helped to initiate; the finely calibrated and limited use of force the Soviet Union hoped for was beyond the capability of a politically weakened Egyptian regime. Nevertheless, the Soviet leadership became alarmed at the prospect of a war between Egypt and Israel and cooperated tacitly and explicitly with the United States for two weeks in an effort to restrain both their allies.

The failure of the United States to restrain Israel was due in large part to its inability to "manage" the crisis that Israel confronted. On the contrary, the regional crisis intensified with each passing day. There was little American or international enthusiasm for a flotilla to break the blockage: mired in Vietnam, the president was reluctant to commit American military personnel without extensive and time-consuming consultation with the Congress, and the Pentagon considered a limited use of naval force ill-advised and dangerous. Only the State Department supported the proposal. Even more to the point, as the United States attempted to prevent a use of force and Israel attempted to secure American support, the nature of the crisis changed. The proposed naval flotilla that would have been relevant in the initial phase was overtaken by a spiralling process of escalation in the Middle East. Under these conditions, a use of force by Israel was a foregone conclusion.

The United States did not address the fundamentals of the crisis in part because of the difference in its agenda and that of its ally. American officials attached highest priority to avoiding a crisis with the Soviet Union and, consequently, to avoiding a war between Israel and Egypt. It was prepared to accept almost any diplomatic compromise to defuse the crisis; indeed, the president sent his personal envoy, Robert Anderson, to Cairo to negotiate privately with President Nasser. The two agreed to a high-level exchange of visits: Vice-President Zahariyah Muhi-a-Din would come to Washington on 7 June and Vice-President Humphrey would reciprocate soon thereafter. Paradoxically, the prospect of a compromise negotiated between Egypt and the United States increased the sense of urgency in Israel to resort to force.[8] Israel's leaders considered it urgent to break the blockade, to restore their deterrent reputation, and to maximize their capacity for defense. The obvious instrument to meet these objectives was a use of military force. This fundamental difference in political purpose bedeviled the prevention of crisis.

Far less important were the divisions within the American government. In the few days before Israel decided to resort to force, Prime Minister Eshkol sent Meir Amit, the head of Israel's Special Services *(Mossad)*, to assess American attitudes unofficially. A major purpose of his trip was to examine the likely American response should Israel resort unilaterally to force. Amit went not to the State Department but to the Pentagon and the CIA, where opinion diverged considerably from policy in the White House. The Pentagon was vigorously opposed to the proposed naval task force. Military officials worried about the likely American response were Egypt to fire on an American ship and the dangers of an open-ended commitment. Success of a limited use of naval force was far from assured and military officers were concerned about the possibility of escalation. As Secretary of Defense McNamara noted, the multinational fleet was a "military man's nightmare" (Quandt, 1977: 47). Pentagon officials considered it an inappropriate and dangerous solution to Israel's problem of national deterrence and defense. Indeed, some have speculated that the Pentagon preferred to see Israel take independent action to solve its problem.

It was not inadvertent that Amit did not talk with officials in the State Department since its senior officials still strongly supported the naval force and cautioned repeatedly against unilateral military action. Secretary of State Rusk, for example, told Israel's ambassador to Washington that plans for maritime action were proceeding and warned that the issue of who fired first would be extremely important (Quandt, 1977: 59).

Amit met with Secretary of Defense McNamara and CIA Director Richard Helms. Not surprisingly, on his return to Jerusalem he reported that those he had spoken with in Washington "scoffed" at the proposed naval task force (Dayan, 1976: 273). During the two weeks of discussions in Washington, Israel's leaders did become adept at reading the different signals from the different branches of the government. It is not implausible that the prime minister sent his unofficial envoy to Washington to capitalize on these differences and structure the information his colleagues received.

Inadvertently, rather than by design, Israel appears to have "managed" the United States in the prolonged consultations. The paradox is sharp: by engaging in extensive discussions, Israel assured itself of American support for its initiation of war, even though the initiation of war threatened a confrontation with the Soviet Union. The strategy of consultation worked, however, only because the United States could not organize a multinational naval response. If the United States had succeeded in organizing a naval escort, Israel's policy-makers would have confronted an extraordinarily difficult dilemma.[9]

Although organizational incoherence in Washington was a factor, its weight was far less than the fundamental divergence in political purpose between the superpower and its ally. No more than the divergences between the Soviet Union and Egypt, this difference in political agenda could not be transcended by improvements in technical or organizational coordination. The difference in purpose reflected the divergent priorities of a superpower anxious to avoid a regional war that could embroil the two nuclear powers and a regional ally with fundamental strategic and intrinsic interests at stake.

The American attempt to prevent a war between Israel and Syria in Lebanon in 1982 was less vigorous, more differentiated, and more ambiguous than its effort in 1967. The American effort began in earnest in 1976, in the wake of an escalating civil war in Lebanon that had erupted a year earlier. In an attempt to prevent war between Syria and Israel, the United States became heavily involved as a "manager" between the two regional powers who were themselves trying, often unsuccessfully, to constrain their Lebanese allies. Crisis prevention was a multilevel challenge: the United States attempted both to manage its ally, Israel, who was trying to constrain its local ally in Lebanon, and to restrain Syria, the ally of its adversary.

In an effort to prevent a regional war, the United States mediated mutually acceptable limits of military behavior. In a complex three way process, Syria signalled its limited intentions through the United States to Israel who, in turn, agreed to the stationing of Syrian forces in the eastern part of Lebanon as part of an Arab peacekeeping force. In extensive secret negotiations through Henry Kissinger, the two agreed to a set of boundaries: Syria would not deploy its forces south of the Zaharani River; it would not deploy surface-to-air missiles in Lebanon; it would not send its aircraft over Lebanon, except in the northern region; and it would not challenge Israel's air activity over Lebanese air space. These "red lines" circumscribed Syria's capacity to attack Israel through Lebanon (Rabin, 1979: 280 and Evron, 1987).

The mutually agreed-upon limits to the deployment of Syrian forces in Lebanon reassured Israel even as it augmented Syrian capacity to influence the political order throughout most of northern, eastern, and central Lebanon. During the bargaining process, the United States facilitated informal agreement between the two parties; it clarified messages between the two powers, modifying their tone and at times their content (Evron, 1987). Although neither Syria nor Israel wanted war in 1976, the United States was instrumental in promoting a limited regime which reduced the probability of an accidental or miscalculated war.

A renewed threat of war arose not from tension between Israel and Syria, but rather from the escalating military activity across Israel's frontier by PLO forces in southern Lebanon and Israel's retaliatory raids. In March, 1978, responding to the hijacking of a civilian bus by Palestinian commandoes and the killing of their passengers, Israel's army crossed the frontier to attack PLO forces in the southern part of Lebanon. It structured its military operations within the framework of the agreed-upon limits with Syria: the scope of the advance was carefully limited to a depth of 10 kilometers along a 100 kilometer front. Military leaders hoped to create a "security zone" along the border in which friendly Christian militias would operate.

In an effort to limit the collateral damage and to avoid unintended escalation, Israel communicated directly to Egypt, through its military mission in Cairo, its limited purposes. It also informed the United States of its intention not to engage Syrian forces and its intent to withdraw as soon as appropriate security arrangements were put in place. The

Carter Administration, heavily preoccupied with the future of the Egypt-Israel relationship and concerned about the possibility of a widening war with Syria, immediately put a draft resolution to the Security Council proposing the creation of a peacekeeping force to be deployed in southern Lebanon. At the same time, President Assad signalled his intention to avoid a wider war; Syria, he said, would "not be dragged into a risky position" (1978).

Responding to Syrian reassurance and to direct pressure from the United States to cease its military operations immediately, as well as to indirect American pressure through the United Nations, Israel's leaders decided to exploit the limited time remaining to send their forces further north as far as the Litani, well south of the Zaharani River. The advance was completed within twenty-four hours and Israel then accepted the Security Council resolution, agreed in principle to the deployment of a peacekeeping force in Lebanon south of the Litani River, and declared its intention to withdraw.

Throughout, Israel, Syria, and the United States, as well as Egypt, were agreed: none wanted a wider war. Nevertheless, the United States again played an important facilitating role. It signalled clearly to both Israel and Syria its expectation that Israel would withdraw and it supported internationally supervised security arrangements for southern Lebanon. Although these security arrangements, predictably, were not terribly satisfactory, the Carter administration accomplished its central purpose; it avoided a wider war and prevented crisis.

In 1981, the Reagan administration came to office with a reduced emphasis on the dangers of the Arab-Israel conflict and a commensurately greater concern with the role of the Soviet Union in the Middle East. It hoped to build a "strategic consensus" among friendly Arab governments and Israel to counteract Soviet ambitions. Very quickly, however, a crisis between Syria and Israel, which arose from the actions of Israel's Lebanese ally in April 1981, again embroiled the United States as "manager." One year after Bashir Jumayyil unified Maronite military forces under his command, the leader of the Phalange military forces deliberately provoked Syrian forces in eastern Lebanon. He did so hoping to extract military support from Israel: in October 1978, the Begin government had promised it would use its air power to defend Christian enclaves were they to be attacked by the Syrian airforce and General Eitain, the Chief of Staff of the Israel Defense Forces, reiterated that pledge when he visited Jumayyil in Junieh in December 1980.[10]

The Phalange sent a unit to Zahle, a predominantly Christian town, situated on the Beirut-Damascus road, on the western slope of the Bekaa where most of the Syrian forces were deployed. In response, Syria shelled Zahle heavily, attacked a Maronite position in the Senin mountains in the core of the Maronite enclave, and, in a tacit signal to Israel, prepared ground emplacements near Zahle suitable for SAM missiles. They did not, however, deploy the missiles which would have violated a central component in the agreement reached in 1976.

Israel's military and political leaders were deeply divided about the appropriate response. The prime minister recalled the promises of air support but military intelligence and the *Mossad*, which had special responsibility for liaison with Jumayyil's forces, considered that the leader of the Phalange militia had deliberately provoked the confrontation to embroil Israel in a war with Syria.[11] While the internal debate was ongoing, Syria used attack helicopters against Christian positions in Mount Senin. Israel's Air Force then attacked and destroyed two Syrian helicopters; after the fact, military leaders learned that these were cargo helicopters transporting soldiers. Very quickly, Syria introduced surface-to-air missiles into the prepared emplacements, in violation of a central component of the tacit agreement negotiated in 1976.

Military escalation between Israel and Syria seemed possible to Washington. Indeed, the prime minister of Israel decided on an air strike against Syrian missile emplacements, scheduled for 30 April (Schiff and Ya'ari, 1984: 34–35). The Reagan administration expressed its strong opposition to a strike against the missile sites and offered to send Philip Habib to mediate the crisis. Largely because political leaders in Israel were divided, the prime minister acceded to American pressure and postponed indefinitely an air strike against the missiles. In a speech to Israel's *Knesset* a month later, Begin explained Israel's inaction: "The government of Israel saw no reason for changing its earlier decision not to be drawn into war with Syria except on the basis of its own considerations"(1981). Helped by the strong divisions within Israel's political elite, the United States was nevertheless instrumental in moving Syria and Israel back from the edge of the precipice. Despite intensive effort, however, Habib did not succeed in mediating an agreement between Israel and Syria.

Only three months later, escalating tensions between Israel and the PLO once again drew the United States in as manager in an effort to prevent a wider war. After intense shelling by the PLO across the border and a spiralling series a retaliatory raids by Israel, President Reagan again sent Philip Habib to mediate a ceasefire. This time, complex, prolonged, tacit, multiparty negotiations orchestrated by the United States led to a ceasefire between Israel and the PLO in the summer of 1981 (Schiff and Ya'ari, 1984: 36).

By this time, the United States had both extensive experience as a "manager" between Israel, Syria, and the PLO in Lebanon and considerable interest in controlling escalation, containing the ongoing violence in Lebanon at low levels, and preventing a wider war. In effect, three American administrations had separated their management of the Israel-Syrian relationship in Lebanon from the wider context of the Arab-Israel conflict. They did so because they gave priority to war avoidance and crisis prevention.

A change in government in Israel in July, 1981 brought Ariel Sharon to the ministry of defense and with him, an attempt to change Israel's strategy from one of avoiding war with Syria to one of deliberate engagement of Syrian forces. Almost immediately, he ordered preparation of two military plans: one for a large-scale invasion of Lebanon to destroy PLO forces and engage Syrian forces to the east and a second, more limited plan to push PLO forces 40 kilometers back from Israel's border and remove PLO artillery from within range of Israel's border towns (Schiff and Ya'ari, 1984: 42–44).

As early as October, 1981, Prime Minister Begin broached the possibility of a limited invasion to Secretary of State Alexander Haig but he met with strong opposition. In words reminiscent of President Johnson, Haig warned: "If you move, you move alone." In a revealing addendum, however, he continued: "Unless there is a major, internationally recognized provocation, the United States will not support such an action" (Haig, 1984: 326). The message from the secretary was equivocal.

American opposition was not decisive. On 20 December, despite his discussion with Haig, the prime minister brought to Israel's cabinet a formal proposal to launch a large-scale military operation in Lebanon. In the face of considerable opposition from his colleagues, Begin decided to withdraw the proposal temporarily (Schiff and Ya'ari, 1984: 47–48). Nevertheless, Begin dispatched General Saguy, the head of Israel's military intelligence to Washington in February, 1982 to meet with Haig and build support for an attack against PLO forces (Schiff and Ya'ari, 1984: 67).

Over the course of the winter, the secretary of state gradually agreed that a serious violation of the ceasefire by the PLO would constitute sufficient cause for a limited attack. Although the necessary scope of the violation and its context remained undefined, Haig indicated that the United States would "not oppose" a limited military operation by Israel if it were provoked. He did reiterate his strong objections to more than a limited use of force (Haig, 1984: 332).

Officials at the State Department were far more reserved than was the secretary about a use of force by Israel. Officers with expertise in the Middle East argued that an invasion by Israel would exacerbate political tension and make economic and political reconstruction in Lebanon more difficult. Members of the National Security Council expressed their concern that even a limited use of force by Israel in

Lebanon would jeopardize the peace treaty between Egypt and Israel and derail the final withdrawal of Israel's forces, scheduled for April, 1982. They anticipated that military action by Israel would so antagonize moderate governments in the Arab world that it would facilitate Soviet penetration and strengthen its position in the Arab world.[12] The Pentagon was even more strongly opposed to a limited military operation by Israel. Officials worried about the possibility of unintended escalation, the involvement of Syrian forces in a wider war, a demand for American forces, and the possibility of a wider confrontation with the Soviet Union.

Sharon and the Chief of Staff, Raful Eitan, continued to press the prime minister and the cabinet to approve large-scale military action. Predisposed to use force, they interpreted Secretary Haig's reservation within the larger context of the administration's emphasis on the Soviet "threat," both directly and through its allies in the Middle East (Schiff, 1983: 84). In March, at an informal meeting in Begin's home, they urged authorization of an attack against PLO forces before the final withdrawal from the Sinai, in order to test Egyptian intentions; most of the ministers present rejected the strategy as too risky (Schiff and Ya'ari, 1984: 52–53).

When the proposal was put yet again to a cabinet meeting in early April, eleven members voted in favor of an air strike and authorized the prime minister to establish a committee of six members to choose the date. Nevertheless, Begin still faced strong opposition to large-scale military action, particularly from the intelligence community. Not only Military Intelligence, the most authoritative voice in the intelligence network, but also *Mossad* expressed grave doubts about the reliability of Jumayyil as an ally in any large-scale military action. Members of the cabinet were aware as well that an air strike could easily provoke counteraction by PLO forces and escalate quickly into a much larger confrontation.

The Reagan administration also communicated to Israel its strong opposition to the use of force precisely because it feared a disruption of the scheduled withdrawal from the Sinai. The National Security Council staff and the State Department in particular argued that military action by Israel could jeopardize its relationship with Egypt. Responding not only to American pressure but also to consensus in the intelligence community and to serious opposition within his cabinet, the prime minister withdrew his support of a large-scale attack (Schiff and Ya'ari, 1984: 53–54). More than American pressure, the dissension among his senior ministers ultimately led Begin to abandon his commitment to a large-scale military operation in Lebanon. The prime minister so informed his minister of defense and the chief of staff. Even a more limited air strike, however, continued to meet with opposition in the cabinet. As the six senior ministers continued to debate the timing of the air attack, the division of opinion within this core group became so obvious that the prime minister did not proceed with the authorized attack.

After Israel completed its withdrawal from the Sinai as scheduled on 23 April, 1982, American officials voiced their opposition to military action less frequently. In May, Israel's minister of defense met with the secretary of state in Washington and again discussed a limited military operation. Considerable controversy has arisen about what was said during that meeting, but both Sharon and Haig insist that the secretary approved only a limited military reaction proportional to the provocation.[13]

Notwithstanding the loss of prime ministerial support, Sharon and Eitan directed the General Staff to prepare for extensive ground and air action in Lebanon. Knowing full well the opposition of his cabinet colleagues to a large-scale use of force, the minister of defense nevertheless continued to prepare for a military operation that would escalate to engage Syrian forces to the east and PLO forces to the north far beyond the accepted limit of 40 kilometers.

On 4 June, after the attempted assassination of Israel's ambassador to London, Chief of Staff Eitan yet again proposed air strikes against PLO strongholds in Beirut and southern Lebanon. After requesting a reduction in the scale of the bombing in and around Beirut, the cabinet unanimously approved the request. It also empowered the prime minister to mobilize reserves if necessary and to authorize an attack against the "sources of fire" should the PLO retaliate. Nevertheless, activation of ground units would require further approval by the cabinet. In anticipation of a precisely such a request, the prime minister scheduled a meeting of cabinet for the evening of 5 June.

At that meeting, the prime minister, the minister of defense, and the chief of staff proposed a military attack limited to southern Lebanon, with no advance to Beirut or against Syrian forces to the east. Israel's forces were to advance no further than the Zaharani River to the north and Hasbaia to the east. They were to try at all costs to avoid engaging Syrian troops, their advance was to be limited to 40 kilometers from the border, and the operation was to take no longer than forty-eight hours. Even then, some members of the cabinet registered concern both about the scope and the unintended consequences of the proposed ground operation. After considerable discussion, only two members of cabinet abstained; the rest approved a limited military attack (Feldman and Rechnitz-Kijner, 1985: 10–12).

When Israel began its air attacks on 4 June, the Reagan administration immediately changed its strategy. Despite its prior approval of a limited military action, it now gave priority to crisis prevention and attempted at the last moment to prevent a use of force. Late on 5 June, the American ambassador to Israel, Samuel Lewis, transmitted an urgent message to Prime Minister Begin asking him not to initiate hostilities. Again, early on the morning of 6 June, a special message arrived from President Reagan asking Israel to refrain from a use of force.

Not surprisingly, Israel proceeded with the planned military operation. Within three days, without the approval of Israel's cabinet, acting on the orders of General Sharon, Israel's forces engaged the Syrian army and advanced well beyond the forty kilometers to the north. Alarmed, Secretary-General Brezhnev wrote to President Reagan of the dangerous possibility of escalation and on 9 June, the president wrote to Prime Minister Begin, insisting on an immediate ceasefire.[14]

This attempt by a superpower to restrain its ally is qualitatively different from the other three cases. A senior member of the Reagan administration did approve a limited use of force; in none of the other cases was this so. When the Reagan administration took office in January 1981, it gave priority in the Middle East not to crisis prevention but to containment of the Soviet Union. Despite several "successful" attempts by the Reagan administration to avoid war between Syria and Israel, Israel's minister of defense and chief of staff nevertheless anticipated that, in the prevailing political climate in Washington, military action against Syria and the PLO, the two principal allies of the Soviet Union in the core of the Middle East, would not meet with strong opposition from the United States.

Moreover, Secretary of State Haig did approve limited military action and approval of even a limited use of force could be read as permissive of larger-scale military action. In the "fog of war," it is often difficult to control military units and prevent unintended escalation; this indeed was the pervasive concern of senior Pentagon officials who opposed entirely the use of force. Approval of a limited use of force compounded the difficulties of crisis managers attempting to control escalation and terminate the fighting in the days immediately following the outbreak of war.

The plans of Israel's minister of defense made concern with unintended escalation irrelevant. Sharon, who had intentionally planned a wider war with Syria, was able to deceive his cabinet, order military action contrary to their expressed preferences, and secure approval after the fact for military operations that were in progress or had already taken place (Schiff and Ya'ari, 1984 and Feldman and Rechnitz-Kijner, 1985). The deliberate deception of the cabinet as a whole, including the prime minister, multiplied further the difficulties of controlling military action. Communication from the United States went, of course, to the prime minister who was not kept abreast of developments in the field. Before escalation could be controlled, Israel's cabinet had to control its minister of defense.

To explain the American failure to prevent a war between Israel and Syria by faulty communication or by organizational incoherence is not entirely satisfactory. Certainly there was organizational incoherence, both in Washington and in Jerusalem, which greatly facilitated the purposes of Sharon who intended a wider war and frustrated those in the Reagan administration who wished to avoid such a war.

Nor was communication as complete as it might have been. There was no direct exchange, for example, between the prime minister of Israel and the president of the United States before Begin authorized a limited use of force; there was only an ambiguous letter on 28 May from the secretary of state (Schiff and Ya'ari, 1984: 75). Indeed, most of the important discussion occurred with Secretary of State Haig who grudgingly approved a limited war. In the crucial meeting in May, Sharon met not with his counterpart in the Pentagon, who strongly opposed a use of force, but with Secretary of State Haig. That meeting was extraordinarily unrepresentative of opinion in Washington and in Jerusalem.

It is doubtful, nevertheless, that more broadly based communication could have overcome the determination of Defense Minister Sharon to proceed with a wider war and his willingness to deceive his colleagues to circumvent their opposition. Only strong and concerted opposition to any use of force, communicated directly and vigorously to the prime minister of Israel, arguably might have succeeded. Once limited military action was approved by the United States and authorized by the cabinet, Defense Minister Sharon had sufficient leeway to execute his plans.

In 1982, some of Israel's leaders saw the opportunity to defeat the PLO and Syria. Unlike 1967, they were responding not to the fear of loss but to the expectation of gain. Precisely because its ally was neither frightened nor desperate, the United States might have succeeded in preventing a use of force had it tried seriously. The Reagan administration did not share to the same degree the fears of its predecessor administrations of regional war and escalation to confrontation. By the time it actively tried to prevent a use of force, it was too late.

Management Reconsidered

The evidence we have just considered is sobering. We have reviewed four attempts by the United States and the Soviet Union to prevent their allies from initiating war. Although they did not try equally hard in all four cases, they failed in all four despite their estimate that the initiation of war might well lead to a dangerous confrontation with the other superpower. Our evidence suggests, moreover, that in the critical task of crisis prevention, the "managers" were often managed.

The critical differences between the two superpowers cannot in and of themselves account for their common failure to prevent war. Their fundamental differences in systems of governance, in decision-making procedures, in styles of negotiation, in the form and financing of military aid to regional allies, do not explain their shared difficulty in restraining two very different allies. Nor do the special characteristics of the relationship between Israel and the United States, the transnational links between the two societies, explain the inability of the United States to prevent Israel from resorting to force. The evidence also does not support the proposition that the cultural differences between the Soviet Union and Egypt created distinct problems which differed in kind from the relationship between the culturally more similar Israel and the United States. Finally, the scale of force appears to have little impact on the capacity of the superpowers to exercise restraint; both the United States and the Soviet Union experienced similar difficulty in restraining their allies when regional leaders used limited force (Egypt in 1969 and Israel in 1982) and when they initiated large-scale military action (Israel in 1967 and Egypt in 1973).

Extrapolating from the literature on crisis management, we identified two variables which seem especially relevant to the task of crisis prevention: first, political control and organizational coherence in the government of the superpower, and, second, frequent communication between superpower and ally (Richardson, 1987). We looked at the impact of these two factors across the four cases and find them to be relevant only in two of the cases. They were important contributing factors to the inability of the United States to restrain Israel but not relevant to the failure of the Soviet Union to dissuade Egypt from a use of force.

When Israel's leaders became aware of political differences in the inner circles in Washington, as they did both in 1967 and 1982, they were able to exploit these differences to work around those who objected to the use of force. It is extraordinarily difficult in an open system like that of the United States to encourage "multiple advocacy" and simultaneously to maintain close political control in dealing with an ally. The better informed allied leaders are, the more familiar they are with the nuances of political leadership in Washington, the more difficult they will be to manage.

In one of the four cases, it was the absence of political control in an allied government that posed a serious obstacle to effective crisis prevention. When the absence of political control in an allied government is not obvious before the fact, as it was not in Jerusalem in 1982, there is little that a superpower can do to compensate for political and organizational incoherence in its ally.

Maintenance of adequate lines of communication appears to be less significant in enhancing superpower capacity to prevent war. The Soviet Union communicated frequently with Egypt's leadership through political and military channels, yet extensive communication did not reduce divergence between their two perspectives. Israel's representatives succeeded at times in structuring the pattern of communication so that they talked to those whom they knew would tell them what they wanted to hear. It was not so much the presence or absence of communication but the pattern that was critical; communication became a resource for the ally to exploit.

Organizational incoherence and skewed patterns of communication did have some impact in two of the cases, more so in 1982 than in 1967, but much more important were asymmetries in the balance of interests between superpower and ally and the consequent differences in their agendas. In all four cases, the principal explanation of the failure of the superpowers to restrain their allies was the profound differences in their priorities. The ally was attracted to the use of force to protect or enhance basic political and strategic interests while the superpower was motivated largely, though not exclusively, by the desire to avoid a confrontation with a rival patron. In a fundamental sense, there was often a dialogue of the deaf.

This analysis is consistent with other studies of the failure to deter war (George and Smoke, 1974; Lebow, 1981; Jervis, Lebow, and Stein, 1985; and Lebow and Stein, 1987). A recent examination of American attempts to extend deterrence to its allies in the Middle East finds that when challengers are motivated primarily by "vulnerability" rather than by "opportunity," when they feel a compelling need to redress an intolerable situation, when they estimate that the costs of inaction are greater than the costs of military action, they will go to war even if they consider themselves militarily inferior (Stein, 1987). If leaders who find the status quo intolerable or threatening are not deterred by the prospect of military loss, they are unlikely to be deterred long by the opposition of their patron.

In three of these four cases, regional leaders were driven primarily by their sense of "vulnerability." Only in 1982 did Israel's leaders see the opportunity to make significant gains against the PLO and Syria. Because Israel's leaders were motivated largely by the prospect of gain rather than by the fear of loss, in this case the United States had the greatest opportunity to exercise restraint successfully. Paradoxically, it made much less of an effort in 1982 than it did in 1967 when the stakes were far greater for Israel's leadership. In the other three cases, the leaders of Israel and Egypt saw themselves as threatened and weak, vulnerable to growing domestic political opposition at home or military attack from abroad. Under these conditions, it is highly doubtful that any strategy of restraint would have worked.

An explanation of the failure of crisis prevention must also evaluate the quality of the attempts by the superpowers to prevent war. In at least two of the four cases, they did not try as vigorously as they might have to prevent a use of force by their regional ally. In one instance, the American secretary of state was motivated in part by the "opportunity" to inflict a defeat on allies of the Soviet Union and, consequently, approved a limited use of force. In so doing, he gave lower priority to crisis prevention, to the avoidance of loss, than to the prospect of gain. For a brief period, American and Israeli interests coincided until the use of force became imminent and the United States almost reflexively reversed its strategy to focus on crisis prevention. Because the two agendas did coincide briefly, however, the United States was ambivalent and inconsistent in its effort to prevent a use of force. An emphasis on "opportunity" by both Israel and the United States predictably led to war. In 1973, however, the Soviet Union did not pursue crisis prevention as vigorously as it might have because it feared the loss of a strategically important ally. The fear of loss which drives regional leaders to choose force can also constrain a superpower's strategy of crisis prevention.

This study underlines both the limits to the influence of superpowers when they are simultaneously patrons of vulnerable allies deeply enmeshed in regional conflict and the reluctance of the United States and the Soviet Union to face the difficult trade-offs between crisis prevention and alienation of an important regional ally. Its findings are consistent not only with analyses of the limits to extended deterrence in the Middle East but also with investigations of the limits of superpower capability to terminate fighting among their allies in the region.

The Soviet Union and the United States were able to compel their allies to ceasefire in 1967 and 1973 only when an acute crisis between the superpowers seemed imminent. The crisis became acute, however, only when a regional ally confronted imminent military disaster. Only when military action of one ally was politically conclusive were the superpowers able to coerce their clients, but when military action became politically conclusive, crisis and the risk of a confrontation between the superpowers became most acute (Stein, 1980: 518).

The diplomacy of war termination in the Middle East was played by the superpowers at an extraordinarily high threshold of risk because they could not effectively constrain their allies at lower levels. Moreover, as George argues, the tacit norm that impels a superpower to restrain its victorious regional ally does not work automatically; rather, it must be activated by a credible threat of intervention by the defending superpower. In part for this reason, George concludes that " . . . this tacit ground rule *cannot* be regarded as a stable, reliable, basis for enabling superpowers to back their regional client states without being drawn into war with each other"(1985c: 10–11, emphasis in original, and 1985b).

Ours is a pessimistic analysis of the capacity of superpowers to manage their allies in the Middle East. Although thus far they have terminated crises in the region short of war, analysts in both the Soviet Union and the United States are not confident of their capacity to do so in the future. If that record is discouraging—and alarming, their record in preventing crises is far worse. Before exploring the limited policy options that are available to the superpowers, however, a caveat is in order.

It may be that the bias in the selection of cases, the concentration on failure, is skewing the analysis of crisis prevention significantly. A cursory review of the last two decades in the Middle East, however, does not sustain an argument of serious bias. Only one case of "success" in crisis prevention is obvious: the American success in preventing war between Israel and Syria through its mediation in 1976. In 1976, neither Syria nor Israel wanted war, but they needed assistance to break out of the "security dilemma" and the United States provided that assistance. Even then, however, the "success" lasted for only six years, until 1982. American attempts to prevent a use of force by Israel in 1981 again succeeded temporarily but failed shortly thereafter in 1982. Much the same can be said of the Soviet Union; it succeeded in preventing a use of force by Egypt in 1971 and 1972 but indeed only delayed the attack until 1973. It is problematic to consider these cases as examples of successful crisis prevention when the crisis explodes one year later. The evidence suggests that our analysis is not overly pessimistic, that crisis is endemic to superpowers who cohabit an anarchic environment and, consequently, is extraordinarily difficult to prevent (George, 1984a, 1985a, 1985b; and Waltz, 1979).

Scholars have written extensively about the techniques of crisis management and, to a lesser degree, crisis prevention (George, 1983, 1984a, 1985a, 1985b, and 1985c; Lebow, 1987a and 1987b). This analysis of the obstacles to crisis prevention in the Middle East suggests two specific policy implications, one addressed to the "horizontal" relationship between the superpowers and the other to the "vertical" relationship between superpower and ally.

First, superpowers are well-advised to acknowledge the difficulties inherent in crisis prevention and modify their expectations of each other accordingly. Considerable damage was done to the rather fragile relationship between the United States and the Soviet Union in the last decade because of the unrealistic expectations that grew out of "detente" and the adoption of general principles to control competition. In part because Moscow and Washington read the Basic Principles Agreement very differently but also because the objective of crisis prevention could not be realized uniformly across very asymmetric sets of interests in different parts of the world, a general agreement on principles of crisis prevention was almost worse than no agreement whatsoever (Breslauer, 1983; George, 1985a). Because the expectations it created could not be met, the disappointment was predictable as was the consequent increase in suspicion and distrust. If Moscow and Washington were to acknowledge their shared difficulties in managing their allies, if each were to see the other as "managed" as well as "manager," a more realistic set of mutual expectations might govern their relationship. If the superpowers had been sensitive to the capacity of their regional allies to manage them, the damage to their relationship from the October War in 1973 would have been significantly less.

Second, our analysis shows that in three of the four cases, the regional leadership that resorted to force was motivated by a strong sense of vulnerability and of urgency, by an estimate that time was working very much against its interests, and by an expectation that the future would be more intolerable and dangerous than the present. Under these conditions, the most effective strategy available to a superpower is, insofar as possible, to address the underlying issues that are creating the sense of urgency and desperation.

This is very much what the United States attempted to do between Egypt and Israel from 1973 to 1982. It tried to reduce the probability of another, even more dangerous war between the two regional powers: it attempted to reduce Egypt's incentive to attack by securing the return of the Sinai peninsula to Egyptian sovereignty and to enhance Israel's security by designing and sponsoring appropriate security arrangements. Its strategy in the Middle East during those years is best understood not as one of conflict resolution but rather as a strategy of war avoidance between Egypt and Israel. Ironically, Henry Kissinger considered the exclusion of the Soviet Union a necessary component of a strategy of war avoidance. If there has been "success" in crisis prevention in the Middle East, it has been a unilateral American success in reducing the probability of a war between the two most important military powers in the region, a war most likely to engage the superpowers.

Not all conflicts are, in Zartman's apt phrase, "ripe for resolution" (1985a, 1987). Leaders must be pessimistic about the future benefits of a resort to force and anticipate an ongoing and dangerous stalemate. These critical conditions held between Egypt and Israel only after 1973

(Stein, 1983). Even when conflicts are not fully "ripe," however, the superpowers can still attend to the issues that fuel the conflict and, together or individually, examine the agendas of their allies. If they cannot resolve the conflict, and in most cases they are unlikely to be able to do so, they may nevertheless be able to reduce the intensity of those conflicts that are most likely to explode into war. If the superpowers are to prevent as well as manage crises, it will not do only to manage their allies; they must also attend to their allies' fears and insecurities and meet their needs.

Notes

1. Anwar el-Sadat recalled that President Nasser started and continued the war of attrition against the wishes of the Soviet Union (Sadat, 1977: 196).

2. For a penetrating analysis of the impact of the military defeat in 1967 on Egyptian intellectuals and society, see Ajami, 1981.

3. Anwar el-Sadat told an interviewer in April 1973: " . . . the Russians are providing us with everything that is possible for them to supply and I am now quite satisfied" (1973).

4. In an aide-memoire to Israel's ambassador to the United States, Secretary of State Dulles undertook " . . . to exercise the right of free and innocent passage [in the Straits] and to join with others to secure general recognition of this right" (Dulles, 1957). In May 1967, President Johnson contacted President Eisenhower, who confirmed that in 1957 the United States had recognized that if force were used to close the Straits, Israel would be within her rights under Article 51 of the Charter to respond with force (Johnson, 1971: 291).

5. Eban reflected privately on the contradiction between Israel's request to the United States to deter military action by Egypt and its demand for American support of preemptive action by Israel (1977: 352).

6. Paradoxically, the appeal was prompted by Israel's transmission to Washington of its estimate of an imminent Arab attack. The United States in turn asked the Soviet Union to restrain Egypt and the Soviet Union then delivered simultaneous messages to both Cairo and Jerusalem.

7. In a eulogy to President Johnson six years later, Eban disclosed the great weight given to the personal relationship with the president in the expectation that he would deter the Soviet Union: "After so many days of contact with him, in writing and in speech, we could all feel that if Israel took up its own responsibility and emerged intact, it could count on him not to support or even permit a policy of international intimidation" (Eban, 1973).

8. Quandt (1977: 57) notes that, from 31 May on, the State Department was searching for a diplomatic compromise to end the crisis.

9. For an analysis of the irrationalities of Israel's decision-making process in 1967, see Stein and Tanter, 1980.

10. Prime Minister Begin revealed the pledge publicly in a speech to the *Knesset* on 3 June, 1981: " . . . the security and the survival of the Christians

and the preservation of a non-hostile Lebanon are vital to Israel's security." General Eitan denies that he repeated the pledge of air support in December, 1980. (See Schiff and Ya'ari, 1984: 24).

11. Interview with member of Military Intelligence, December, 1983.

12. Interview with member of the National Security Council staff, Washington, February 1982 and with officials in the Department of State, November 1982.

13. Some analysts contend that Haig approved a more extended military operation. See Schiff, 1983 and Quandt, 1984: 239–240. Quandt acknowledges, however, that the United States did not endorse a military operation against Syria or the protracted battle for Beirut. Most convincing is Sharon's denial of American approval, since he would have benefited greatly from American endorsment of the major military operation which he initiated without the approval of Israel's cabinet. See Sharon, 1982 and Haig, 1984: 335.

14. On 9 June, President Reagan wrote to the prime minister of Israel, Menachem Begin, urging a ceasefire. In his letter, he expressed his concern about the possibility of escalation, and alluded to a letter he had received that morning from Secretary-General Leonid Brezhnev (Interview with official in the Foreign Ministry of Israel, December 1983). The Secretary-General had written to the president to express his concern about the possibility of escalation. Secretary of State Alexander Haig described the Soviet message as "frank" but "not threatening" (*The New York Times*, 6 June 1982).

9

Alternative Attempts at Crisis Management: Concepts and Processes

I. William Zartman

The most misleading feature of current work on crisis and negotiations is the presentation of the phenomena as single, shortlived events rather than as moments in a longer evolving context. Crises can only be understood and handled well as part of a general process of ripening and unripening to the point where they burst or fall, with the components of power and interest taking on a new form in the next phase. This is not the same as saying that one must understand the historical background of a conflict in order to be able to resolve it, although it does recognize that the shape of a crisis is determined by its history. Nor does it mean to imply that conflict has a course of its own that is impervious to damming, although it does emphasize that the effectiveness of the dam is determined as much by the currents and banks as by the skills of the engineer and his choice of materials. It does assert that crises are the product of a course of events and not an isolated event of their own, and that crisis management involves a particular manipulation of the power and interests of the parties to the conflict in the course of their evolution.

However, all moments in that evolution are not equally propitious for dealing with conflict and crisis. Ripe moments, or windows of opportunity, can be identified in their essential characteristics and then recognized in the event; once recognized they can be seized upon to move the conflict toward management and even resolution. Ripe moments are associated with crises but are not identical to them; they tend to come before or after but not usually during a crisis. If they can be identified, they can also be created, or at least the conditions for their creation can be identified, even if they may be difficult to bring about in reality (Zartman, 1985). Identifying the ripe moment, seizing it, and creating it are not unambiguous actions, just as the ripening process or the appearance of ripe moments are not unambiguous events. There is likely to be lots of "dirt" in the product and noise in the channels, and countertendencies of some strength are certain to be vying for control of the flow of events.

But timing and ripening are not enough, either. For the crisis to be surmounted and the conflict managed, if not resolved, the interests of the parties must be clearly understood and then shaped into a common understanding of the problem and its solution—a formula which can both frame the problem within a common notion of justice and provide a guideline for implementing details (Zartman, 1978; Zartman and Berman, 1982). Finding a formula for agreement is a product of negotiating skill, but it is also a function of the evolving currents of conflict. The negotiator takes the issues and interests of the parties in conflict and fashions them into an agreement. Even if he fails, his efforts leave those strands of the conflict twisted in new directions, and often-repeated failures—partially ineffective attempts at success—are necessary before a final effective attempt at success can be achieved. Success at one of these earlier moments would not be possible, even if agreement were reached among the parties, because the position of the parties—the elements of the conflict—had not evolved enough to provide the basis of a lasting solution. There is no appropriate way of conceptualizing the "distance" between parties' positions; therefore it is hard to deal with the commonplace impression that parties can sometimes find formulas to bridge a large gap while other parties remain unable to overcome the remaining small space that divides them. Hence, the challenge of formulation is not a mechanical test but one of innovative and creative skill.

It may help, in connection with the ideas of ripening and of formulation, to evoke the concept of "regime" which is currently much in use (Krasner, 1983). Regime can be considered a set of international rules and institutions governing relations around an issue. Conflicts may arise within a regime but the institutions are generally established to handle disputes within the given relations. If not satisfactorily handled, the conflict may then turn to challenge the regime itself, since it is inadequate to take care of the new turn in relations. The Hay-Bunau-Varilla Treaty on Panama, crown colony status for Rhodesia, colonial status for the Falklands and for Cyprus were all regimes governing the structure of power in these four territories, for example. Conflict arose either to challenge these regimes and/or to establish new power structures within a replacement regime. Power, its relations and its distribution were in flux before the actual collapse of the *ancien régime*, and it was the shifting power relations which had to be taken into account in the successor. The key, then, to a successful new regime which would resolve the conflict was to contain and reflect the new power relations among the interested parties.

In some ways, a formula resembles a regime in that it provides a general framework for an agreement. However, there are many formulas: each party comes to the conflict with one or more in hand, and the two (or more) parties may even agree to a joint formula without actually resolving the conflict. Furthermore, parties may agree on the ultimate regime for the conflict area but not agree on how to get there. In these cases, it is the transition formula that is most necessary. Since politics is taken up with the meanwhile, transitions often overshadow final solutions. To keep matters straight, "regimes" here will refer to the power arrangements in place, and "formulas" will refer to the various proposals—adopted or not, resolving or not—which are put forward to create agreement.

Frequently, parties to the conflict are unable to perfect their evolution or find their formulas for agreement on their own. The pressures of the conflict remain too powerful to allow them the necessary momentum and creativeness to overcome their differences. At such times, a mediator is needed (Jackson, 1952; Young, 1967; Rubin, 1981; Touval, 1982; Touval and Zartman, 1985). The amount of mediation necessary may vary, but the mediators' presence does not change the nature of the management and resolution process. It merely introduces an additional player—an interested catalyst who helps the process along without being a party to the conflict, but who almost invariably has an interest in ending the conflict, even if not in any particular way. From the process point of view, effective negotiators can be thought of as mediators in their own conflict, since as individuals they may be interested above all in solutions, but may have to deal with home teams and issues which are more closely wedded to the maintenance of conflict, or at least those positions which produce conflict. When conflict and crisis are powerful enough to keep negotiators ineffective, catalysts are needed to make the management process work.

These four notions—ripening conflict, ripe moment, formula, mediation—are the basic elements in an analysis of recent significant conflicts. The cases used as a data base are Panama, Rhodesia/Zimbabwe, Cyprus, and Falklands/Malvinas (Bendamane and McDonald, 1986; Zartman, 1986). Two of these cases were successful. Negotiations between Panama and the U.S. ended 13 years of open conflict on 10 August, 1977 by establishing a new regime for the Panama Canal; the agreement was signed on 10 September and ratified after much difficulty on 16 June, 1978. It replaced the regime created by the 1903 treaty by shifting sovereignty over the canal from the U.S. to Panama, and worked out defense and operations relations for a fixed period of this new regime (Jorden, 1984; Scranton and Furlong, 1984; Linowitz, 1985; Habeeb, 1986). Negotiations among the Rhodesian parties in the presence of the British ended 15 years of conflict on 21 December, 1979 by establishing conditions for an independent regime, Zimbabwe; the elections were held in April, 1980 and independence was declared on 18 April. The agreement shifted sovereignty from the British, and away from the Rhodesian Front's unilateral claims of independence in 1965, to the new independent state and its Patriotic Front majority government, and it provided some conditions for the operation of the new state (Davidow, 1983; Davidow, 1984; Low, 1985.). Quite obviously, both new situations contained some continuing elements of conflict, but the major issue— in both cases the vital issue of sovereignty—was solved (and many minor issues with it) and a new set of relations among the parties was created.

Two other cases were apparent failures. Negotiations between Great Britain and Argentina during the southern hemisphere winter of 1982 failed to prevent the Argentinian take-over of the Falkland Islands (which triggered the last phase of negotiations), the British reconquest, and the embittered return to the status quo which underlay the conflict. Negotiations had begun in 1966, but the resort to violence 16 years later destroyed apparently ripening chances for a change in regime through a shift in sovereignty, and provided no future procedures for handling the problem. Its most immediate impact was to topple the government in the defeated party, Argentina. Similarly, negotiations have been a continuous if intermittent event in Cyprus, but the latest round in 1985 broke down, leaving unresolved the status quo created by the Turkish invasion 11 years earlier. Negotiations brought independence to Cyprus in 1960 and a cease-fire in 1967, but the resulting regime was not stable, and the attempt to change the status quo in 1974 by Greece brought a new status imposed by Turkey. Again, the most immediate impact was the fall of the Greek regime (Dobell, 1967; Weintal and Bartlett, 1967; Harbottle, 1980; Polyviou, 1980.).

Clearly, both Falklands and Cyprus do not represent final failures of conflict resolution or crisis management, but landmarks in the evolution of the problem, making it more difficult to resolve but also changing the power relations between the sides and demanding new solutions. The basic questions, for analysts and practitioners alike, can be applied to both cases: How was the conflict handled at the time of crisis or resolution? and, why was it not handled earlier to provide resolution and forestall crisis? To find these answers, the analysis will turn to the four parameters already introduced before returning to aggregate responses to the questions.

Formulas, Regimes, and Ripening

The concepts of formula and ripening conflict will have to be taken together because the whole ripening process is part of a search for an appropriate formula to resolve the conflict. The notion of a search should not be taken to imply that what may eventually be the formula for resolution was never mentioned until that time. Indeed, to the contrary, it is most likely that the idea itself was mentioned occasionally earlier on but was never seriously considered—at least not seriously enough to be adopted—by the parties. This fact only heightens the importance of the original question, for if the idea was in the air, why was it not adopted earlier? Part of the answer, to be examined in this section, is that the parties were simply too far apart in their own notions of formula during the earlier stages of the conflict to be able to make the big jump that the resolving formula would have required. But the answer may (although need not) be seen as tautological: The parties were too far apart because they were too far apart. Independent variables will therefore be sought to provide better answers, in this and the following sections.

For over half a century the Panama Canal was governed by a formula or regime established in the Hay-Bunau-Varilla Treaty of 1903. Unilateral American control, exercise of sovereign rights, perpetuity and payment of rent to Panama were the elements of the regime under which the Canal was operated. The 1955 implementation agreement was the last U.S.-Panama treaty to embody the 1903 elements, and it was soon challenged by the 1958–59 demonstrations over the question of Panamanian flags. The U.S. reaffirmed Panama's "titular sovereignty" and proceeded to implement a two-flag policy, which was then challenged in bloody riots in January 1964 that began with American Zonians' challenge to the policy and ended with Panamanians' rebellion against it. Before the end of the next year, new guidelines were issued by the two governments which formed the basis of a new formula. The Johnson-Robles Guidelines of 1964 called for a new treaty to replace the 1903 regime, linking the Panama Canal administration to the construction of a new sea-level canal, but not specifying the new regime. The formula was completed in the 1967 treaties negotiated between the two countries, which established a joint defense, justice and administration for the Canal on the basis of Panamanian sovereignty. Initialed on 20 June, 1967, the treaties were never signed and never submitted for ratification; the election of a hostile Panamanian government in part on the Canal issue showed that the proposed regime did not contain a resolving formula.

Negotiations resumed in 1971 and quickly ran aground on very differing formulas of jurisdiction, the U.S. demanding longterm rights to operate and defend the Canal and the Panamanians calling for a shorter treaty and effective sovereignty. The American-proposed formula was a reversion toward the 1903 formula from the 1967 regimes, since the escape provided by the sea-level possibility had proven unworkable. Two quotes from the two sides frame the issue: The U.S. negotiator indicated the U.S. wanted to go "as far as we can go" but not "from 100 to 0," while the Panamanian negotiator answered that "your proposal does not resolve the causes of the conflict" (Jorden, 1984: 156). Panama then took the issue to a special meeting of the U.N. Security Council in Panama City, forcing the U.S. to veto the resolution. There was a complete stalemate. There was no avenue left for resolution; the threat of violence and crisis was increasing, but without any possibility of bringing its own resolution, and the parties were wise enough to grasp this situation.

The result of this stalemate was the negotiation of the Kissinger (Bunker)-Tack Principles of 1974 which set the basic formula for the final resolution: sovereignty and jurisdiction would revert to Panama, perpetuity would be replaced with fixed-duration agreements, defense and administration would be handled jointly, and Panama was to receive a just and equitable share of benefits recognizing the Canal as its principal resource. On this basis negotiations were conducted from June, 1974 to March, 1975. In the process they carried each of the eight principles as far as possible from general agreement into details, ending in "threshold agreements" in November and then a status of forces agreement. When the implementing details aroused opposition in the home capitals, the negotiators returned for more detailed instructions, including a two-treaty formula that allowed for different durations for operations and defense agreements. Negotiations were interrupted from September, 1975 to February, 1977 to allow for the American presidential campaign. Six months after resumption, the negotiations were completed on the two treaties. In the Panamanian case, there was an unusual coda to the movement, in that negotiations then shifted from the executive to the legislative branch over the following ten months. The negotiations were among the most hostile of the whole conflict, but it is important to note that, conceptually, they were never able to shake the formula that resolved the issue between the two parties. Details were renegotiated, but the regime of 1974, refined in 1975 and 1977, stuck.

Thus, the four rounds of negotiation—1965–67, 1971–72, 1973–75, 1977–78—represent a ripening of the conflict in terms of formulas, in which various types of replacement regimes were tried and either did not receive joint agreement or did not resolve the causes of the conflict. The concept introduces an unusual notion in discussions of conflict resolution, for it suggests that agreement between parties is not enough: the formula must satisfy the demands of the conflict as well if it is to be a resolving formula. The 1971–72 negotiations produced no agreement and it is easy to see why, in these terms. The parties actually backtracked from their previously agreed positions. But the 1967 agreements would not have resolved the conflict either, even though there was a joint decision. The longterm defense commitment, the joint jurisdiction as well as administration, the administrative autonomy, and the sea-level canal tie-in were all elements which would have continued the conflict despite the agreement. But a 1977 agreement was not obtained ten years earlier and by all indications was not obtainable. On the other hand, the 1967 and 1972 terms had to be tried out before they could be discarded. More broadly, alternative solutions—of which these two were the most prominent—had to be considered and discarded and the particularly prominent one tried before being discarded. Thus, by trying to find and apply agreement on the two prominent alternatives, the negotiation ripened the process and cleared the way for a final resolution of the conflict.

The same process is visible even more fully in Zimbabwe. The regime under which Rhodesia was governed was established in 1923, when it received self-governing crown colony status for its white minority, and was changed little by its incorporation into the Central African Federation in the late 1950s. When the Federation collapsed in 1963 as its other members proceeded to independence under majority rule, Rhodesia was confronted with the conflict between the divergent implications of its own status: either self-government should be extended to all citizens, or it should be carried to independence under minority rule. The latter was chosen in 1965, leaving the former colonizer and the African majority allied in opposition to the Rhodesian Front's Unilateral Declaration of Independence. Britain and the majority declared their position to be NIBMAR—No Independence Before Majority African Rule. When U.K. tried to negotiate something less, an outcome between the two parties' positions, it was rejected by the UDI government first, as in the *Tiger* talks in 1966 and the *Fearless* talks in 1968, or by the nationalist organizations, as before the Pearce Commission in 1972. During this period, the UDI government was in a strong position and its option had not yet been disproven; the African movements could not accept the compromise that the U.K. sought to offer. After 1974, the tables began to turn, as Rhodesia now became encircled by independent territory and the national liberation struggle heated up, as a result of the fall of the Portuguese empire. But it took time for this change to become apparent, even though it raised the commitment and expectations of the African parties. Therefore, direct negotiations in 1974–75 sponsored by South Africa and Zambia collapsed as well; the Rhodesian government was still too strong to compromise and the Zimbabwean nationalists were too weak to agree. In 1976, the mediator was American and the formula involved majority-rule independence in two years with a joint transitional government in exchange for economic support from the U.S. But the formula was not clear, the endpoint was obliterated by the transition, the mediators had spent their leverage just to get a hearing for their proposals, and the effort failed.

UDI as a regime was losing its ability to appear as a solution but a new regime remained to be tested—an internal settlement with an appearance of power-sharing but an effective maintenance of the Rhodesian government. This was tried in 1978–79. It was clearly doomed to failure, since conflicting formulas for not sharing power could not be bridged by a formula for sharing power. But under the circumstances it had to be tried so that it could be disproven in fact, as it was in logic, or proven in fact against all logic. It was the first that happened, opening the way for the final Lancaster House negotiations. They returned the conflict to the early 1960s, but with all the competing alternative regimes now ruled out. Under restored British auspices, a democratic constitution and a one-man-vote election (NIBMAR), proceded by a brief transition and a cease-fire, provided the temporary and permanent regimes for the transfer and exercise of sovereignty.

In the Zimbabwean case, the resolving formula was in the air nearly two decades before it was finally adopted, but the conflict had to catch up with it. That ripening process of the conflict involved both trying and discarding alternative formulas and also undergoing power shifts to approximate more closely the positions of the parties in the final regime. Unlike Panama, there was never any agreement among the parties on an insufficient alternative. The possible exception was the internal settlement, but it does not qualify because it did not involve enough of the parties to constitute a resolution of the conflict. Somewhat like Panama, however, the resolving formula was even more advanced than the initial demands of the newly benefitting side; the original NIBMAR formula focused more on a transition than the final settlement, but the fifteen to twenty years lost in the evolution of the conflict more than absorbed the time of transition. Thus the conflict ripened to the point where a stable resolving formula could be negotiated. In this light, none of the failed negotiations actually represented a step backwards, but rather were used, and perhaps were necessary, to clear the way for the step forward constituted by the final negotiated settlement.

This interpretation—and the case—raises as many new questions as it answers. Ripening involves elimination of salient alternatives, but which alternatives are salient is a matter of judgment. Internal settlement is clearer in its saliency than in its viability as an alternative, yet it had to be tried to be discarded. Ripening carries the conflict to the point where parties are confronted with a resolving formula, but does it preclude earlier resolution? A close examination of the conflict shows at least four periods when a similar regime (probably with a different transition) might have been negotiated, although such insights are impossible to prove. In the early 1960s, at the breakup of the Federation and then at the time of UDI, a firmer British response might have been conclusive. In the late 1970s, at the end of 1975 and the end of 1978, the parties were very close to agreement. Yet the fact that these moments did not produce resolution indicates at least that their lesson is not absolute. They may tell us something about ripe moments *per se*, or about mediators, both examined below, but they do not refute the notion that reality unfortunately requires a ripening process or that its components involve parties' positions, viable formulas, and parties' power.

The Cyprus question in its modern version has been a problem in search of a regime for thirty years. The Cyprus question is complicated by the fact that there is still no firm agreement on the nature of the problem—whether it is a dispute between Greece and Turkey, or a dispute between the two Cypriot communities. From 1960 to 1974, there was ostensible agreement on the second, but the first interpretation rose to upset the regime which had been unsteadily established as an answer to the wrong question. Both problems were joined in the independence regime, which defeated an alternative concept of majoritarian rule with civil rights guarantees in favor of a bicommunal government linked with treaties of guarantee ("alliance" and "establishment") to the two neighboring countries and to Britain. Within a few years, bicommunalism had destroyed unitary government operations. In 1964, civil war greeted the attempt to revise the constitutional regime and American mediation proposed a looser alternative of communal autonomy within a unitary administration. Continued civil war brought effective communal autonomy patrolled by UNICYP troops. Civil war again in 1967 provoked even greater communal separation, utilized then as the basis for intercommunal talks. But the results were neither successful in reaching agreement nor satisfactory in finding a resolving formula for the conflict, and in 1974 the Greek military regime returned the problem to its international dimension by attempting *enosis* (union with Greece). Turkish troops intervened to support the Turkish zone, and effective partition, with a third of the island in Turkish hands, resulted. In 1975, the Turkish Cypriots declared a Turkish Federated State of Cyprus, and negotiations began within a year under U.N. auspices to replace the two-state regime with a one-state federal regime. However, in 1983, the Turkish Cypriots made their unilateral declaration of independence. Not long after, in January 1985, the federal formula was complemented by details on several aspects of its implementation, but talks broke off due to disagreement over the amount of agreement that had prevailed.

The Cyprus dispute includes several crises and, to date, no resolving formula. What appeared to be one in 1960 was undone in practice, both by the Greek-Cypriot-dominated government and then by the Greek military regime. As a result, there has been a conflict ripening away from the bicommunal regime toward a more strongly separated federal regime, still within a single state. Other alternatives—*enosis*, two-state regime—have been tried, as in Panama and Zimbabwe, but unlike these cases, the alternatives have not been fully rejected nor has their experiment served to reinforce the original and remaining regime. To the contrary, a quarter-century experience has shown the original agreement not to be a resolving formula. As of 1985, the parties were tinkering with the details of a new formula, but underneath the dispute over details remains the more basic dispute on the nature of interrelations of the two units: separate and equal, or proportional and cooperating. The sense of justice which is so basic to the nature of a formula and which found expression in the "one-man-one-vote majority rule" notion in Zimbabwe and the "single-sovereignty-and-jurisdiction but joint administration and defense" notion in Panama is still elusive in Cyprus.

Thus, there are two ways in which the ripening can be perceived: one as an "unripening" or exacerbation of conflict away from an initial agreement, and the other as the evolution of the conflict toward a new (but not necessarily final or resolving) regime. The latter is more helpful, because it fits into a broader interpretation and provides insights into the evolution and resolution of conflict and crisis. If the Cyprus problem can be seen as a bumpily evolving conflict, then the independence regime in 1960, the unitarizing reforms of the 1960s, *enosis* in 1974, partition and bi-state status since the mid-1970s, and possibly even the UNICYP patrols since 1964 were all attempts at trying out alternative regimes in an effort to find the one that worked. Negotiation in this type of situation serves two purposes. It not only works to bring the parties' views together on an agreeable (satisfying) formula, as is commonly supposed, but it also seeks to eliminate by logic and persuasion the alternatives other than a resolving formula. It is not enough to bring the parties to agreement; the agreement must also solve the problem, and it must lock the parties into their agreed solution without leaving them leeway or temptation to try out alternatives. In other words, the alternatives must be shown to be logically inoperative, structurally unavailable, and less attractive to the parties than the agreed solution. This is less difficult in a Zimbabwe where one of the parties is corporately dissolved, or even in a Panama, where one party holds sovereignty but where there is an operative interdependence in other fields, than it is in Cyprus where the parties are locked in a position of separable inequality.

These insights add to the understanding gained in the previous cases, particularly in regard to the identification of missed opportunities and also to the identification of resolving, as opposed to merely agreeable, formulas. They reinforce the notion, current in many analyses, that the conflict took a turn for the worse in 1974 because the problem was turned into a Greek-Turkish dispute, a level from which it had been removed in 1960. It was not necessary to try out the *enosis* and invasion alternatives; they had already been firmly excluded when the conflict was defined as an inter-communal. This analysis only establishes the importance of forestalling the events of 1974, not its possibility, which will have to await discussions of the ripe moment in the following section.

In regard to resolving regimes, the Cyprus negotiations show that resolution must take into account the parties involved, their legitimate existence, and their power relations. The 1960 regime did the first admirably, in bringing in British, Greek and Turkish commitment to the settlement along with that of the two Cypriot communities. But the second and third elements were in conflict, since the power of the Greek community in the bicommunal regime threatened the legitimate existence of the Turkish Cypriot community, and the temptation to use the structural basis of that power was not resisted by the Greek Cypriot government. A federal regime seems to meet these requirements more realistically, although aspects of both the formula and the details remain to be negotiated.

Finally, the Falklands conflict illustrates an attempt to move from one regime to another which broke down over the parties' inability to find a formula for the transition. The conflict itself never seems to have ripened. Rather, the old regime appeared more and more anachronistic but never untenable in reality nor weakened in its original justification: basic principles of self-determination would leave the islands in British hands, and only less certain principles of geography would shift them to Argentina. In between, an independence regime lacked the support of a self-determining population or the prospect of viability. Negotiations which began in 1966 reached agreement five years later on the principle of gradual transfer of sovereignty from Britain to Argentina. After a half-decade pause to consider modalities, negotiations resumed in 1977 but no formula for the transfer was discovered. Argentinian impatience rose. In 1981, Britain offered a leaseback formula, with sovereignty to be given to Argentina but the islands leased back to Britain. When Argentina and the Falklanders rejected the idea, formulas for divided sovereignty were considered, then rejected, as negotiations broke down again in February, 1982. After issuing thinly veiled warnings in January and February, Argentina took over the South Georgia Islands in March and the Falklands in April. The issue of the crisis to be resolved now included not only the future regime and the transition but also the liquidation of hostilities. In the subsequent two months, until British troops restored the *status quo ante*, American, Peruvian and U.N. mediators tried to revive negotiations on the basis of various formulas which had been discussed in previous years. In all proposals, liquidation of hostilities was to be accomplished by cease-fire, the withdrawal of forces, and an interim international administration. The American proposal foresaw a condominium as a future regime, whereas the Peruvian and U.N. Secretary General's proposals foresaw merely a commitment to negotiate under some mediating auspices.

Ripening was therefore not characteristic of this conflict and in its absence there was no elimination of alternative regimes. But there was an elimination of the military option, at least for a while. The war put the conflict back on the negotiators' table, with unilateral attempts at solution shown to be unsuccessful on both sides.

Lessons of Formulas and Ripening

It is now possible to pull together some answers to basic questions about formulas and the ripening process. What is the nature of the ripening process? What determines its pace, or why does it not lead to earlier agreement? Does the process proceed on its own? Can there be lost opportunities, and how can one avoid losing them?

The ripening process is composed of four elements: the collapse of the original regime, the elimination of alternative regimes, the readjustment of power relations among the parties, and the identification of a resolving formula (including a transitional formula to a new regime). For the first, "collapse" may be a misleading term for the eroding of the *ancien regime*, since its inadequacies and unworkable nature only become evident gradually. It is this gradual and perceptional nature that is the key to the whole process, since some see the old order as outmoded before it is, while others do not see its passing long after it has happened. As will be seen in regard to other elements in the process, slow, differential, and uncertain learning practiced by human beings is what makes for uneven ripening. As the inadequacies of the old regime appear in perception and in practice, the conflict provides pressure for a new arrangement to meet the parties needs and interests. The cost of maintaining the crumbling regime against attack adds to that pressure. Conceivably, these efforts may succeed in restoring the old order at bearable cost, but if the conflict becomes sufficiently vigorous to be marked by events that cost enough to be termed crises, it is likely to require new solutions that involve the input and agreement of all the parties; that is, it is likely to require negotiations.

The second element of the ripening process serves to eliminate alternative regimes. It may do so by allowing time for reflection, but if that were all it would mark a perfect, philosophical world. As in the case of the old regime, new ones too have to be tried, tested, and fought over in order to be discarded. What is referred to here is a unilateral effort, in which one side proposes, applies, defends, and the other side rejects. There is more involved than merely a matter of floating ideas; breakdown of negotiations or crisis in the field result when one side decides to press a favorite alternative to see whether it can solve the problem and finally win agreement. Thus, *enosis* in Cyprus, UDI in Rhodesia and Cyprus, leaseback in Panama, and also unilateral transition in the Falklands are all attempts to try a different regime to replace the old order. The collapse or defeat of alternatives continues the conflict but it also narrows the possible outcomes. Sometimes it may eliminate the only remaining ones, leaving the parties with no evident way out. The conflict continues, a problem without a solution until new elements appear to make resolution possible.

The third element is the change in power relations. The prospect of the elimination of one party (who therefore wants to make a deal while there is still time, as in Rhodesia) or the gradual equalization of party power (as practiced in Cyprus and Panama, and attempted in the Falklands) are the two apparent forms of power change that characterise the ripening process. In fact, the first blends into the second, since it is the weakening, not the disappearance, of the stronger party, bringing the power structure closer to equality that is propitious for settlement (Zartman, 1985: 235; Zartman, 1985). The negotiation literature is dominated by the notion that equality is best for satisfactory settlements (Rubin and Brown, 1975: 199, 213–222; Deutsch, 1973; Hopmann, 1978), a judgment too stark to be applied strictly to the real world but important enough to provide insights into complex situations (Habeeb, 1986). As will be seen in the following section, it is stalemate that prepares for negotiation, and stalemate means mutually blocking vetos. Turkish Cypriots sought to move toward equality when inequality proved to be the basis of the problem. The rising threat of a Panamanian mob veto on Canal operations pressed the acuity of the Panamanian problem; Panama never was the equal of the U.S. to be sure, but in the Canal

Zone Panama could raise the operating costs so high as to constitute an effective challenge to American power. The African nationalist Patriotic Front and the white settler Rhodesian Front teetered along the line of equality in the late 1970s as the former rose in strength (but not enough to take over immediately) and the latter sank (but not enough to lose its claim to a few privileges and a fair electoral chance before giving up power). One key to the Falklands problem was that there were not such incremental ways of shifting, let alone equalizing, power. Distance helped a bit, as did the wave of anticolonial feelings, but neither was conclusive. All that was left was for Argentina to make a total grab, and the very cost of repulsing it fit the mood of Britain at the time. That is why there was little ripening process in the South Atlantic.

Fourth, the culmination of the ripening process is the emergence of a resolving formula. In the spirit of the other three elements, the right formula is more than a bright idea (although that is the beginning). It is an idea that takes hold, that is considered, discussed, debated, tinkered with, tested, probably even discarded and reinvented as it begins to look better in comparison with alternatives. Again, the accent is on the perceptual, even experiential element, rather than a cold checklist of ingredients. Yet the ingredients of a resolving formula appear from the cases as well. They include a new regime that solves the major problems, a common definition of the issue at conflict, a working relation among the parties involved, an inclusion of the major parties concerned, and a notion of justice underlying the solution. Within these five guidelines, the rest is invention. However, the cases also show the need for an additional element in the settlement, and that is a transitional formula— a way of getting from the current conflict (or the collapsing *ancien regime*) to the new regime. Often this is more crucial than the resolving formula to the settlement of the conflict. One may differ on the percentage of the conflict or solution that lay in the transition in Panama, Rhodesia or the Falklands, but it was at least half, and perhaps all in Cyprus where the 1960 bicommunal regime might have provided a new era if it had worked.

The answer to many of the initial questions is found in the nature of the ripening process. Its pace is determined by the learning and perceiving of the parties, for which there is no fixed rate. Attempts to maintain old regimes or to find alternatives are necessary, but they slow down the evolution of the conflict and their failure often creates bitterness that further slows progress. Yet some alternatives must be tried; confrontation groups are no substitute and simulations are uncertain. Since politics is risk-taking, the trial-and-error nature of the process goes on. Since power relations are a basic and inevitable part of the conflict, as much as is justice, the process goes even further, and since both power and justice are changing and ambiguous, it goes even further yet. The process proceeds on its own, although humans are its agents, pursuers as well as perceivers. It can be accelerated by a pragmatic search for solutions, innovative thinking, quick learning, attention to the components of a formula, and a sense of the ripe moment. It is to the latter that the next section turns.

Ripe Moment

There are times when efforts at resolving conflict are more likely to succeed than others. Since conflict resolution and crisis management mean coming to terms with the opponent and making a joint decision rather than pursuing the conflict unilaterally, it seems logical that certain conditions favor such a shift of perceptions and activities. Such conditions are independent of the distance which separates the positions of the two sides; hence they work on the evolution of the conflict but are outside the previously discussed elements that constitute that ripening process. Professional diplomats often talk in terms of "a ripe moment" or a "window of opportunity," but little attention has been given to more precise identifications that would allow analysts and practitioners to better discern the moment or eventually to create it.

Ripeness is associated with conditions where parties realise that their attempts to solve the problem and pursue their goals alone are unlikely to succeed at an acceptable price. Therefore, they are amenable to looking for jointly established alternatives. The elements of such a moment are a deadlock or blockage to competing unilateral solutions, a high or rising cost, valid spokesmen, and an alternative way out that reduces the cost but achieves an acceptable number of the goals and interests originally sought. A ripe moment may therefore be characterized as a mutually hurting stalemate with a way out. Each of the four elements needs further examination.

The deadlock or plateau in the conflict relations must constitute a longterm stalemate with no prospect of escape through escalation of the conflict. It is the attempt to break out of a stalemate by a sudden raise in the stakes or a grab for the prize that makes a crisis, quite the opposite situation from the deadlock into which the parties are locked without hope of unilateral escape. Parties will consider the chances of effective escalation when they find themselves in stalemate, but a negative conclusion on its cost-effectiveness leads them into a ripe moment for resolution. It is important to emphasize as well the necessity of being "locked in." A situation where neither party has been able to prevail in the conflict but where each has lots of untried alternatives is not a deadlock or statemate; it is simply a situation of unattained goals with many means of achieving them. Stalemate implies that these means are (considered) exhausted.

The deadline or precipice is the element related to cost that turns the stalemate into a ripe moment. People learn to live with stalemates, even unpleasant ones. Therefore the stalemate must actually hurt, so that the parties feel that things can't go on like this and something must be done to find a way out. Pain or cost inherent in the stalemate is one element in this pressing need but it too is not likely to be enough. What is needed is a sharp change in costs, a catastrophe that will make matters much worse if a way is not found to come to agreement. The timing of the catastrophe is the most ambiguous element in the scenario. It would be nice to think that a looming catastrophe—a deadline—would be most effective, since then the threatening situation with all its costs would not have to be played out. Unfortuntely, in the terms previously discussed, looming catastrophes often constitute the last, risky chance a party has to escalate its way out of the stalemate, and as such it may have to be played out to be proven illusory. As in the very nature of threats, effectiveness—and especially cost-effectiveness—is greater if the threat is not used, but threats are not infallible—also by their very nature. Therefore, the catastrophe may well have to be past to be effective in defining the ripe moment. Perhaps most effective is the catastrophe narrowly missed, whose credibility is no longer in doubt but whose actual application is avoided. Thus, the ripe moment comes from a stalemate that is both costly and related to a sharp increase in cost without any corresponding escapability.

The third component is as obvious as the others but nevertheless crucial—the existence of valid spokesmen for each side. Even when dealing with two sovereign states, the institutional spokesmen may be so constrained by a hostile or divided domestic setting that they become unable to enter into the give and take that diplomacy requires. In such a case—and such a case is present to some extent in almost any governmental situation—it becomes necessary for the opponent to enter the other party's domestic politics. This does not mean subversion, the physical entry into political interaction, but it does mean careful consideration of the way in which each party's moves are viewed by and affect the political actors on the other side. In addition to putting across its own point, each party must try to provide the opposing leader with a position that can be sold at home, or that can help build a constituency and consolidate a position as valid spokesman for the other side. Often this involves tradeoffs, different levels of emphasis, and careful language, but sometimes two different positions must be cut out of the same issue, a delicate job. The problem is obviously more complicated when one side or another is composed of many parties. Then, one of the functions of the whole process may be to create a valid spokesman so that negotiations can begin.

The fourth element requires less discussion since it has already been covered. A ripe moment needs to have the possibility of a way out. Locked in a worsening stalemate with no way out, parties can turn desperate and irrational, seizing unreal opportunities for escalation that only make matters worse. This element may actually reinforce the notion of a precipice, but it needs to be complemented with the possibility of a joint solution. This consideration returns the analysis to the question of a resolving formula, discussed above.

The Falkland situation in March, 1982 illustrates the concept well. The negotiated deadlock was perceived as total and was painful, but only to one side. The moment was scarcely ripe because of the asymmetry, and the thinly veiled threats from Argentina implying that the cost for Britain was rising were not believed. Furthermore, there was no attractive way out, in this case no appealing transitional formula that bridged the two competing ideas of justice. A number of putative formulas were floated, however, and might have constituted a range of resolving formulas had the moment been ripe.

But the Falklands also show ways of manipulating reality and changing perceptions. The problem in creating the ripe moment was the absence of symmetry and credibility; even Secretary of State Alexander Haig could not convey the threat of a British recapture persuasively. However, had the Argentines effected only a symbolic capture, making their own threat credible but not a direct invitation to its own undoing, the hurting quality of the stalemate would have been shared, and the ripe moment created. This would have required something like a unilateral withdrawal by the Argentines, except perhaps for a token police force in the post office, accompanied by a public invitation to complete the negotiations. Another possibility would have been public occupation—to complete the "private" take-over—of the South Georgia Islands, followed by the same sort of invitation providing a way out.

The third lesson of the Falklands is that moments can be riper after the crisis than before. Argentina and Britain had both shown that they could take the Islands, albeit with some heavy cost. The virility of each was demonstrated, at appropriate pain (virility shows best with a bit of pain). However, the cost and pain was enough to cause doubts about a repeat adventure on either side; the castatrophe was more effective past than looming, and once an appropriate face-saving time had passed, private and then even official contacts could be revived. But they have not been pursued with any urgency, and have died. The last caution on past catastrophes, therefore, is that their memory fades and their effectiveness dims as time goes on. Ripe moments are indeed often only moments.

A similar ripe moment was missing but might have been created in Cyprus in 1974. Again, the threat of invasion was not credible, this time because it was so illegitimate, the same barrier which reduced the threatened power of a Turkish invasion. But external intervention to eliminate the invasion before it occurred or immediately thereafter could have capitalized on the catastrophe to create a propitious time for revising the regime or reinforcing its workability. Since then, ripeness has been elusive and the concept indicates why. There is nothing really painful about the stalemate to the two sides. Greek Cyprus learns to live with its reduced size, Turkish Cyprus learns to live with its lack of recognition. Only the first element of the ripe moment is present but the second is missing, and indeed the threats have all been played out, leaving no catastrophes on the horizon.

Other near moments occurred in Cyprus with some of the same characteristics as early 1974, when there was practically an agreement among Cypriots that was turned down by one or both of the neighboring capitals in hopes of a better deal. For example, in July, 1978, a proposal to break the deadlock on Varosha was turned down by the Greek Cypriots until it was too late, in the hopes of getting a better offer. In January, 1985, when Turkish pressure had gotten a U.N. Turkish-Cypriot agreement on the new federal formula, the framework was rejected by the Greek Cypriots in hopes of negotiating better details, a manifest confusion of formula and detail. The Turkish Cypriots then pressed Ankara for a constitution and elections, further steps toward sovereignty. The moment remained propitious for agreement, even if some of the elements of ripeness were still absent, as discussed. But the prevailing spirit of haggling—failing to see that the alternative to a given agreement is not better, but no agreement at all—defeats even the ripest moments.

The two successful cases are full of lessons about ripeness, not only in regard to the success of the resolution attempts themselves but also to earlier opportunities. In Zimbabwe, the ripeness of the moment in the fall of 1979 was classic: the suspended threat of the Thatcher government to recognize the internal settlement, the temporary success of Smith's anti-guerrilla offensive, and the combined pressure of the local and distant allies of both sides focused on the moment as the last chance for a while, with a prospect of uncertainty and serious worsening for both sides if it failed. The orchestration of Lancaster House by the British chair, Lord Carrington, applied the concept of ripeness in detail. Conditions were nearly ready but not quite so in early 1976 and mid-1978, suggesting that ripeness builds up in at least some instances. In 1976, the threat of guerrilla escalation was the impending catastrophe, but it was not yet credible enough before being demonstrated. A Nkomo-Smith internal settlement would have been the result, although it is not certain that it would have been any more than a transitional formula, just as the Muzorewa-Smith internal settlement turned out to be. In 1978, the problem was the weakness of the British Labour Government, since parties and even mediators must be in a presently strong, if prospectively threatened position, for the time to be ready.

Conditions were also ripe in a different set of circumstances in 1963 and 1965, but at those times it was more a question of British authority than of negotiation among conflicting parties. The African nationalist organizations were not yet strong enough to be equal parties to a stalemate or even to a conflict (much like SWAPO in Namibia for a long period into the 1980s). At least they needed an ally to even up the sides, something that Angola was able to do for SWAPO but that even Britain could not do very well for the Rhodesian movements of the time. Conditions were therefore ripe for crisis, if the British had not abdicated their authority, but crisis and conflict were needed before management and resolution could be considered.

Finally, Panama brings a special angle on the idea of the ripe moment. Analysts agree that there was a window of opportunity that the negotiators had to seize, composed of such elements as the post-Vietnam reactions, the bipartisan adoption of the Canal issue, the liberal reaction of the first half of the Carter administration, Torrijos' patience and commitment and also the temporary abeyance of his critics, and the rising wave of American opposition to a new treaty. The conjunctural nature of this opening meant that ratification required an all-out fight, squeaked through as the window began closing, and almost certainly never would have made it after 1979. Yet for all its chanciness, that ripe moment was remarkably durable while it lasted, even bridging two opposite administrations. Happily, the Carter administration did not do in Panama what it did in SALT—substitute a different formula for the one of the previous administration; instead, it pursued the momentum and even kept the same negotiators, measures that took the best advantage of the fragile opening. By the same token, it is hard to see earlier-missed opportunities, since the ripening process had not yet played its course at earlier times. As seen, even the earlier times of agreement—1967, 1972—did not contain resolving formulas and did not occur at moments of ripeness.

In sum, the cases show a richness in the actual occurrence of ripeness that makes it difficult to describe in terms more precise than "plateau, precipice, and outcome." In all instances, where there was a degree of circumstantial propitiousness for agreement, a hurting stalemate or blockage of the parties' efforts at unilateral solution, even by escalation, was present and was uncomfortable or unstable as a resting place for the conflict. When the moment was not ripe, there was frequently a stalemate, but a stable or comfortable one. Furthermore, there was always a catastrophe hanging around, somewhere near the moment of ripeness. Sometimes that escalation of discomfort came from a recent or impending crisis, and sometimes it was merely a general or specific feeling that if the current opportunity or disposition of the parties to find a solution were let slip, the conflict would pick up again in a worse form, to the greater detriment of its own settlement and of the parties. These are matters that reinforce both the social science analysts' claims that concepts can be identified, and the practitioners' claims that recognition is a matter of skill, feel, and experience. Finally, it should be noted that each time the moment was ripe, the evolution of the conflict itself had brought the dispute to the point where there was a way out, a negotiable outcome that could be seized upon by the parties to lift them out of the mess and carry the conflict through transition to resolution.

Mediation

Frequently, parties are so absorbed by the conflict or so locked in the crisis that they cannot seize the moment or the outcome without the help of a mediator. The mediator is a catalyst, an agent required to make the negotiation process take place, and therefore mediated crisis management or conflict resolution involves the same process and components as unmediated negotiation. Catalyst is misleading in one sense, however, in that it implies that the mediator must be merely an unchanged presence which makes the operation take place without "giving" anything of itself. The image rejoins the legal notion of the mediation as a narrow function distinct from conciliation or good offices (or negotiation or arbitration) and the psychological notion of the mediator as a neutral or impartial presence. As a political operation in the real world, mediation encompasses a range of activities. The mediator is inspired by some interests of its own (if only an interest in success for its reputation as a mediator), and it may be closer to one party than to another without harming its function if it handles that closeness properly (Douglas, 1955; Touval, 1975; Touval and Zartman, 1985: 15, 255).

The mediator's range of roles covers three functions: the mediator as a communicator (the most neutral), the mediator as a formulator, and the mediator as a manipulator (the most engaged). Mediation may be limited to simply carrying messages and overcoming the procedural barriers that the parties have erected between themselves. It is more likely to involve some shaping and thinking of the mediator's own, overcoming some of the substantive barriers of the parties to even speaking and hearing proposals in terms worthy of consideration. It may even actively pressure the parties or help create a stalemate (by strengthening the weaker or threatening the stronger) or even impose a deadline. Although the last is tricky business, it is often part of mediation and it still leaves the mediator in a different position than one of the parties. The mediator may have an interest in an outcome (one that satisfies the parties and resolves the conflict) and it may have interests in relations with the parties, but only when the third party is part of the conflict with a share in the outcome does it cease to be a mediator and become one of the parties.

The mediator is usually a most unwelcome intruder into the conflict. Mediation has to be sold to the parties; parties in international conflicts usually do not hire a mediator. The mediator, like the parties, suffers from the effects of the conflict and frequently has more to lose from continuing conflict than the parties. It tries to end the conflict, or help the parties end it, since that is the only way it will end and stay ended. Recognition of this situation helps an understanding of the basic means of leverage of the mediator: leverage comes as an acceptable formula. The challenge of the mediator is to help the parties produce a solution to the conflict (including a management of the crisis or conflict) that will achieve both sides' agreement, or in a more disarticulated form, to extract from each party a proposal attractive to that party and also assured of winning the other party's agreement. The challenge is formidable, and it explains the patience and open-minded creativity needed to be a mediator.

If this is an unusual notion of leverage, it is insightful but not complete. Mediation often involves some sort of pressure as well, as part of leverage. Mediated negotiation is more than just an intellectual exercise, where the fit of the formula sells itself. Frequently, the parties may confront a fitting—even a resolving—formula and still hope to improve it or to escalate their way into a more attractive outcome. Since a joint solution is by definition second best to an ideal unilateral solution for each party, the mediator is often required to reinforce the blockage to unilateral solutions, strengthen the stalemate, or seal a deadline in order to have a resolving formula appear attractive. The triple roles of the mediator, the question of partiality, and the dual aspects of leverage can all be examined and exemplified in the cases. In three of the four cases, the parties were unable to seize the moment on their own and instead needed a mediator. (Some might suggest that Panama too was a case of mediation, with the negotiators bridging the gap between the Panamanian government and the U.S. Congress. But that would be to substitute imagery for analysis, and to confuse complex domestic components of international negotiations with third-party mediation). Cyprus has had a series of mediators: Dean Acheson in 1964, Cyrus Vance in 1967, the U.N. after 1974, with various other parties trying their hands at each round. The Falklands also saw a succession of would-be mediators: Alexander Haig, then the government of Peru, then Perez de Cuellar of the U.N., all in the short space of a few months. Zimbabwe, like Cyprus, had a long period of mediation, but it was primarily dominated by Britain which slipped from a party to a mediator as the conflict evolved, joined by the U.S. from 1976 to 1978, before becoming the sole and successful mediator in 1979.

Some distinctions can be made among these experiences. Vance in 1967 and the Falklands mediators were crisis managers, and among them Vance succeeded. He focused on providing a ceasefire to the communal strife, not on bringing a resolving formula (which he did not provide); the Falklands mediators failed to do either. All were more than communicators and acted as formulators; all had their degress of partiality or impartiality. In Zimbabwe there was a long escalating conflict, or a crisis-in-length. Britain (and the U.S.) acted in reasonable impartiality, although each side thought the mediator partial to the other. By the time of Lancaster House, Britain was acting not as just a communicator or a formulator but, in addition to these, as a manipulator. Indeed, it carried the threat of legitimizing one of the sides by recognition, a manipulation that Haig could not sustain in the Falklands. To try to draw some conclusions on keys to the role of the mediator means eliminating a number of cases for cause. As seen, in Panama there was no mediator. In the Falklands, there was no formula and no stalemate, and so the mediator provided neither of the two ingredients which were necessary to his job. In Zimbabwe, there was both formula and stalemate, and the mediator in the end helped hold the parties to the formula by reinforcing the stalemate with threats of his own, including the threat to stop the mediation. Cyprus then is the test case and it is eloquent: there was a succession of formulas as the conflict evolved through its various crises, but, particularly after 1967 (operatively, after the end of 1973), the mediator was a failure because of an inability to reinforce the stalemate that would keep the parties on track and force them to agree to the fitting formula—perhaps even resolving formula—at hand instead of trying to bargain or to escalate a better deal. The U.N. by its nature was unable to do so; the U.S. in 1974 was unwilling.

Many other cases outside of these four (Chad, Namibia, Lebanon, Nicaragua) would show that the difference between their failure and success was the inability (unwillingness) of the mediator to constrain the parties to agree to the resolving formula offered them, instead of trying to run or stall in hopes of a better deal (Day, 1986; George et al, 1983). The conclusion should lay to rest the notion that merely the communicator is enough, when in fact, in a political world of risk-takers, the mediator as a manipulator is often needed. It should scarcely need to be added that this is not the same as simply imposition and *diktat* on the part of the third party, but that all the previous insights about ripening conflicts and resolving formulas need to be included in the mediator's job as well. By the same token, when the resolving formula does not imply the disarming or elimination of one side, as was done in Zimbabwe and as was not done in Panama, it is best that the parties reach their own agreement on a new regime, without the interference of a third party, since they will be around to contest the agreement if it would not continue to satisfy them.

Crisis and Conflict Management

In none of these cases of crisis were both superpowers the protagonists. They all took place within the Free World, and they all were serious enough to attract the attention of one superpower, the head of the "Free World family." No doubt the danger that the conflict if continued might attract the attention of the other superpower was a motivating factor, although questions can be expressed about the reality of the danger (Day, 1986). Basically, it was the conflict itself that was intrinsically costly and destabilizing, and where there was a mediator role for a superpower, it was because of the third party's concern for its friends, not for fear of its enemies. Crisis, conflict management, and mediation have much wider applicability as concepts and problems than just in relation to superpowers. (And happily so, one might add, since reliance on superpower crises alone would give a much smaller number of cases from which to learn, and yet ones that would be more catastrophic.)

In addition to the conceptual framework for the analysis of conflict and conflict management which has been presented here, some specific conclusions can be drawn about the role of crisis.

1. Crises come from attempts to impose a stalemate (block the other party's attempts to apply its unilateral solution in the conflict) or to escalate out of a stalemate. They are not isolated or freestanding accidents independent of the evolution of the conflict, but are part of the shift from an old regime of relations to a new one. The Falklands Crisis of 1982 and the Cyprus Crises of 1960, 1964, 1967, and 1974 were all attempts to escalate out of a stalemate with a sudden decisive move, and they failed. The Panamanian Crisis of 1964 was an attempt to impose a stalemate and challenge the old regime. Thereafter, Panama, and Zimbabwe as well, may be considered to be ongoing crises rather than the single explosions that marked the Falklands and Cyprus, although the purposes were the same. Crises mark shifts or attempts to shift in

relations between the parties but they are rarely successful in bringing about new regimes.

2. Crises can help conflict resolution by eliminating options or providing stalemates. They are costly means of achieving what more clearsighted people might be able to do in their minds, but that can be said of many human events (with no agreement among presumably clearsighted people over which ones). The most useful point, however, is that the crises should be understood and acted upon in terms of their relation to the larger process of resolving the conflict (finding new, resolving regimes), rather than being reacted to as isolated events.

2a. However, to say that crises need to be integrated into conflict management is not to suggest that they are either efficient or necessary ways of eliminating alternatives or even producing stalemate. Furthermore, it should be emphasized that almost invariably, crises do not resolve conflict, and frequently they only eliminate alternatives that most people thought or wished were already eliminated. Optimists may find some such value in the Falklands crisis, in the internal settlement in Rhodesia, or even in the precipitating riots in Panama in 1964, but it is hard to find much that is positive in the various Cyprus crises.

3. Conflict management efforts should begin when crises break out (if not before) so as to be in operation when the crisis is ready to be managed. Once in a crisis, the parties must make their point and are unlikely to desist without either a symbolic outcome or exhaustion. Conflict management efforts—cease-fire, separation of forces, cooling off, ending hostile propaganda—are unlikely to be accepted before the current phase is played out, but the efforts should begin earlier.

4. Threatened crises as well as recent crises create ripe moments for conflict resolution. A forestalled crisis or a crisis just brought under control are alternative ways of providing the hurting stalemate and the narrowing of options that provide opportunities for mediators and the parties themselves to search for better outcomes. Of the two, threatening crises are more cost-effective but unfortunately may be less credible.

5. Mediating third parties work better to suspend threatening crises and urge conflict resolution; failing that, they should seize on the crisis past to press the same goal. This is a role that both superpowers as well as lesser actors would do well to cultivate.

Acknowledgments

This paper was originally presented at the XIIIth World Congress of the International Political Science Association. A similar version of this study has appeared in Diane Bendahmane and John W. McDonald Jr., eds. *Perspectives on Negotiation: Four Case Studies and Interpretations* (Washington: Government

Printing Office, for the Center for the Study of Foreign Affairs, Foreign Service Institute of the Department of State). The case material for this study has come from a project of the Center for the Study of Foreign Affairs in which the author is involved. The analysis has also benefitted from the author's participation in similar projects by the United Nations Association of the U.S.A. and the International Peace Academy, and by the Conflict Management and Security Program at the Johns Hopkins School for Advanced International Studies.

10

Conclusion

Gilbert R. Winham

In the Introduction it was argued that changes in the balance of power between the United States and the Soviet Union have put increased pressure on crisis management in the 1980s and beyond. In keeping with this analysis the papers in this volume are not optimistic about the superpowers' capacity to manage serious political crisis. The thrust of this book is thus consistent with the "new tone of urgency in strategic analyses of the 1980s" which James Richardson mentions in the concluding paragraph of Chapter Two.

A common theme in the chapters is the fear of loss of control in crisis situations, that is, an inability to manage an intense conflict short of violence. As was mentioned in the Introduction, crisis management involves treading a very careful line between coercion and accommodation in one's strategy, in order to maximize the interests of one's nation on the one hand while avoiding war on the other. The situation is one of great delicacy, both in conception and in execution, and loss of control is an understandable concern. It was previously observed that policy-makers engaged in crises are frequently fearful of losing control of the situation, and this concern is apparently also reflected in the more detached writing of academics.

Loss of control is explictly raised in Ned Lebow's chapter, and he analyzes three factors—civil military relations, emotion, and sabotage—that could threaten a government's control over its strategic response. Control is a central concern for Joseph Nye and William Ury in their elaboration of the concept of "owls," for as they put it: "Owls worry primarily about loss of control." The contributions by Charles Hermann, and Karen MacGillivray and Gilbert Winham focus on the issue of crisis instability, and they emphasize the potential for loss of control due to weapons characteristics and the deployment plans of the two superpowers. A more political perspective on the problem of control is presented in the chapter by Alexander George, which emphasizes the frequent mis-calculations that occur as the superpowers try to determine and com-municate their interests in crisis situations. Finally, Janice Stein analyzes the capacity of superpowers to control their regional allies, and concludes with the memorable assertion that "the managers are the managed." In sum, the authors collectively recognize that crisis management is, in Lebow's words, a "blunt instrument," and there is general concern that this instrument may not be adequate to the task of maintaining control of political crises in the future.

Although control may be questionable in any future crisis, it remains difficult, as argued by Nye and Ury, to describe a plausible scenario for starting a major nuclear war. William Zartman's useful concept of "ripening" conflict, meaning the progressive elimination of salient op-tions, could be used to describe a path to war as well as crisis resolution. However, this general model still leaves many gaps to be filled, for even with many options foreclosed it is improbable that national leaders would ever intentionally choose nuclear war as a means to achieve national interests. With regard to other paths to war, such as accidental war, the "Avoiding Nuclear War Project" reported in Nye and Ury has found that the risks of purely accidental nuclear war are lower today than they were two decades ago. The same is also true for "catalytic" wars, which are wars caused intentionally or otherwise by third parties.

While the path to nuclear warfare is not easy to predict, one way to approach this problem is to examine previous cases of crisis and warfare. Two such cases, the Peloponnesian War and World War I, are briefly summarized in the Introduction. In both cases a war that involved the major powers of the day started between smaller actors allied to the major powers. Hostilities between the smaller countries invoked the interests of the major powers and then created an atmosphere of tension and crisis. Commitments were made by the major powers, and when these were challenged, the sense of threat escalated. Defensive actions were taken, but in the context of crisis such actions can easily appear as offensive to the other side. Particularly in 1914, the mechanisms of strategic alert and partial mobilization served to deepen the crisis. At some point war was judged to be inevitable, whereupon war became the rational and even the conservative decision to take. Both wars were wars of preemption, although there is no evidence that this preemption took place in any great haste in the case of the ancient Greeks. But for the European powers, the technology of mobilization created enormous haste, and placed European leaders in the circumstances aptly summarized by Von Der Goltz: "The Statesmen who, knowing his instrument to be ready, and seeing War inevitable, hestitates to strike first is guilty of crime against his country."[1] These leaders, perceiving no alternative, declared war.

The great difference between these historical cases and the modern situation is that nuclear weapons vastly increase the costs of war. For the ancient Greeks, war appeared to be an acceptable cost of the practice of interstate politics. For the Europeans, the costs of war were greater, but they still could be introduced into a rational calculation of the national interests. Today, the costs of nuclear war are estimated to be so staggering that it is difficult to imagine they could be integrated into rational calculations of costs and benefit. And yet, and leaving aside all non-rational considerations, the basic politics of crisis escalation between nation-states have changed very little from the time of the ancient Greeks; they operate, at least in the early stages, largely independent of the costs of war. And once a crisis is deeply engaged, the mechanics of preemption take account mainly of the likelihood of war, not the costs of war. If war were to become perceived as inevitable in the modern era, whether it were conventional or nuclear, the advice of the generals would very like be the same. As Steinbruner (1984: 47) has stated: "If war should ever appear unavoidable, military commanders on both sides charged with executing their assigned missions would inevitably seek authority to initiate an attack, whatever prior national-security policy may have been. They would do so with a forcefulness that would depend directly on the intensity of the crisis." Thus, as difficult as it may be to predict a path to nuclear war, one cannot dismiss the concern for preemptive war, and one cannot consider cases like the Peloponnesian War or 1914 irrevelant to nuclear crisis management in modern times. On this subject then, what do the papers in this volume have to say?

The expectations that violence is nearly unavoidable creates a watershed in crisis management. Prior to this point—from the earliest beginning of a crisis until the time when violence becomes probable—a range of diplomatic behaviors will be employed by the parties, including political, military, and even economic. After this point the focus is much more on the military factor, and technical problems like the invulnerability of strategic forces to a first strike become of paramount concern. The papers in this volume divide in their focus on the different stages of political crisis: some are more concerned about how crises arise, and how they are managed politically especially in their early stages; others are more concerned with the stability of crisis management as a crisis becomes intense and violence becomes more probable.

The chapter by Alexander George examines the circumstances in which crises originate. It is a continuation of the work by George and his colleagues (e.g., George, 1983) on crisis prevention, a recent extension of the sub-field of crisis management. The assumption of crisis prevention is that the best way to manage crisis between the superpowers is to prevent them from arising in the first place. This can be done through either formal or informal procedures. Some effort has been made by the superpowers in the past to negotiate formal rules of conduct, and to this end a Basic Principles Agreement was concluded between President Richard Nixon and Secretary General Leonid Brezhnev in 1972. However, subsequent disagreements over the meaning of this accord did not reduce, and may even have exacerbated, Soviet-American competition in areas like Africa and the Middle East. As a result, the attention of George and others has turned to how the superpowers might establish informal norms of competition to restrain their behavior in areas where their interests clash. The implicit model for this work is the informal rules of accommodation that helped make the balance of power system an effective mechanism for preserving peace in the 19th century.

Two variables figure prominently in George's analysis: the strength and the symmetry of superpower interests. These variables provide a means for categorizing different geographical areas where superpower interests might come into conflict, such as an area of high interest asymmetry (e.g., East Europe), or low interest symmetry (Africa). When categorized in this way, it is obvious that major crises occurring in areas of high interest (whether symetric or assymetric) would constitute maximum danger to international peace. However, it is precisely those areas where the superpowers have had greater success in accommodating their interests. Where disputes are more likely to arise are in areas of low interest symmetry, or in areas of disputed interest symmetry (e.g., Middle East) where the superpowers do not agree on the relative balance of their interests. In these cases there is an uncertainty about the scope of superpower interests, and uncertainty provides an incentive for competition.

As competition between the superpowers is engaged, interests tend to grow and commitments are expanded. In any exchange where prestige is committed or costs are incurred, future policy then carries the burden of justifying past decisions. This in turn can cause a minor conflict to snowball into a serious crisis. The value of George's analysis is that it demonstrates how disputes can arise between the superpowers, and why it is difficult to establish "norms of competition" to restrain their behavior.

Janice Stein goes one step further in analyzing relations between superpowers and their allies in the context of regional crises that are already underway. In the four cases of Middle East crisis described by Stein—two involving the United States and two involving the USSR—it is clear that regional allies are often not interested (any more than was Austria in 1914) in avoiding war. These allies are nations with critical vulnerabilities for whom military inaction can be a more serious cause for alarm than military action. Whereas at an early stage the superpowers might have had an interest in encouraging hostilities between their allies, as a crisis escalates they quickly find they face a trade-off between managing the crisis at reasonable levels of conflict, or losing influence with an ally that is seeking to escalate the crisis, or to settle matters through force of arms. Thus at certain points in a regional crisis, dependent allies appear to have more capacity to manipulate their patrons than the reverse.

One mechanism the superpowers used to manage regional crises was to allow the crisis to escalate to high levels of risk because, as Stein notes, "they could not effectively constrain their allies at lower levels." Needless to say this is an exceptionally dangerous form of crisis management, which in the 1973 war in the Middle East led the United States to make use of a general strategic alert (DEFCON 3) to reinforce its bargaining position. At worst, Stein's analysis describes a mechanism whereby a regional conflict could turn into a much wider war; at best, it reveals the inherent difficulty in managing crisis in areas where regional actors are intensely hostile to each other, and where the interests of superpowers are uncertain or disputed. Since, as George notes, these are areas where confrontations are most likely to arise, it seems the prospects for avoiding serious crisis in the future are not encouraging.

Once a crisis is underway, the outcome is as dependent on the process of crisis management as on the substance of dispute. Process issues are the stock-in-trade of the crisis management literature, and Richardson's review of them takes the form of a series of principles gleaned from much previous research. These principles are extracted largely from research on the Cuban Missile Crisis, which continues to provide much of the conventional wisdom on superpower decision-making and communication during crisis.

By comparison, William Zartman examines crisis behavior outside the U.S.-USSR context, and his analysis provides an interesting counterpoint to the literature on crisis management which is mainly oriented towards superpower relations. Zartman's cases of crisis are of a longer duration than would likely occur in crises between superpowers, and this leads him to develop concepts like "hurting stalemate" and "ripe moment" to emphasize the importance that proper timing plays in crisis management. Another variable is "catastrophe," which Zartman finds is helpful in establishing a ripe moment for crisis resolution. This variable for obvious reasons would be inappropriate in superpower crisis, where nuclear weapons are involved. Finally, Zartman examines the value of mediation in crisis, which again is a factor that is unlikely to play a role in superpower crisis. The result of comparing the analyses of James Richardson and William Zartman brings one to the realization that the range of behaviors in superpower crisis management is very much circumscribed by the preponderant power of the two nations, and by the relationship in which they are enmeshed. In any serious crisis between the superpowers the scope for creative diplomacy would be minimal, and the pressures toward immobility of response would be substantial.

Crises reach a turning point when the parties begin to believe that hostilities are probable. One would expect this to be an extremely tense period in any crisis, but under certain circumstances it could be a point of an extreme instability in a nuclear crisis. Charles Hermann has laid out in stark terms the conditions that would lead to nuclear crisis instability: (i) a perception by political authorities that war (especially nuclear) is inevitable; (ii) a belief that one's own forces are vulnerable and would not survive an enemy's first strike; and (iii) a belief therefore that a decisive advantage could be had in attacking first with nuclear weapons. If these conditions were met, decision-makers would be under great pressure to launch a preemptive strike before the enemy did so. Whereas previously decision-makers might have attempted to slow down the crisis in order not to force precipitated action, once Hermann's conditions were met their reaction time would be greatly foreshortened and speed in decision-making would be essential. Ned Lebow has used the term "superconductivity" to describe a state where ordinary human and institutional friction no longer offers any resistance to the runaway escalation of a crisis. It would seem "superconductivity" is an appropriate concept to describe the kind of behavior that could occur in conditions of crisis instability.

The main element in crisis instability is the weapons themselves, particularly their nature and the plans for their deployment. Hermann's paper argues strongly that both superpowers have eroded nuclear crisis stability with their strategic decisions over the past decade. For example, procurement decisions (especially the deployment of MIRVs) have increased the offensive capability of both superpowers to the point where a large portion of the strategic forces on both sides are at risk from the other's first strike. Further developments have been made by both sides in anti-satellite capabilities, which could be used to attack vital communications and intelligence functions necessary to insure a crisis remained under control. Furthermore, decision time and reaction time have been vastly reduced by a new generation of intermediate and medium range weapons.

The potential instability from the characteristics of weapons, however, is further compounded by the vulnerability of command and control in any nuclear exchange. Vulnerability itself is a fact that could lead to pressures to preempt an adversary in a nuclear crisis. Additionally, attempts to reduce or control for this vulnerability has led to decision structures (such as "predelegated authority") that would further reduce stability in a nuclear crisis. Hermann warns of an "eroding decision control" in severe crises, and the possibility that parties might resort to a form of automated decision processes to get around some of the problems of short decision time and disrupted organizational control. Especially worrisome is the prospect that both sides might try to overcome their own weaknesses vis-a-vis the other by planning a preemptive decapitation strategy against the other's command centers. Such a plan would have disastrous consequences for crisis stability. Hermann concludes from his analysis that both sides have pursued policies over the past one and one-half decades that make it more difficult to end an acute crisis without war, and therefore, one would assume the risks of nuclear war have increased.

Other factors besides characteristics and deployment of weapons can effect crisis stability. Once a crisis becomes intense, there are both human and organizational factors that can contribute to loss of control, and hence a movement toward war. Joseph Nye and William Ury describe some of these as non-rational factors, and include examples such as misperception, deterioration of decision-making under stress, the problem of controlling large organizations and the dangers of accident or unintended consequences of actions. One problem they note especially is that multiple events often arise simultaneously in crisis, a point which is confirmed by Hazlewood's (1977: 98) statistical findings that over 35 percent of crisis involving the United States occurred when U.S. leaders were handling another crisis. Analyses like this tend to discredit the view that crisis decision-making would be a neat or well organized affair. In this sense, American decision-making in the Cuban Missile Crisis, which did have the appearance of effective organization, may be (as Richardson notes) an overly optimistic guide to future crisis decision-making.

Lebow examines some of the same factors as Nye and Ury, from a Clausewitzian perspective that acknowledges the emotional dimensions of war. The fact that Clausewitz' analysis was far more penetrating than other strategists who attempted to reduce war to abstract formulas lends some credence to Lebow's argument. His analysis of the emotional and organizational factors in nuclear crisis management—such as anger or sabotage—leads him to suggest that these factors may become more problematic in crises that reach high levels of escalation. Thus at the same point where Hermann claims crises might become unstable due to technical factors, Lebow is suggesting that human and political factors could work in the same direction. All of this of course may be nothing new, and may simply be part of what makes an intense crisis intense. Nevertheless, it is sobering to observe analysts who approach nuclear crisis management from entirely different perspectives reach similarly pessimistic judgments about the capacity to avoid hostilities as a crisis intensifies. This does not inspire confidence in crisis management. The main lesson may be for U.S. and Soviet leaders to avoid crisis confrontation in the first place.

It was argued in the introduction to this volume that underlying conditions in the international system and particularly a shift in power between the superpowers increased the likelihood of political confrontation between the United States and Soviet Union. This is therefore a time when the procedures for managing crisis, especially nuclear crisis, should be improving, not deteriorating. However, the papers in this book suggest that improvements are not occurring. If there is any one message to be taken from this volume, it is that we cannot be sanguine about the capacity of the superpowers to manage the kinds of crises that the East-West rivalry could easily generate in the next decade. Both sides must confront the issue of crisis instability, which as the chapter by Karen MacGillivray and Gilbert Winham argues has not been addressed in the predominant form of superpower dialogue, arms control negotiations. The chapters by Hermann and Nye and Ury propose a series of measures—both unilateral and bilateral—which would improve crisis management while at the same time would be consistent with national security. These recommendations should be approached from the perspective that war itself between nations armed with nuclear weapons is the greatest security threat facing the West, and that the apparent deterioration of the capacity to manage crisis is a factor which could lead to an unwanted war.

Notes

1. Von der Goltz's statement is quoted in Colonel Maude's introduction to Clausewitz (1968, 1832: 85).

About the Contributors

Alexander L. George is Graham H. Stuart Professor of International Relations, Stanford University. His first book, *Woodrow Wilson and Colonel House* (1956), written with his wife, Juliette L. George, is widely regarded as a classic study of the role of personality in politics. He has also authored or co-authored *Deterrence in Foreign Policy* (1974), which won the 1975 Bancroft Prize; *The Limits of Coercive Diplomacy* (1971); *Propaganda Analysis* (1959); *The Chinese Communist Army in Action* (1967); *Presidential Decisionmaking in Foreign Policy* (1980); *Force and Statecraft* (1983); and *Managing U.S.-Soviet Rivalry* (1983).

Charles F. Hermann is Director of the Mershon Center and Professor of Political Science at The Ohio State University. Under his direction, the Mershon Center has included among its concerns a new emphasis on Soviet international behavior and local citizenship participation in international affairs. Before coming to Ohio State in 1970, Dr. Hermann worked on the National Security Council staff for Dr. Henry Kissinger and taught at Princeton University. He has written extensively on international crises and foreign policy decision-making, and is currently working on Soviet policy-making in national security.

Richard Ned Lebow is Professor of Government and Director of the Peace Studies Program at Cornell University. He previously served as Professor of Strategy at the National War College and Scholar-in-Residence in the Central Intelligence Agency. Among his published works are *Nuclear Crisis Management: A Dangerous Illusion* (1987), *Psychology and Deterrence*, co-authored (1985), and *Between Peace and War: The Nature of International Crisis* (1981).

Karen Patrick MacGillivray is a Ph.D. student in the Department of Political Science at Dalhousie University. She received an M.A. (with distinction) in International Affairs from Carleton University in 1983. Her M.A. thesis on international technological negotiations won the Drayton Award and was published by the Centre for Foreign Policy Studies at Dalhousie University. Her Ph.D. dissertation is on comparative case studies of arms control.

Joseph S. Nye, Jr., is director of the Center for Science and International Affairs at Harvard University. He was Deputy to the Undersecretary of

State for Security Assistance, Science and Technology and chaired the National Security Council Group on Nonproliferation of Nuclear Weapons. He is co-author of *Living with Nuclear Weapons*. His recent books include *The Making of America's Soviet Policy* (1984); *Hawks, Doves, and Owls: An Agenda for Avoiding Nuclear War* (coedited with Albert Carnesale) (1985); and *Nuclear Ethics* (1986).

James L. Richardson is Professorial Fellow in International Relations at the Australian National University. His previous positions include: Research Associate, Center for International Affairs, Harvard; member of the Arms Control and Disarmament Research Unit, Foreign Office, London; and the Department of Government, University of Sydney. His interests include Germany and European security, the cold war and detente, arms control and crisis diplomacy; and he has written *Germany and the Atlantic Alliance*, (1966) and *Arms Control in the Later 1980s*, (1986).

Janice Gross Stein is Professor in the Department of Political Science at the University of Toronto. She has been Vice President of the Canadian Political Science Association, and a member of the Editorial Boards of *International Organization*, *Etudes Internationales*, *Canadian Journal of Political Science*, and *Negotiation Journal*. She has co-authored *Rational Decision Making: Israel's Security Choices 1967* (1980) and *Psychology and Deterrence* (1985).

William L. Ury is Associate Director of the Avoiding Nuclear War Project at the Kennedy School of Government, where he directs a joint study group on crisis prevention with scholars and officials from the United States and the Soviet Union. He co-founded and serves as Associate Director of Harvard's Program on Negotiation. He co-authored (with Roger Fisher) *Getting to Yes: Negotiating Agreement Without Giving In* (1981). His recent work includes *Beyond the Hotline: How Crisis Control Can Prevent Nuclear War* (1985).

Gilbert R. Winham is Professor and Chairman of the Department of Political Science at Dalhousie University. He previously served as Director of the Centre for Foreign Policy Studies and Research Coordinator of the Royal Commission on the Economic Union and Development Prospects for Canada. He specializes in the analysis of international negotiation, and his recent work includes *International Trade and the Tokyo Round Negotiation* (1986).

I. William Zartman is Professor of International Politics and Director of African studies at the Johns Hopkins School of Advanced International Studies in Washington, D.C., and past president of the Middle East Studies Association. He is the author of *Ripe for Resolution* (1985) and co-author of *The Practical Negotiator* (1982) as well as co-author and editor of *The Negotiation Process* and *The 50% Solution,* (1976). He helped establish the international negotiating seminar for the International Peace Academy. Dr. Zartman is a consultant for the State Department and has written a number of works on the Middle East and African politics.

Bibliography

Abel, Elie (1966) *The Missile Crisis*. Philadelphia: J.B. Lippincott.

————. (1966) *The Missiles of October: The Story of the Cuban Missile Crisis 1962*. London: MacGibbon and Kee.

Adelman, Kenneth L. (1984/85) "Arms Control With and Without Agreements," *Foreign Affairs* 63: 240–263.

Adomeit, Hannes (1982) *Soviet Risk-Taking and Crisis Behaviour: A theoretical and empirical analysis*. London: George Allen & Unwin.

Ajami, Fouad (1981) *The Arab Predicament*. Cambridge: Cambridge University Press.

Albertini, Luigi (1952) *The Origins of the War of 1914* (trans. Isabella M. Massey). Oxford: Oxford University Press.

Allison, Graham T. (1971) *Essence of Decision: Explaining the Cuban Missile Crisis*. Boston: Little, Brown.

American Committee on East-West Accord (1982) *Basic Positions*. Washington, D.C.

al-Assad, Hafez (1978) Speech Broadcast by Radio Damascus, 18 March, *Foreign Broadcast Information Service*, 20 March.

Ball, Desmond (1983) *Targeting for Strategic Deterrence*, Adelphi Papers No. 185. London: International Institute of Strategic Studies.

Bar-Siman-Tov, Yaacov (1980) *The Israeli-Egyptian War of Attrition, 1969–1970*. New York: Columbia University Press.

Beatty, Jack (1987) "In Harm's Way: America's Scary, and Expensive, New Naval Strategy," *Atlantic* 259: 37–53.

Begin, Menachem (1981) Speech to the *Knesset*, 3 June 1981, *Divrei Ha-Knesset*.

Bell, Coral (1986) "Managing to Survive," *The National Interest* 2:36–45.

————. (1982) "Crisis Analysis," in D. Ball (ed.) *Strategy and Defence: Australian Essays*. Sydney: George Allen & Unwin.

————. (1979) "Crisis Diplomacy," in Laurence Martin (ed.) *Strategic Thought in the Nuclear Age*. Baltimore, Maryland: The Johns Hopkins University Press.

————. (1978) "Decision-making by governments in crisis situations," in D. Frei (ed.) *International Crises and Crisis Management*. Farnborough: Saxon House.

————. (1971) *The Conventions of Crisis: A Study in Diplomatic Management*. London: Oxford University Press.

Bendahmane, Diane and John W. McDonald, Jr. (eds.) (1986) *Perspectives on Negotiation: Four Case Studies and Interpretations*. Washington, D.C.: Government Printing Office.

Berman, Robert P. and John C. Baker (1982) *Soviet Strategic Forces: Requirements and Responses*. Washington, D.C.: Brookings Institution.

Betts, Richard K. (1985a) "Surprise Attack and Preemption," in Graham Allison, Al Carnesale, Joseph S. Nye, Jr., (eds.) *Hawks, Doves and Owls: An Agenda for Avoiding Nuclear War*. New York: W.W. Norton and Company.

———. (1985b) "A Joint Nuclear Risk Control Center," in Barry M. Blechman (ed.) *Preventing Nuclear War*. Bloomington, Indiana: University of Indiana Press.

———. (1977) *Soldiers, Statesmen, and Cold Warriors*. Cambridge: Harvard University Press.

Blair, Bruce G. (1985) *Strategy Command and Control: Redefining the Nuclear Threat*. Washington, D.C.: Brookings Institution.

Blechman, Barry M. (ed.) (1985) *Preventing Nuclear War*. Bloomington, Indiana: University of Indiana Press.

———. (1983) "U.S.-Soviet Nuclear Risk Management Centers," in Hilliard Roderick with Ulla Magnussan (eds.) *Avoiding Inadvertent War*. Austin, Texas: Lyndon B. Johnson School of Public Affairs, University of Texas.

——— and Douglas M. Hart (1982) "The Political Utility of Nuclear Weapons: The 1973 Middle East Crisis," *International Security* 7:132–156.

Bloomfield, Lincoln and Amelia Leiss (1969) *Controlling Small Wars*. New York: Knopf.

Bracken, Paul (1985) "Accidental Nuclear War," in Graham Allison, Al Carnesale, Joseph S. Nye, Jr. (eds.) *Hawks, Doves and Owls: An Agenda for Avoiding Nuclear War*. New York: W.W. Norton and Company.

———. (1983) *The Command and Control of Nuclear Weapons*. New Haven: Yale University Press.

Brecher, Michael (ed.) (1978) *Studies in Crisis Behavior*. New Brunswick, New Jersey: Transaction Books.

———. (1977) "Toward a Theory of International Crisis Behavior," *Jerusalem Journal of International Relations* III, 2 and 3.

———. (1975) *Decisions in Israel's Foreign Policy*. New Haven: Yale University Press.

——— and Jonathan Wilkenfeld (1982) "Crises in World Politics," *World Politics* 34:380–417.

——— with Benjamin Geist (1980) *Crisis and Decision: Israel 1967, 1973*. Berkeley: University of California Press.

Breslauer, George W. (1983) "Why Detente Failed: An Interpretation," in Alexander George (ed.) *Managing U.S.-Soviet Rivalry*. Boulder, Colorado: Westview Press.

Broad, W.J. (1985) "Experts Say Satellites Can Detect Soviet War Steps," *New York Times*, 24 January.

Buchan, Alistair (1966) *Crisis Management: The New Diplomacy*. Boulogne-sur-Seine, France: Atlantic Institute.

Buchheim, Robert W. and Dan Caldwell (1986) "The U.S.-USSR Standing Consultative Commission: Description and Appraisal," in Paul R. Viotti (ed.) *Conflict and Arms Control*. Boulder, Colorado: Westview Press.

Bull, Hedley (1977) *The Anarchical Society.* London: MacMillan.

Burt, Richard (1981) "The Relevance of Arms Control in the 1980s," *Daedalus* 110: 159–177.

Caldwell, Dan (1985) "The Standing Consultative Commission," in William G. Potter (ed.) *Verification and Arms Control.* Lexington, Massachusetts: Lexington Books.

————. (1978) "A Research Note on the Quarantine of Cuba, October 1962," *International Studies Quarterly* 22:625–53.

Camps, Miriam (1974) *Management of Interdependence.* New York: Council on Foreign Relations.

Carnesale, Albert, and Joseph S. Nye, Jr. (eds.) (1985) *Hawks, Doves, and Owls: An Agenda for Avoiding Nuclear War.* New York: Norton.

Carnesale, Albert, Joseph S. Nye, Jr. and Graham T. Allison (1985) "An Agenda for Action," in Graham T. Allison, *et al* (eds.) *Hawks, Doves, and Owls.* New York: Norton.

Carter, Rosalynne (1984) *First Lady from Plains.* New York: Fawcett.

Chang, King-Yuh (1982) "Practical Suggestions for Crisis Management: An Inventory," in D. Frei (ed.) *Managing International Crises.* Beverly Hills: Sage.

Clausewitz, Carl von (1976) *On War.* (ed. and trans. Michael Howard and Peter Paret). Princeton: Princeton University Press. *and* (1968, 1832) Anatol Rapoport (ed.) Harmondsworth, England: Penguin Books.

Cohen, Eliot A. (1986) "Why We Should Stop Studying the Cuban Missile Crisis," *The National Interest* 2:3–13.

Cohen, Raymond (1981) *International Politics: The Rules of the Game.* London: Longman.

Colton, Timothy J. (1979) *Commissars, Commanders, and Civilian Authority: The Structure of Soviet Military Politics.* Cambridge: Harvard University Press.

Costa-Mendez, Nicanor (1986) Interview. 21 October.

Cox, Arthur Macy (1982) *Russian Roulette: The Superpower Game.* New York: Times Books.

Craig, Gordon A. (1964) *The Politics of the Prussian Army, 1940–1945.* London: Oxford University Press.

Davidow, Jeffrey (1984) *A Peace in Southern Africa.* Boulder, Colorado: Westview Press.

————. (1983) *Dealing with International Crises: Lessons from Zimbabwe.* Muscatine, Iowa: Stanley Foundation Occasional Paper 34.

Dawisha, Karen (1980–81) "Soviet Decision-Making in the Middle East: The 1974 October War and the 1980 Gulf War," *International Affairs,* 57:43–59.

Day, Arthur and Michael Doyle (eds.) (1986) *Escalation and Intervention: Multilateral Strategy and its Alternatives.* Boulder, Colorado: Westview Press.

Dayan, Moshe (1976) *The Story of My Life.* New York: William Morrow.

Dessouki, Ali E. Hillal (1982) "The Middle East Crisis: Theoretical Propositions and Examples," in D. Frei (ed.) *Managing International Crises.* Beverly Hills: Sage.

Deutsch, Morton (1973) *The Resolution of Conflict.* New Haven: Yale University Press.

Dinerstein, Herbert (1976) *The Making of a Missile Crisis.* Baltimore: Johns Hopkins Press.

Dismukes, Bradford and James M. McConnell (eds.) (1979) *Soviet Naval Diplomacy.* New York: Pergamon Press.

Dobell, M.W. (1967) "Division over Cyprus," XXII *International Journal* 2:287–292.

Douglas, Ann (1955) "What can research tell us about mediation?," VI *Labor Law Journal* 8:550.

Downs, George W. and David M. Rocke (1987) "Tacit Bargaining and Arms Control," *World Politics* 39: 297–325.

Dowty, Alan (1984) *Middle East Crisis: U.S. Decision-Making in 1958, 1970 and 1973.* Berkeley: University of California Press.

Drell, Sidney D. and Theodore J. Ralston (1985) "Restrictions on Weapon Tests as Confidence-Building Measures," in Barry M. Blechman (ed.) *Preventing Nuclear War.* Bloomington, Indiana: University of Indiana Press.

Druckman, Daniel (1986) "Stages, Turning Points, and Crises: Negotiating Military Base Rights, Spain and the United States," XXX *Journal of Conflict Resolution* 2:327–360.

Duffy, Gloria (1983) "Crisis Prevention in Cuba," in Alexander L. George (ed.) *Managing U.S.-Soviet Rivalry.* Boulder, Colorado: Westview Press.

Dulles, John Foster (1957) "Aide-Memoire to Israel's Ambassador to the United Nations," *United States Senate Documents,* February 11, Document 14.

Dyson, Freeman (1984) *Weapons and Hope.* New York: Harper & Row.

Eban, Abba (1977) *Abba Eban: An Autobiography.* New York: Random House.

————. (1973) Speech to a Memorial Meeting for Lyndon Johnson, 25 January. Broadcast on *Kol Yisrael,* 27 January.

Eberwein, Wolf-Dieter (1978) "Crisis Research—The State of the Art: A Western View," in D. Frei (ed.) *International Crises and Crisis Management.* Farnborough: Saxon House.

Edwards, John (1982) *Super Weapon: The Making of the MX.* New York: Norton.

Ellis, Richard H. (1980) "Building a Plan for Peace: The Joint Strategic Target Planning Staff," Offut Air Force Base: Joint Strategic Target Planning Staff, mimeo, pp. 6–7.

Evron, Yair (1987) *War and Intervention in Lebanon: The Israeli-Syrian Deterrence Dialogue.* Baltimore: The Johns Hopkins University Press, forthcoming.

————. (1979) "Great Powers' Military Intervention in the Middle East," in Milton Leintenberg and Gabriel Sheffer (eds.) *Great Power Intervention in the Middle East.* New York: Pergamon Press.

Fahmy, Ismail (1983) *Negotiating for Peace in the Middle East.* Baltimore: The Johns Hopkins University Press.

Fallows, James (1984) "What Good is Arms Control?," *Atlantic* 25:6.

Feldman, Shai and Heda Rechnitz-Kijner (1985) *Deception, Consensus, and War: Israel's Intervention in Lebanon.* Tel Aviv: The Jaffe Center for Strategic Studies.

Fisher, Roger (1978) *Points of Choice.* Oxford: Oxford University Press.

Fiske, S.T., F. Pratto, and M.A. Pavelchak (1983) "Citizen's Images of Nuclear War: Content and Consequences," *Journal of Social Issues* 39:41–65.

Frei, Daniel (1983) *Risks of Unintentional Nuclear War.* Totowa, New Jersey: Rowman and Allanheld.

————. (ed.) (1982) *Managing International Crises.* Beverly Hills: Sage.

————. (ed.) (1978) *International Crises and Crisis Management.* Farnborough, England: Saxon House.

Garthoff, Raymond L. (1985) *Detente and Confrontation: American-Soviet Relations from Nixon to Reagan.* Washington, D.C.: Brookings Institution.

————. (1978) "SALT I: An Evaluation," *World Politics,* 31:1–25.

Garwin, Richard L., Kurt Gottfried, and Donald L. Hafner (1984) "Anti-Satellite Weapons," *Scientific American 250* (June):45–55.

George, Alexander L. (1987) "U.S.-Soviet Global Rivalry: Norms of Competition," in this volume.

————. (1985a) "Problems of Crisis Management and Crisis Avoidance in U.S.-Soviet Relations," Paper presented to the Nobel Institute Symposium on War and Peace Research, Oslo, Norway, June.

————. (1985b) "U.S.-Soviet Global Rivalry: Norms of Competition," Paper presented to the XIIIth World Congress of the International Political Science Association.

————. (1985c) "Mechanisms for Moderating Superpower Competition," *Foreign Policy and Defense Review* 6, 1 (Summer). Washington: American Enterprise Institute.

————. (1984a) "Political Crises," in Joseph S. Nye, Jr., (ed.) *The Making of America's Soviet Policy.* New Haven: Yale University Press.

————. (1984b) "Crisis Management: The Interaction of Political and Military Considerations," *Survival* 26:223–234.

————. (ed.) (1983) *Managing U.S.-Soviet Rivalry: Problems of Crisis Prevention.* Boulder, Colorado: Westview Press.

————. (1982) "Case Studies and Theory Development," Paper presented to the Second Annual Symposium on Information-Processing in Organizations, Carnegie-Mellon University, October.

————. (1980) *Presidential Decision-making in Foreign Policy.* Boulder, Colorado: Westview Press.

————. (1972) "The Case for Multiple Advocacy in Making Foreign Policy," *American Political Science Review* 66:751–785.

————. and Richard Smoke (1974) *Deterrence in American Foreign Policy: Theory and Practice.* New York: Columbia University Press.

————, David K. Hall and William R. Simons (1971) *The Limits of Coercive Diplomacy: Laos, Cuba, Vietnam.* Boston: Little Brown.

Gilbert, Arthur N. and Paul Gordon Lauren (1980) "Crisis Management: An Assessment and Critique," *Journal of Conflict Resolution* 24:641–664.

Glaser, Charles L. (1984) "Why Even Good Defenses May Be Bad," *International Security* 9: 92–123.

Golan, Galia (1977) *Yom Kippur and After: The Soviet Union and the Middle East Crisis.* Cambridge: Cambridge University Press.

Golan, Matti (1976) *The Secret Conversation of Henry Kissinger: Step-by-Step Diplomacy in the Middle East.* Chicago: Quadrangle.

Goldman, Kjell (1969) "International Norms and Governmental Behavior," *Cooperation and Conflict* 4, 3.

Gordon, Michael R. (1987) "U.S. Officials Look to Geneva Talks, but Critics are Skeptical on Prospects," *New York Times* October 14:A11.

Gowa, Joanne and Nils H. Wessell (1982) *Ground Rules: Soviet and American Involvement in Regional Conflicts.* Philadelphia: Foreign Policy Research Institute.

Groom, Arthur John Richard (1978) "Crisis management in long-range perspective," in D. Frei (ed.) *International Crises and Crisis Management.* Farnborough: Saxon House.

Habeeb, Mark (1986) *Power in Asymmetrical Negotiations.* Washington: The Johns Hopkins University Press.

Haig, Alexander (1984) *Caveat: Realism, Reagan, and Foreign Policy.* New York: MacMillan.

Halloran, John (1986) "How Leaders Think the Unthinkable," *New York Times* 2 September :12.

Harbottle, Michael (1980) "The Strategy of Third Party Intervention," XXXV *International Journal* 1:118–131.

Hart, Douglas M. (1984) "Soviet Approaches to Crisis Management: The Military Dimension," *Survival* 26:214–223.

Hazlewood, Leo, John J. Hayes and James R. Brownell, Jr. (1977) "Planning for Problems in Crisis Management: An Analysis of Post-1945 Behavior in the U.S. Department of Defense," *International Studies Quarterly* 21:75–106.

Heikal, Mohamed (1975) *The Road to Ramadan.* New York: Quadrangle Books.

Herken, Gregg (1985) *Counsels of War.* New York: Knopf.

Hermann, Charles F. (1987) "Enhancing Crisis Stability: Correcting the Trend Toward Increasing Instability," in this volume.

————— . (1985) "The Ultimate Crisis in the Nuclear Era," Paper presented at XIII International Political Science Association Congress.

————— . (ed.) (1972) *International Crises: Insights from Behavioral Research.* New York: Free Press.

Hersh, Seymour M. (1986) *The Target is Destroyed: What Really Happened to Flight 007 and What America Knew About It.* New York: Random House.

Hilsman, Roger (1969) "An Exchange on the Missile Crisis," *New York Review of Books* 12:37–38.

————— . (1967) *To Move a Nation: The Politics of Foreign Policy in the Administration of John F. Kennedy.* Garden City, New York: Doubleday.

————— . (1964) "The Cuban Crisis: How Close We Were to War," *Look* 28: 17–21.

Hoetzendorff, Franz Conrad von (1921–25) *Aus Meiner Deinstzeit.* (5 vols.), IV:152.

Holst, Johan J. (1983) "Confidence-Building Measures: A Conceptual Framework," *Survival* (January/February).

Holsti, Ole R. (1972a) *Crisis, Escalation, War.* Montreal: McGill-Queens University Press.

————. (1972b) "Time, Alternatives and Communications: The 1914 and Cuban Missile Crises," in C. Hermann (ed.) *International Crises: Insights from Behaviorial Research*. New York: Free Press.

Hopmann, Terrence (1978) "An Application of a Richardson Process Model," in William Zartman (ed.) *The Negotiation Process*. Beverly Hills, Calif.: Sage Press.

Horelick, Arnold and Myron Rush (1966) *Strategic Power and Soviet Foreign Policy*. Chicago: University of Chicago Press.

Jabber, Paul and Roman Kolkowicz (1981) "The Arab-Israeli Wars of 1967 and 1973," in Stephen S. Kaplan *Diplomacy of Power: Soviet Armed Forces as a Political Instrument*. Washington, D.C.: Brookings Institution.

Jackson, Elmore (1952) *Meeting of Minds*. New York: McGraw-Hill.

Jervis, Robert (1976) *Perception and Misperception in International Politics*. New Jersey: Princeton University Press.

————. (1978) "Cooperation Under the Security Dilemma," *World Politics* 30, 2.

————, Richard Ned Lebow and Janice Gross Stein (1985) *Psychology and Deterrence*. Baltimore: The Johns Hopkins University Press.

Johnson, Lyndon Baines (1971) *The Vantage Point: Perspectives of the Presidency, 1963–1969*. New York: Holt, Rinehart, and Winston.

Joint Chiefs of Staff (1980) Special Operations Review Group, *Rescue Mission Report*. Washington, D.C.: Joint Chiefs of Staff.

Jönsson, Christer (1984) *Superpowers: Comparing American and Soviet Foreign Policy*. London: Frances Pinter.

Jorden, William (1984) *Panama Odyssey*. Austin: University of Texas Press.

Kael, Paul (1983) *Unspoken Rules and Superpower Dominance*. London: Macmillan.

Kahan, Jerome H. and Anne K. Long (1972) "The Cuban Missile Crisis: A Study of Its Strategic Context," *Political Science Quarterly* 87:564–90.

Kalb, Marvin and Bernard Kalb (1974) *Kissinger*. New York: Dell. *and* Boston: Little, Brown and Company.

Kaplan, Fred (1983) *The Wizards of Armegeddon*. New York: Simon & Schuster.

Kaplan, Stephen S. (1981) *Diplomacy of Power: Soviet Armed Forces as a Political Instrument*. Washington, D.C.: Brookings Institution.

Kennedy, Paul (1983) "Arms Races and the Causes of War, 1850–1945," in Paul Kennedy *Strategy and Diplomacy, 1870–1945*. London: George Allen and Unwin.

Kennedy, Robert (1969a) *Thirteen Days: The Missile Crisis*. London: Pan.

————. (1969b) *Thirteen Days: A Memoir of the Cuban Missile Crisis*. New York: Norton.

Kinder, Donald R. and Janet A. Weiss (1978) "In Lieu of Rationality: Psychological Perspectives on Foreign Policy Decision Making," *Journal of Conflict Resolution* 22:707–735.

Kissinger, Henry A. (1982) *Years of Upheaval*. Boston: Little, Brown.

————. (1981) *For the Record: Selected Statements, 1977–80*. Boston: Little, Brown.

Kolkowicz, Roman (1981) "The Arab-Israeli Wars of 1967 and 1973," in Stephen S. Kaplan, *Diplomacy of Power: Soviet Armed Forces as a Political Instrument*. Washington: Brookings Institution.

Kramer, B.M., S.M. Kalicki, and T.A. Milburn (1983) "Attitudes Toward Nuclear Weapons and Nuclear War: 1945–1982," *Journal of Social Issues* 39:7–24.

Krasner, Stephen (ed.) (1983) *International Regimes.* Ithaca: Cornell University Press.

Kruzel, Joseph (1985) "What's Wrong with the Traditional Approach," *Washington Quarterly* 8: 121–132.

LaFeber, Walter (1979) *The Panama Canal.* New York: Oxford University Press.

Landi, Dale M. and others (1984) "Improving the Means for Intergovernmental Communications in Crisis," *Survival* 26:200–214.

Lauren, Paul (ed.) (1979) *Diplomacy.* New York: Free Press.

Lebow, Richard Ned (1987a) "Clausewitz, Loss of Control, and Crisis Management," in this volume.

————. (1987b) *Nuclear Crisis Management: A Dangerous Illusion.* Ithaca: Cornell University Press.

————. (1985a) "Practical Ways to Avoid Superpower Crises," *Bulletin of the Atomic Scientists* 41 (January).

————. (1985b) "Miscalculation in the South Atlantic: The Origins of the Falkland War," in Robert Jervis, Richard Ned Lebow, and Janice Gross Stein *Psychology and Deterrence.* Baltimore: Johns Hopkins University Press.

————. (1984) "The Soviet Offensive in Europe: The Schlieffen Plan Revisited," *International Security* 9:44–78.

————. (1983) "The Cuban Missile Crisis: Reading the Lessons Correctly," *Political Science Quarterly* 98:431–58.

————. (1981) *Between Peace and War: The Nature of International Crisis.* Baltimore: Johns Hopkins University Press.

———— and David S. Cohen (forthcoming) "Cognitive Versus Motivational Models of Attitude Change: The Carter Administration's Reaction to Afghanistan."

————, and Janice Gross Stein (1987, forthcoming) "Beyond Deterrence: Alternative Approaches to Conflict Management," *Journal of Social Issues.*

Leintenberg, Milton and Gabriel Sheffer (eds.) (1979) *Great Power Intervention in the Middle East.* New York: Pergamon Press.

Levy, Jack S. (1986) "Organizational Routines and the Causes of War," *International Studies Quarterly* 30:193–222.

Lichterman, Martin (1963) "To the Yalu and Back," in Harold Stein (ed.) *American Civil-Military Decisions.* New York: Twentieth Century Fund.

Linowitz, Sol (1985) *The Making of a Public Man.* Boston: Little, Brown and Co.

London *Sunday Times* Insight Team (1974) *The Yom Kippur War.* Garden City, New York: Doubleday.

Low, Stephen (1985) "Anglo-American Mediation in Zimbabwe," in Saadia Touval and I. William Zartman (eds.) *International Mediation in Theory and Practice.* Boulder, Colorado: Westview Press.

Luttwak, Edward and Walter Laqueur (1974) "Kissinger and the Yom Kippur War," *Commentary* 58:33–40.

MacGillivray, Karen Patrick and Gilbert R. Winham (1987) "Arms Control Negotiations and the Stability of Crisis Management," in this volume.

Matheson, Neil (1982) *The 'Rules of the Game' of Superpower Intervention in the Third World.* New York: University Press of America.

McNamara, Robert S. (1983) "No Second Use—Until," *New York Times* 2 February.

McWhinney, Edward (1964) *Peaceful Coexistence and Soviet-Western International Law.* Leyden: A.W. Sijthoff.

Mearsheimer, John J. (1986) "A Strategic Misstep: The Maritime Strategy and Deterrence in Europe," *International Security* 11:3–57.

Meyer, Stephen M. (1985) "Soviet Perspectives on the Paths to Nuclear War," in Graham T. Allison, Albert Carnesdale, and Joseph S. Nye, Jr. (eds.) *Hawks, Doves, and Owls: An Agenda for Avoiding Nuclear War.* New York: Norton.

Milburn, Thomas (1972) "The Management of Crises," in C. Hermann (ed.) *International Crises: Insights from Behavioral Research.* New York: Free Press.

Miller, Gerald E. (1986) "Who Needs Arms Control?," *U.S. Naval Institute Proceedings* 112: 39–42.

Morgenthau, Hans J. (1961) *Politics Among Nations* (3rd edition) New York: Knopf.

Napper, Larry C. (1983) "The Ogaden War: Some Implications for Crisis Prevention," in Alexander L. George (ed.) *Managing U.S.-Soviet Rivalry.* Boulder, Colorado: Westview Press.

————. (1983) "The African Terrain and U.S.-Soviet Conflict," in George (ed.) *Managing U.S.-Soviet Rivalry.* Boulder, Colorado: Westview Press.

Nasser, Gamel Ab'dul (1968) Interview, *The New York Times*, 29 December.

————. (1969) Interview, *Al-Ahram*, 21 January.

Neuhold, Hanspeter (1978) "Principles and Implementation of Crisis Management: Lessons from the Past," in D. Frei (ed.) *International Crises and Crisis Management.* Farnborough: Saxon House.

Neustadt, Richard (1964) "Afterword: 1964," in *Presidential Power.* New York: Mentor.

New York Times. (1962) 12 September:1.

Nitze, Paul H. (1985) "Arms Control: The First Round in Geneva," *Atlantic Community Quarterly* 23:53–50.

Nixon, Richard (1978) *RN: The Memoirs of Richard Nixon.* New York: Grosset and Dunlap.

Nunn-Warner Working Group (1985) "A Nuclear Risk Reduction System: The Interim Report," in Barry M. Blechman (ed.) *Preventing Nuclear War.* Bloomington, Indiana: University of Indiana Press.

Nye, Joseph S. Jr., (1986) "Farewell to Arms Control?" *Foreign Affairs* 65:1–20.

————. (1984a) "U.S.-Soviet Relations and Nuclear-Risk Reduction," *Political Science Quarterly* 99 (Fall).

————. (ed.) (1984b) *The Making of America's Soviet Policy.* New Haven: Yale University Press.

———— and William L. Ury (1987) "Approaches to Nuclear Risk Reduction," in this volume.

———— and William L. Ury (1985) "Approaches to Nuclear Risk Reduction," Paper presented at XIII International Political Science Association Congress.

Organski, A.F.K. (1961) *World Politics.* New York: Knopf.

Osgood, Charles E. (1962) *An Alternative to War or Surrender.* Urban, Illinois: University of Illinois Press.

Pflanze, Otto (1963) *Bismarck and the Development of Germany: The Period of Unification, 1815–71.* Princeton: Princeton University Press.

Polyviou, Polyvios G. (1980) *Cyprus: Conflict and Negotiations 1960–1980.* New York: Holmes and Meier.

Porter, Bruce D. (1984) *The USSR in Third World Conflict: Soviet Arms and Diplomacy in Local Wars, 1945–1980.* Cambridge: Cambridge University Press.

Posen, Barry (1982) "Inadvertent Nuclear War? Escalation and NATO's Northern Flank," *International Security* 7:28–54.

Powers, Thomas (1982a) "Choosing a Strategy for World War III," *Atlantic.* 250:82–110.

————. (1982) *Thinking About the Next War.* New York: Alfred A. Knopf.

Primakov, Ye. M. (1978) *Anatomiya blizhnevostochnogo konflikta [The Anatomy of the Near East Conflict].* Moscow: Nauka.

Pruitt, Dean G. and Kenneth Kressel (eds.) (1986) *The Mediation of Conflict,* special issue of *Journal of Social Issues* XXXXI, 2.

The Public Agenda Foundation (1984) "Voter Opinions on Nuclear Arms Policy," *Time,* 2 January.

Quandt, William (1984) "Reagan's Lebanon Policy: Trial and Error," *Middle East Journal* 38, 2:237–255.

————. (1977) "Soviet Policy in the October Middle East War," 2 parts, *International Affairs* 53:377–89, 587–603.

Rabin, Yitzhak (1979) *The Rabin Memoirs.* Boston: Little, Brown, and Company.

Reagan, Ronald (1986), "Text of Reagan's Broadcast Address on Talks with Gorbachev in Iceland," *New York Times* 14 October:A10.

Richardson, James L. (1987) "Crisis Management: A Critical Appraisal," in this volume.

————. (1979) "Crisis Management versus Crisis Diplomacy," Paper presented to the conference of the Australasian Political Studies Association, Hobart.

Ritter, Gerhard (1970) *Sword and Sceptor: The Problem of Militarism in Germany.* (trans. Heinz Norden) Coral Gables: University of Miami Press, 4 vols., II:239–63.

Robinson, James A. (1972) "Crisis: An Appraisal of Concepts and Theories," in C. Hermann (ed.) *International Crises: Insights from Behavioral Research.* New York: Free Press.

Rosenberg, David A. (1980–81) "A Smoking Radiating Ruin at the End of Two Hours: Documents on American Plans for Nuclear War with the Soviet Union," *International Security* 6:3–38.

Rowen, Henry (1985) "Catalytic Nuclear War," in Graham Allison, Al Carnesale, Joseph S. Nye, Jr. (eds.) *Hawks, Doves and Owls: An Agenda for Avoiding Nuclear War.* New York: W.W. Norton and Company.

Rubin, Jeffrey (ed.) (1981) *The Dynamics of Third-Party Intervention.* New York: Praeger.

————, and Bert Brown (1975) *The Social Psychology of Bargaining and Negotiation.* New York: Academic.

Russett, Bruce and Fred Chernoff (eds.) (1985) *Arms Control and the Arms Race.* New York: H.W. Freeman and Company.

Sadat, Anwar (1977) *In Search of Identity.* New York: Harper and Row.

————. (1973) Interview by Arnaud de Borchgrave, *Newsweek* 9 April.

Safran, Nadav (1978) *Israel the Embattled Ally.* Cambridge: Harvard University Press.

Sagan, Scott D. (1985) "Nuclear Alerts and Crisis Management," *International Security* 9:99–139.

Saunders, Harold (1985) *The Other Walls.* Washington, D.C.: American Enterprise Institute.

Schelling, Thomas C. (1985/86) "What Went Wrong with Arms Control?" *Foreign Affairs* 64:2.

————. (1984) "Confidence in Crisis," *International Security* 8:55–66.

————. (1966) *Arms and Influence.* New Haven: Yale University Press.

————. (1960) *The Strategy of Conflict.* Cambridge, Massachusetts: Harvard University Press.

Schiff, Ze'ev (1983) "The Green Light," *Foreign Policy* 50, Spring.

———— and Ehud Ya'ari (1984) *Israel's Lebanon War.* New York: Simon and Schuster.

Schlesinger, Arthur M. Jr. (1965) *A Thousand Days: John F. Kennedy in the White House.* London: Deutsch.

Schmemann, Serge (1986) "Gorbachev Terms Reagan too Timid: Says President Lacked Will to Make a 'Turn in History'," *New York Times* 15 October:A1.

Schneider, William (1985) "Peace and Strength: American Public Opinion on National Security," in Gregory Flynn and Hans Rattinger (eds.) *The Public and Atlantic Defense* London: Croom-Helm.

Schroeder, Paul W. (1974) "Review of O. Holsti, Crisis, Escalation, War," *Journal of Modern History* 46:537–540.

Scranton, Margaret and William Furlong (1984) *Dynamics of Foreign Policy Making.* Boulder, Colorado: Westview Press.

Sharon, Ariel (1982) Interview by Jack Anderson, *Jerusalem Post* 15 August.

Shlaim, Avi (1983) *The United States and the Berlin Blockade, 1948–1949: A Study in Crisis Decision-Making.* Berkeley: University of California Press.

Shubik, Martin (1971) "The Dollar Auction Game: a Paradox in Noncooperative Behavior and Escalation," *Journal of Conflict Resolution* 15: 109–111.

Sloss, Leon and M. Scott Davis (eds.) (1986) *A Game for High Stakes and Lessons Learned in Negotiating with the Soviet Union.* Cambridge, Massachusetts: Ballinger Publishing Co.

Snyder, Glenn H. (1961) *Deterrence and Defense.* Princeton, New Jersey: Princeton University Press.

————, and Paul Diesing (1977) *Conflict Among Nations: Bargaining, Decision Making and System Structure in International Crises.* Princeton, New Jersey: Princeton University Press.

Snyder, Jack (1984a) *The Ideology of the Offensive: Military Decision Making and the Disasters of 1914.* Ithaca: Cornell University Press.

————. (1984b) "Civil-Military Relations and the Cult of the Offensive, 1914 and 1984," *International Security* 9.

Sorensen, Theodore (1965) *Kennedy*. New York: Harper and Row.

Spanier, John (1965) *The Truman-MacArthur Controversy and the Korean War*. rev. ed., New York: Norton.

Steel, Ronald (1969) "The Kennedys and the Missile Crisis," *New York Review of Books* 12:15–22.

Stein, Harold (ed.) (1963) *American Civil-Military Decisions*. New York: Twentieth Century Fund.

Stein, Janice Gross (1987) "Extended Deterrence in the Middle East: American Strategy Reconsidered," *World Politics*. 39, 3:326–352.

————. (1987) "The Managed and the Managers: Crisis Prevention in the Middle East," in this volume.

————. (1985) "Calculation, Miscalculation, and Conventional Deterrence I: The View from Cairo," in Robert Jervis, Richard Ned Lebow, and Janice Gross Stein *Psychology and Deterrence*. Baltimore: The Johns Hopkins University Press.

————. (1983) "The Alchemy of Peacemaking: The Prerequisites and Corequisites of Progress in the Arab-Israeli Conflict," *International Journal* 38, 4: 531–555.

————. (1980) "Proxy Wars: How Superpowers End Them," *International Journal* 35, 3.

————, and Raymond Tanter (1980) *Rational Decision Making: Israel's Security Choices, 1967*. Columbus: Ohio State University Press.

Steinbruner, John D (1985) "Arms Control: Crisis or Compromise," *Foreign Affairs* 63: 1036–1049.

————. (1984) "Launch under Attack," *Scientific American* 250: 37–47.

————. (1981–82) "Nuclear Decapitation," *Foreign Policy* 45:16–28.

————. (1978) "National Security and the Concept of Strategic Stability," *Journal of Conflict Resolution* 22 (September).

Szulc, Tad (1978) *The Illusion of Peace: Foreign Policy in the Nixon Years*. New York: Viking.

Tanter, Raymond (1975) "Crisis Management: A Critical Review of Academic Literature," *Jerusalem Journal of International Relations* 1:71–101.

Tate, Raymond (1980) "Worldwide C³I and Telecommunications," Seminar on Command, Control, Communications, and Intelligence. Cambridge: Program on Information Resources Policy, Harvard University.

Tatu, Michael (1968) *Power in the Kremlin: From Khrushchev to Kosygin*. London: Collins.

Thucydides (1954) *The Peloponnesian War*. (trans. Rex Warner.) Harmondsworth, England: Penguin Books.

Time. (1976) 12 April.

Touval, Saadia (1982) *The Peacebrokers*. Princeton: Princeton University Press.

————. (1975) "Biased Intermediaries: Theoretical and Historical Considerations," *Jerusalem Journal of International Relations* 1:51–69.

————, and I. William Zartman (eds.) (1985) *International Mediation in Theory and Practice*. Boulder, Colorado: Westview Press.

Tsou, Tang (1963) *America's Failure in China, 1941–1950*. Chicago: University of Chicago Press.

Turner, L.C.F. (1968) "The Russian Mobilization in 1914," *Journal of Contemporary History* 3:65–88.

Ury, William L. (1986) "A 'Warm Line' to Avert War," *New York Times* 27 August Editorial Page.

————. (1985) *Beyond the Hotline: How Crisis Control Can Prevent Nuclear War.* Boston: Houghton Mifflin.

————, and Richard Smoke (1984) *Beyond the Hotline.* Cambridge: Harvard Law School Nuclear Negotiation Project.

Valenta, Jiri (1982) "Toward Soviet-U.S. Prevention of Crises at the Soviet Periphery," Paper presented at the International Political Science Association, 12th World Congress, Rio de Janeiro, August.

Van Evera, Stephen (1984) "The Cult of the Offensive and the Origins of the First World War," *International Security* 9.

Vick, Alan J. and James A. Thomson (1985) "The Military Significance of Restrictions on the Operations of Strategic Nuclear Forces," in Barry M. Blechman (ed.) *Preventing Nuclear War.* Bloomington, Indiana: Indiana University Press.

Vogele, William B. (1986) "Negotiating Arms Control Agreements: The Conditions for Success in U.S.-Soviet Arms Control Negotiations, 1954–1980," Paper presented at the 1986 Annual Meeting of the American Political Science Association, Washington, D.C.

Waltz, Kenneth (1979) *Theory of International Politics.* Reading: Addison-Wesley.

Weintal, Edward and Charles Bartlett (1967) *Facing the Brink.* New York: Scribners.

Whiting, Allen S. (1960) *China Crosses the Yalu: The Decision to Enter the Korean War.* New York: Macmillan.

Wilkenfeld, Jonathan and Michael Brecher (1982) "Superpower Crisis Management Behavior," in C.W. Kegley and P.J. McGowan (eds.) *Foreign Policy: US/USSR, Sage International Yearbook of Foreign Policy Studies, VIII.* Beverly Hills, California: Sage.

Williams, Phil (1976) *Crisis Management: Confrontation and Diplomacy in the Nuclear Age.* New York: Wiley.

Young, Oran R. (1968) *The Politics of Force: Bargaining During International Crises.* Princeton: Princeton University Press.

————. (1967) *The Intermediaries.* Princeton: Princeton University Press.

Young, Robert A. (special editor) (1977) "A Special Issue on International Crisis," *International Studies Quarterly* 21.

Zartman, I. William (1987) "Alternative Attempts at Crisis Management: Concepts and Processes," in this volume.

————. (1986) "Practitioners' Theories of International Negotiation," II *Negotiation Journal* 3:299–310.

————. (1985a) *Ripe for Resolution: Conflict and Intervention in Africa.* Oxford: Oxford University Press.

————. (1985b) "Alternative Attempts at Crisis Management: Concepts and Processes," Paper presented at XIII International Political Science Association Congress.

————. (1985c) "Negotiating from Asymmetry: The North-South Stalemate," I *Negotiation Journal* 2:121–138.

Zartman, I. William (ed.) (1978) *The Negotiation Process*. Beverley Hills: Sage
    Press.
Zartman, I. William and Maureen Berman (1982) *The Practical Negotiator*. New
    Haven: Yale University Press.
Zumwalt, Elmo R., Jr. (1976) *On Watch: A Memoir*. Chicago: Quadrangle.

Index

Abel, Elie, 20
ABM Treaty. *See* Anti-Ballistic Missile Treaty
Accidents Agreement (1971), 159, 163
Accidents at Sea Agreement (1972), 70, 159, 163
Acheson, Dean, 220
Afghanistan, 48, 62, 87, 101, 148n
Agnew, Spiro, 57
Agreement on Prevention of Nuclear War (1973), 68, 141, 159
Alerts, strategic (inc. DEFCON), 42, 43, 57, 61, 127–129, 132, 139, 148n, 226, 229
"ratchet effect," 60
Allison, Graham T., 41, 63n, 147n, 166n
American Committee on East-West Accord, 68, 69, 72, 88n
Amit, Meir, 182–183
Anderson, George (Admiral), 19, 41
Anderson, Robert, 182
Angola, 82, 217
Anti-ballistic missiles. *See* Weapons, anti-ballistic missiles
Anti-Ballistic Missile Treaty (1972) (ABM Treaty), 70, 95–97, 102, 104, 105, 107–108, 140
Anti-satellite systems. *See* Weapons, anti-satellite systems
Arab-Israeli conflict. *See* October War; Six Day War; War of Attrition
Argentina, 61, 202, 209–210, 212, 215
Arms, types of. *See* Weapons

Arms control, 90–92, 101–107, 137–138
goals of, 117n
problems with, 107–111, 113–117
See also Anti-Ballistic Missile Treaty; Crisis management, and arms control; SALT I; SALT II; Verification of forces
Arms race, 92, 153. *See also* Counterforce matching; Deterrence strategy; Escalation of conflict
al-Assad, Hafez, 185
Australia, 36n
Austria, 38, 50, 156–157, 229. *See also* Austria-Hungary
Austria-Hungary, 1–2
Austrian State Treaty (1955), 69, 79

Balance of power, 7, 9, 94, 225, 228
theories of, 7–9
See also Spheres of influence
Balfour, Arthur James, 79–80
Bargaining. *See* Crisis diplomacy
Basic Principles Agreement (1972), 67–68, 86, 141, 159, 196, 228
Bay of Pigs, 46
Begin, Menachem, 186–191, 197n, 198n
Belgium, 2
Bell, Coral, 15, 21, 23, 27
Bendahmane, Diane, 222n
Berlin, 27, 48, 122
Berlin Quadripartite Agreement (1971), 70, 79
Bethmann-Hollweg, Theobald von, 45, 50

Betts, Richard K., 124, 137, 152
Bismarck, Otto, 40, 46
Blair, Bruce G., 133, 136
Bonaparte, Napoleon, 39. *See also*
Napoleonic Wars
Bosnia-Herzogovina, 2, 157
Bracken, Paul, 60, 130, 131, 132, 151,
154
Bradley, William, 160
Brecher, Michael, 33, 148
Brezhnev, Leonid, 54, 55, 56, 67–68,
78, 82, 86, 94, 99, 141, 177, 190,
198n, 228
Britain. *See* United Kingdom
Brownell, James R., Jr., 35n
Bulow, Bernhard, 45
Bundy, McGeorge, 46

C³I. *See* Command, Control,
Communications and Intelligence
Caldwell, Dan, 63n
Carnesale, Albert, 147n, 166n
Carrington (Lord), 216
Carter, Jimmy, 48, 71, 86, 99, 101
Casey, William, 63n
Castro, Fidel, 75
Central African Federation, 205, 207
Chad, 220
Chamberlain, Neville, 27, 156
Chang, King-Yuh, 19, 23
Chernoff, Fred, 113
China, 29, 51, 93, 121
Churchill, Winston, 79
Clausewitz, Carl von, 37–41, 45–46,
48, 58–61, 63, 231
Cohen, Eliot A., 27
Cohen, Raymond, 89n
Colby, William, 57
Cold War, 3, 7, 23, 32, 69, 74, 81,
84, 93
Command, Control, Communications
and Intelligence (C³I), 129–133,
136, 151. *See also* Command
centres
Command centres, vulnerability of,
114–115, 129–131, 135–136, 138,
139, 230–231

Communication (esp. during crisis),
22, 34, 51, 83, 91, 114, 115, 176,
184, 191, 193. *See also* Hotline
Competition, U.S.-USSR. *See* U.S.-
Soviet relations
Concert of Europe, 32
Control, loss of, 6–7, 37, 41, 42, 62–
63, 91, 130, 133, 134, 153–154,
225–226, 231
Costa-Mendez, Nicanor, 61
Counterforce matching, 113
Crimean War, 24, 25
Crises, international, 3, 33, 122–124,
221–222
definition of, 122
types of, 4–7
Crisis control. *See* Crisis management
Crisis diplomacy, 15, 22, 28, 29, 31,
32, 33, 34, 214. *See also* Crisis
management
Crisis management/control
and arms control, 112–117
criticisms of, 25–29
definitions of, 4, 14–17, 24–25,
35n, 91, 116, 158, 213
improvements in (past and future),
158–161, 162–166, 232. *See also*
Crisis stability, proposals for
improvement
use of mediator in, 201, 206, 210,
218–221
use of military in, 9, 35n
principles of/rules of, 18–23, 25–
27, 33, 192–193, 221–222
resolving formula, 200–201, 203,
204, 205, 207, 208–209, 212,
215, 219, 220
risks of, 162
and stability, 91–92, 166
study of, 3–4, 10, 23–24, 33–35,
45, 146–147, 227–232
superpower-ally management, 173,
191–197, 226, 228–229
U.S., 178–191
USSR, 175–178, 181
See also Crisis prevention; Crisis
stability; Cuban Missile Crisis;

Emotion during crises; Ripe moment
Crisis prevention, 194, 228, 232
difficulties of, 171–172, 176–177, 195–196
"Crisis slide," 27, 33. *See also* Escalation of conflict
Crisis stability, 112, 114, 115, 116, 123–125, 143–147, 166
definition, 123
proposals for improvement, 133–143, 145–146. *See also* Crisis management, improvements in
and strategic alerts, 127–129
and weapons systems/arms control, 125–127, 129–133, 139, 140, 158, 230–231
Cuba, 2–3, 70, 71, 75, 89. *See also* Cuban Missile Crisis
Cuban Missile Crisis (1962), 2–3, 5, 17, 18–22, 26–27, 28, 33, 36n, 41, 42, 43, 46–48, 49, 51, 58–60, 62, 63n, 64n, 70–71, 75, 122, 128, 129, 154, 158–159, 166, 229, 231
Cyprus, 200, 202, 207–209, 211, 212, 216, 219–220, 221, 222
Czechoslovakia, 75, 152

Dartmouth Conference Task Force on Regional Conflicts, 86, 88
Dean, John, 108
de Cuellar, Perez, 220
DEFCON. *See* Alerts, strategic
Dessouki, Ali, 16
Détente, 67, 68, 74
Deterrence strategy, 5, 67, 98, 114, 115, 121, 132, 147, 153, 167n
and arms control, 93, 97
criticisms of, 134
and defense systems, 102, 103
stability of, 91, 92, 112, 123
in world wars, 157
See also Crisis stability; Preemption; Verification of forces
Diesing, Paul, 4, 5, 6, 14, 15, 29, 30, 167n

Dinerstein, Herbert, 89n
Dinitz, Ambassador, 53, 55
Direct Communications Link. *See* Hotline
Dulles, John Foster, 197n

East Germany, 122. *See also* Germany
Eban, Abba, 179, 197n
Egypt, 121, 192–196, 197n
and Lebanon, 184, 185, 188
and October War, 53–56, 68, 128, 173, 176–178
and Six Day War, 173, 178–182
and war of attrition, 78, 174, 175–176
Eisenhower, Dwight D., 121, 197n
Eitan, Raful, 185, 188, 189, 198n
Ellis, Richard H., 42
Emotion during crises, 21, 26, 30–31, 45–50, 61–63, 63n, 122, 124, 126, 154, 175, 231–232
Escalation of conflict, 20, 35n, 38, 42, 43, 48, 59, 60, 61, 62, 80, 81–82, 85, 122, 127, 128, 133, 134, 147n, 152, 164, 165, 176, 190, 213, 227, 229, 230, 231. *See also* Graduated response
Eshkol, Levi, 180, 182
Ethiopia, 69

Fahmy, Ismail, 176, 177
Falkland-Malvinas war, 61, 200, 202, 209–210, 211, 212, 215, 220, 221, 222
Fallows, James, 107
Fashoda crisis, 28
Ferdinand, Franz, 1
First strike, 121–122, 124, 125, 127, 129, 135. *See also* Preemption
Flexible response. *See* Graduated response
Four Power Agreement (1971). *See* Berlin Quadripartite Agreement
France, 24, 103, 104, 175
in WWI, 2, 50

in WWII, 152, 156
Freedom of choice, 20. *See also*
    Graduated response
Frei, Daniel, 13
French Revolution, 40, 61

Garthoff, Raymond L., 64n
Garwin, Richard L., 126
GATT. *See* General Agreement on
    Trade and Tariffs
General Agreement on Trade and
    Tariffs (GATT), 108
George, Alexander L., 15, 29, 30,
    35n, 142, 171, 194–195, 226,
    227–228, 229
Germany, 39, 155
    in WWI, 2, 6, 38, 50, 124, 157
    in WWII, 27, 79
Gilbert, Arthur N., 24, 25
Golan, Matti, 64n
Gorbachev, Mikhail, 87, 102, 106–
    107, 121
Graduated Reduction in Tension
    (GRIT), 137
Graduated response, 20, 25
Greece, 8, 202, 207–209. *See also*
    Peloponnesian War
GRIT. *See* Graduated Reduction In
    Tension
Gromyko, Andrei, 87, 103, 104, 175
Groom, John, 27
Guam, 57

Habib, Philip, 186
Haig, Alexander, 54, 57, 187–191,
    198n, 215, 220
Hall, David K., 15
Harman, Ambassador, 181
Harvard-Soviet group on Prevention
    of International Political Crises,
    86, 88
Hay-Bunau-Varilla Treaty, 200, 203
Hayes, John J., 35n
Hazlewood, Leo, 35n, 231
Helms, Richard, 183
Helsinki Accord/Helsinki Final Act
    (1975), 79, 159

Herken, Gregg, 64n
Hermann, Charles F., 225, 230, 231,
    232
Hersh, Seymour M., 63n
Hilsman, Roger, 19, 63n
Hitler, Adolf, 16, 17, 152, 156, 157
Holsti, Ole R., 21, 23
Hotline (Direct Communications
    Link), 22, 147, 158–159, 160,
    161, 162, 163, 165
    use in Six Day War, 77, 173
Howe, Jonathan, 57
Humphrey, Hubert, 182
Hungary, 75. *See also* Austria-
    Hungary
Hussein, Ibn Talal, 78

ICBMs. *See* Weapons, ballistic
    missiles
India, 80
Iran, 44
Iran hostage crisis, 38
Israel, 64n, 173, 192–196, 197n, 198n
    and October War, 52–56, 68, 78,
        173, 176–178
    and Six Day War, 77, 173, 178–
        183, 197n
    and war in Lebanon, 183–191
    and war of attrition, 77–78, 174,
        175–176

Jackson, Henry, 140
Japan, 49, 155, 157
Jervis, Robert, 79, 167n
Johnson, Lyndon B., 178, 179–180,
    187, 197n
Johnson-Robles Guidelines of 1964,
    203
Jomini, Baron Antoine-Henri, 46
Jordan, 78, 180
Jumayyil, Bashir, 185, 188

KAL 007 incident, 48, 49–50, 62,
    63n, 122, 148n, 163
Kalb, Bernard, 93
Kalb, Marvin, 93

Kennedy, John F., 19, 20, 21, 22, 43, 46–49, 51, 58–59, 60, 63n, 69, 70–71, 154, 159, 166
Kennedy, Robert, 18, 20, 21, 22, 47
Khrushchev, Nikita, 20, 21, 22, 46, 47, 48, 59, 69, 70–71, 89n, 121, 151, 159, 166
Kissinger, Henry, 8, 35n, 42, 44, 47, 52–58, 63, 64n, 78, 94, 184, 196
Kissinger-(Bunker)-Tack Principles (1974), 204
Korea/Korean War, 29, 51. *See also* North Korea; South Korea
Kosygin, Aleksei, 77–78, 94, 178, 180
Kruzel, Joseph, 113

Landi, Dale M., 143
Laos, 69
Launch under attack, 131–132, 134, 135
Lauren, Paul, 24, 25
Law, international, 23, 35n, 70, 96
Lebanon, 122, 174, 198n, 220
  war in (1982), 183–191
Lebow, Richard Ned, 5, 6, 27, 28, 29, 31, 32, 136, 138, 143, 148n, 225, 226, 230, 231
LeMay, Curtis, 51, 52, 64n
Lewis, Samuel, 190
Libya, 122
Loss of control. *See* Control, loss of
Luxembourg, 2

MacArthur, Douglas, 51, 52
McDonald, John W., 222n
MacGillivray, Karen, 225, 232
McNamara, Robert, 13, 19, 20, 44, 49, 182, 183
Mediation. *See* Crisis management, use of mediator in
Meir, Golda, 54–55
Meyer, Stephen, 44, 152
Middle East, 89n, 172, 228. *See also* Arab-Israeli conflict; *individual countries*
Milburn, Thomas, 19, 23

MIRV. *See* Weapons, multiple independently-targeted reentry vehicle
"Missile gap," 2, 3
Missiles, nuclear. *See* Weapons
Moltke, Helmuth von, 44, 46, 50
Moorer, Thomas, 57
Muhi-a-Din, Zahariyah, 182
Mutual and Balanced Force Reductions Talks, 108–109
Mutual assured destruction. *See* Deterrence strategy

Namibia, 217, 220
Napoleonic Wars, 45, 61
Nasser, Gamal Abdel, 77, 175, 178–179, 182, 197n
National interest, concept of, 84
National Security Council, 18, 187, 188
NATO. *See* North Atlantic Treaty Organization
Neuhold, Hanspeter, 15, 23
Nicaragua, 75, 220
Nicholson, Arthur D., 163
Nixon, Richard, 47, 53, 54, 57, 58, 67–68, 77, 82, 86, 94, 141, 177, 228
Non-Proliferation Treaty (1968), 92
North Atlantic Treaty Organization, 101, 104, 106
North Korea, 46, 84
Nuclear weapons. *See* Weapons
Nunn, Sam, 140, 143, 160
Nye, Joseph, 113, 137, 142, 147n, 166n, 225, 226, 231, 232

OAS. *See* Organization of American States
OAU. *See* Organization of African Unity
October War (1973), 43, 44, 52–58, 62, 68, 77–78, 122, 128, 173, 176–178, 196
Ogaden, 69

Options, range of options,
    maintaining options. *See*
    Graduated response
Organization of African Unity
    (OAU), 165
Organization of American States
    (OAS), 165
Organski, A.F.K., 8
Osgood, Charles E., 137, 148n

Paleologue, Maurice, 50
Palestine Liberation Organization
    (PLO), 193
    in Lebanon, 174, 184, 186–191
Panama, 200, 201–202, 203–205,
    206, 209, 211–212, 217, 219, 220,
    221, 222
Peace movement, 13
Peloponnesian War, 1, 3, 8, 226, 227
Peru, 220
PLO. *See* Palestine Liberation
    Organization
Poland, 156
Power, Thomas, 44, 51
Preemption, preemptive strategy, 9,
    43, 114, 125, 127, 130, 132–133,
    134, 140, 143, 144, 147n, 151,
    152, 226, 227, 230, 231

Quandt, William, 197n, 198n

Reagan, Ronald, 34, 63n, 86–87, 102,
    104, 105–106, 110, 121, 160–161,
    190, 198n
Regime, definition of, 200
Reykjavik summit (1986), 104–107,
    115
Rhodesia. *See* Zimbabwe/Rhodesia
Richardson, James, 225, 229, 230,
    231
"Ripe moment," "ripening conflict,"
    196–197, 199–200, 203, 204–205,
    207, 208–209, 210–218, 226, 229
Roosevelt, Franklin Delano, 79
Rostow, Eugene, 179, 181
Rowen, Harry, 152

Rusk, Dean, 181, 183
Russett, Bruce, 113
Russia, 155
    in WWI, 2, 6, 50, 124, 157

Sadat, Anwar, 56, 176–178, 197n
Safran, Nadav, 55, 64n
Sagan, Scott, 167n
Saguy, General, 187
Sakhalin, island of, 49
SALT I, 70, 92–97, 108, 113, 115
SALT II, 71, 86, 97–101, 107–109,
    217
Saturday Night Massacre, 54, 57
Schelling, Thomas C., 114, 157
Schlesinger, Arthur, 19, 20
Schlesinger, James, 53, 57
Schlieffen Plan, 2, 41, 45
Schroeder, Paul W., 24, 25
Scowcroft, Brent, 57
SDI. *See* Strategic Defense Initiative
Seabeds Arms Control Treaty (1971),
    108
Serbia, 1, 2, 50, 124
Sharon, Ariel, 187–191, 198n
Shevardnadze, Eduard, 104
Shultz, George, 63n, 87, 103, 104
Simons, William R., 15
SIOP options, 42, 44
Six Day War (1967), 77, 173, 178–
    183
Smoke, Richard, 29, 30, 167n
Snow, C.P., 151
Snyder, Glenn H., 4, 5, 6, 14, 15,
    29, 30, 167n
Snyder, Jack, 44
Somalia, 69
Sorensen, Theodore, 46
South Africa, 206
South Korea, 84
Spheres of influence, 23, 72–82
Stalin, Josef, 79
Standing Consultative Commission,
    96, 141, 159
START talks, 101
Steel, Ronald, 63n

Stein, Janice Gross, 226, 228–229
Steinbruner, John D., 133, 227
Strategic alerts. *See* Alerts, strategic
Strategic Defense Initiative (SDI), 34, 95, 102–104, 105–107, 108, 110, 134, 139
Stremlau, John, 88n
Suez Canal, 55, 174, 175
Suez crisis, 19
Superpower relations. *See* U.S.-Soviet relations
SWAPO, 217
Syria, 78, 178, 179, 181, 193, 195, 198n
  and Lebanon, 122, 174, 183–191
  and October War, 53, 56, 173, 176
Szulc, Tad, 53

Tanter, Raymond, 30
Thomson, James A., 148n
Thomson, Llewellyn, 21
Toynbee, Arnold, 1
Turkey, 202, 207, 209, 216

United Kingdom, 19, 24, 103, 104, 155, 165, 175
  and Cyprus, 207, 209
  and Falklands war, 61–62, 202, 209–210, 212, 215
  in WWI, 2
  in WWII, 152, 156
  and Zimbabwe/Rhodesia, 202, 205–207, 216–217, 220
United Nations, 55, 87, 88, 160, 165, 178, 179, 180, 185, 204, 207, 208, 210, 216, 220
United States, 14, 31, 206, 210, 220
  and Cold War, 7
  and Cuban Missile Crisis, 2–3, 5, 22, 36n, 41, 42, 43, 46–48, 51, 58–59, 62, 70–71, 231. *See also* Kennedy, John F.
  and KAL 007 incident, 49–50, 62
  and Korean War, 29, 51, 84
  and Lebanon, 183–191
  and military strategy, 26, 44, 67. *See also* Cuban Missile Crisis;

U.S.-Soviet relations, interests, principles, values; Deterrence strategy
  and October War, 52–58, 128, 173, 177–178, 196
  and Panama, 201–202, 203–205, 217
  and Six Day War, 173, 178–183
  and Vietnam War, 25
  and war of attrition, 174, 175
  and WWII, 155, 157
  See also U.S.-Soviet relations
Ury, William L., 117, 225, 226, 231, 232
U.S.-Soviet relations, 225
  agreements, understandings, 23, 68–72, 86–88, 107, 113, 141–142, 159, 164, 228. *See also* Arms control; Basic Principles Agreement
  with allies. *See* Crisis management, superpower-ally management
  competition and crisis, 6, 8–9, 72–82, 89n, 90, 122–123, 228, 230. *See also* Crisis stability
  effect of arms control on, 107–111, 115–117
  interests, principles, values, 26, 82–86, 106, 122, 161–162, 171–172, 228
USSR, 47, 188
  and Afghanistan, 122, 148n
  and Cold War, 7
  and Cuban Missile Crisis, 2–3, 5, 21, 22, 42, 43, 46, 51, 58–59, 62, 63n, 70–71
  and KAL 007 incident, 49–50, 62, 148n
  and Korean War, 84
  and military strategy, 26, 44–45, 67. *See also* Deterrence; U.S.-Soviet relations, interests, principles, values
  and October War, 52–58, 128, 173, 176–178, 196
  and Six Day War, 173, 179–183

and war of attrition, 174, 175–176,
197n
See also Khrushchev, Nikita;
Russia; U.S.-Soviet relations

Vance, Cyrus, 220
Verification of forces, 95–96, 98, 111,
114, 135, 138, 139, 143, 151
Vick, Alan J., 148n
Vietnam War, 7, 25, 55, 94, 182, 217

War, nuclear, causes of, 122, 147n,
152–157, 167n, 226, 230
Warner, Jack, 140, 143, 160
War of attrition (1970), 77–78, 174,
175–176, 197n
Warsaw Pact, 106
Watergate, 47, 57
Weapons
anti-ballistic missiles (ABM), 93,
94, 112. *See also* Anti-Ballistic
Missile Treaty
anti-satellite systems (ASAT), 102–
103, 125–126, 139, 144
ballistic missiles (inc. ICBMs), 3, 7,
48, 93, 94–97, 98–99, 101–105,
108, 112, 113–114, 123, 126, 130,
131–132, 135, 138
and bargaining power, 6, 109–110
defensive weapons, destabilizing
ability of, 107, 112, 127–128,
140, 148n

multiple independently-targeted
reentry vehicle (MIRV), 93, 98,
108, 112–113, 125, 131
non-nuclear, 59–60
See also Arms control; Crisis
stability, and weapons systems;
Window of vulnerability
Weinberger, Caspar, 160
West Germany, 138. *See also*
Germany
Wilkenfeld, Jonathan, 33
Williams, Phil, 23, 25
"Window of vulnerability," 7, 100,
113
Winham, Gilbert, 225, 232
World War I, 1–2, 8, 24, 27, 38, 40,
50–51, 124, 153, 155, 156–157,
226, 227. *See also* Schlieffen
Plan
World War II, 49, 74, 79, 92, 122,
152, 153, 155, 157

Yom Kippur War. *See* October War

Zambia, 206
Zartman, I. William, 196, 226, 229–
230
Zhukov, Marshal, 52
Zimbabwe/Rhodesia, 165, 200, 202,
205–207, 209, 211, 212, 216–217,
220, 221, 222